CW00554363

COMING HOME

Notes for the Journey

Stephen G Wright

For Jeannie

© Stephen G Wright.

First published 2008 by Sacred Space Publications,
Emmers Farm, Sparket, Cumbria CA11 0NA

All rights reserved. No part of this publication may be reproduced, stored
in a retrieval system, or transmitted in any form or by any means, electronic,
mechanical, photocopying or otherwise, without the prior permission of the
copyright owner, except in accordance with the provisions of the Copyright,
Designs and Patents Act, 1988 or under terms of a licence issued by the
Copyright Licensing Agency, 90 Tottenham Court Road, London W1P 9HE.
Applications for the copyright owner's written permission to reproduce part of
this publication should be addressed to the publisher.

This publication is sold subject to the conditions that it shall not, by any way
of trade or otherwise, be lent, resold, hired out, or otherwise circulated without
the publisher's prior consent in any form of binding or cover other than that in
which it is published and without a similar condition including this condition
being imposed upon any subsequent purchaser.

The moral right of Stephen G Wright to be identified as the author of this
work has been asserted in accordance with the Copyright, Designs and Patents
Act of 1988.

British Library Cataloguing in Publication Data
A catalogue record for this book is available from the British Library.

ISBN: 978-0-9560303-0-6

Some material in parts 3, 4, 5 and 9 was published in editorials for Spirituality
and Health International Volume 7, issues 1-4. Further information on this
journal can be found at
www.interscience.wiley.com/journal/shi.

I am grateful also to the editor of Nursing Standard for her permission to
include extracts from my regular column on spirituality and wellbeing. For
more information on this journal see www.nursing-standard.co.uk

A number of "case" studies are included in this book, taken from the accounts
of individuals who have been with me seeking spiritual direction. In all cases
the names have been fictionalised.

Typeset and Printed on recycled paper by
Reeds Printers Limited
Southend Road, Penrith, Cumbria CA11 8JH
Tel: 01768 864214

Contents

...Stuck to the rock
Afraid of the unknown open sea
The shell domed limpet clings to home
From Home.
Deaf to the call of the ocean "come to me".
Deaf beneath the time hard shield.
Blind: facing stone and stone.
Blind: encased and lightless
In the womb, isolation
In the tomb, salvation
"Oh break me, break me again. Let wind and wave do their will.
Let the Master find the servant
Let the servant leave home for Home."
The choice of god for God.
Choice! In the image of God are we made?
Choice – the bitter call to sweet redemption
the reunification of source with Source
The call forever rilling patiently through the long night
Waiting
To be heard.
We pour out of buildings
Onto blistering black tarmacked sunblasted city streets
In high summer bikeroared and roaddrilled deafening heatflattening
Summer in London or anywhere
Out into the heat
The unashamed unforgiving heat.
We choose to enter the furnace
We choose the heat.
The searing heat (compassion
Cooling the suffering soul),
A brick melting heat; roasting identity.
Heat concealed, in the loving heart.
Heat unleashed the limpet calls "for freedom",
Burning shell from shell
Hearts on fire
Hearts on fire
Bring more oil, bring
More oil...

Part 1

"Home, is where one starts from"[1]

A letter

Dear Unknown Friend,

There is a word on this keyboard, the one I am using to write this letter, to the right of my hand. It says "home" and if I press it the cursor is taken instantly back to the place where it began. If only the spiritual life were that simple! Nonetheless, dear Unknown Friend, this book comes to those who look for that key. The return Home is rarely so rapid; for most of us that longing, that empty space that aches to be filled, that something that we feel in the depths of our being must be that there is "more than this" lurks waiting. Waiting to have the ignition button pressed and for the long, slow, joyful-painful burn to get under way. There comes a time when beneath the protecting or imprisoning shell we get a sense that it's time to break loose, to set out and face the ocean of possibility in calm or storm. For me, it felt like a neck wrenching handbrake turn in an old car, or a sudden scary skid on ice – the loss of control, complete and entire when you end up, if you are lucky, with the deep relief that you can breathe again as you are brought to halt facing the wrong way and all your life has flashed before you and death may be more than facing you. Life after this is never quite the same again.

It certainly was not so when some 25 years ago I hurtled through that particular spiritual crisis known as burnout, cracking the familiar shell of who I thought I was. It could have been countless other things, those moments in time that change us, make us take stock, pull us around to another way of being. Moments when truth and illusion, after vying for authority down a lifetime, break the old truce and one finally gains the upper hand, and the truth is what sets us free. That freedom does not always feel welcome. The chains may be gone, the door of the cell burst wide open, but better the devil you know...A creature long caged may be surprisingly unwilling to run free into the unknown; the cage may be cramped, but it's a safe cage. It keeps things out, as well as in.

It can happen in a moment, it can be the long slow curve of a lifetime, or it may never happen at all, for some never turn while others have never quite moved off in the first place – away from Home. I have encountered many people in my lifetime who seem to have always felt at home in the Friend, the One, the Absolute, God. They appear to have no memory of ever having fallen from that Source and felt no need to search. But for most of us the fall away from Home happens early on, and the quest begins to find our way back at any point in our lives, not necessarily with the spiritual kick to our psyche that a sudden crisis can bring.

This book is about that journey Home, that urge to seek something which we know is there but which has sometimes lain long forgotten at the back of the mind, on the tip of the tongue not quite able to be expressed, some irrepressible urge barely touched upon. Or sometimes driving us on powerfully and unaccountably – where? The search for that "something other", the numinous or the *mysterium tremendum*, seems to be a primary quality of what it is to be human. That sense of a loss of Eden provokes in us all the desire for Home, where we were at one. We are all here to reclaim that Home, it is our birthright.

Much of our secular, materialist, technocratic society regards such a searching in varying degrees along a continuum from toleration, to irrelevant to slightly odd to dangerous. Faith, worship, spirituality, mysticism have been cleansed from our culture in so many ways that it is left mutilated rather than free. Those who pursue such things are often viewed as outdated or deluded. Already dear Unknown Friend, by picking up this book you have marked yourself out as slightly weird, a little odd. The spiritual search is not for the faint-hearted and it is certainly not seen as relevant in many dominant parts of our culture. The spiritual seeker commonly feels somewhat alien to prevailing mores, at least at the beginning, until the work of maturation and integration enable us to live in the world with equanimity, compassion and understanding. Spiritually mature persons may be judged quite crazy by the rest of society, because their values often stand in contrast to what the rest of the world says is true. Film star Bette Davies remarked[2] that "Old age ain't no place for cissies" – the same might be said of the place of spiritual enquiry. However, dear Unknown Friend, welcome to the deviants' club! But know that millions of others, who do not speak of it, are searching too. You are not alone. To want to see beyond the self may be regarded as beyond the pale in some quarters, but in others to not want to see is the madness.

I recall feeling at Home as a child, a sense of being safe and at one with the world that was only in part cultivated by the safe working class background into which I was born. In 1949, England was still emerging from the aftermath of war, but it was a time for working class kids like me of unprecedented opportunity rooted in a diminution of fear. For millions of kids from poor backgrounds the great reforming Labour government of the post war era was creating opportunities on a scale unimagined. For the first time, huge numbers of parents like mine no longer had the same relentless financial anxieties associated with homelessness, ill health, lack of education, unemployment and other dark horses that lurked in the psyches of the poor – for the state was building houses, providing health care, education and social benefits at hitherto impossible levels. Kids like me were to grow up in a world transformed because fear of finding the money to pay for schooling or health and other basic needs no longer depended on savings, if you had them, or charity, if you could find it.

And at the same time the freedom from fear was to be part of the breaking down of the old order that was to see decades of social transformation under way. The certainties of my parents – of knowing your place, of being defined by what the established order of class or religion or government and other part of the establishment furnished you with; all these were to begin their dissolution. For more people than ever before the influences of change in the decades to follow, still running their course to the present day, moved millions of people from defining themselves objectively, by what society told us we were, to subjectively, by using our own feelings to define who we were. This subjective turn[3] unleashed and was itself unleashed by forces at work in the world that were to affect above all the religious/spiritual backdrop into which I and millions of others emerged. The search for the "I am" in this post-modern world was to be found less and less in the givens of a particular religion into which you might be born, but by the fruits of a personal interior search and often outside that religion.

My mum always said I was a daydreamer, for I recall hours as a child spent just staring at the sky, or the trees in the garden or lying in the grass. I could not explain then, but I was not daydreaming, my mind was not wandering off into some fantasy land; I was simply feeling utterly present in those moments. I did not have the words to express that I was feeling completely at Home, at one with everything, in Love - the presence of something that was both within and without me. In this Presence, the world continued around me and I felt both part of it and witness to it. I thought everybody felt like this, experienced the world like this, but if they did they never said so. We are here to remember that we are bearers of that Presence, One, God. This too is our birthright.

At the time, on the few occasions I attempted to explain what was going on in me, I was dismissed or judged strange, until I began to think that it must be me that was in the wrong, that the way others saw the world must be the right way, simply because they said so and they were grown ups and there were more of them than me. When I grew up and shared these intimations the response in some quarters was the same, except by then, armed with psychology or physiology, it was more barbed – that it was something to do with my poor parental relationships, or the search for a loving father I did not really have at home, or a flush of endorphins in the brain. So I learned to shut up about it, and even forget about it. Thus the seeds of separation were sown, the road to Home-lessness set down. Only later in life, as I met many seekers along the way, did I discover that what I felt as a child was felt by many others too. That for all kinds of reasons the "I" that I was to become (or who I thought I was) and the world had conspired to push or pull me away from Home - for a while.

In the Jewish mystical tradition it is said that we know God in the womb and then start to forget after we are born. We fall at birth, or maybe not long after, into forgetting or perhaps are pushed there by life's painful experiences or the demands of simply growing up and learning to fit in. The essence of this book will be in exploring how we remember. How as we shift into adulthood, our own personal story determines how we respond to that forgetting and to the world, with love or fear, with hope or despair with a consciousness of Yes or No. Often our social and educational systems reinforce the forgetting, knocking us ever more into the No place instead of the Know place where we drown out the original wisdom embedded in us. However, a point of disillusionment sooner or later turns up in our lives, the point when we start to seek new answers. The old way of being, seeing and doing no longer suffices and the seeds of the soul are stirred, pushing up to a new life, so that we may start to expand beyond the limitations that our personhoods have incubated.

This book is rooted, dear unknown Friend, not only in my personal experience of the collapse of who I thought I was and the tentative awakening to who I might be (with the passage through the times of stillness and turbulence in the journey between the two) but also the many others with whom I have shared and worked down the years. Each passed in their own unique way along the same trajectory. It was in part their promptings, dear Unknown Friend, that suggested this book if written might help others. In the mountains where I live the wise person does not set off without map and compass. Beautiful as they are, they can be dangerous.

So this book comes to you based on the richness of experience and a diverse range of approaches to spiritual awakening grounded in the wisdom of the perennial philosophy. I'm not so sure, dear Unknown Friend, that I will be saying anything new. Truth is truth, but each generation must express this truth in its own way, for its time, in the eternal search. For some of us that search for Home is a deepening in life of something we have never lost, for others it is seeking something new when our earliest sense of home no longer fulfils, to others it is a return to what was known, but seen again and known differently.

This book is also for those like me who are or have been in exile. Who might feel no allegiance to or feel cut off from a particular tradition, yet are seeking heartfully nonetheless. Perhaps you are on the threshold of spiritual enquiry or of a religion, or feel cut off completely. It can be hard to be associated with religion these days; it gets such a bad press and is blamed for all the ills of the world. And true, religious organisations have often become corrupted and fed that perception. Religions can seek to serve God; but the will to power, which can mask itself as religion, can corrupt the soul's longing into its own ego ends. Much of "Old Age" religion reeks of this while much of the "New Age" movement is about building up the power of the ego, not demolishing it. We will explore more about these issues later as well as, dear Unknown Friend, even looking at the pros and cons of being part of a religion or otherwise in the search.

Meanwhile, perhaps you have done a lot of spiritual work, but are wondering now "what next", or have become disheartened. Perhaps you are looking for something new, or to deepen and strengthen what is already yours. Whatever your hope, dear Unknown Friend, my hope is that these notes made along my own way may inspire and nourish you along yours. Simone Weil writes of those who are "unable to cross the threshold"[4] of faith, the "immense and unfortunate multitude of unbelievers" who are by accident or design on the margins of religions, and questing sincerely nonetheless. I hope this book may help you, dear Unknown Friend, to get clearer about the way for you, about what barriers to cross, what thresholds if any to step over. Some, as we shall see, see the spiritual seeker as someone trying to find comforters to dull the pain of being in the world. But to call somebody spiritual does not invoke some mysterious non-natural way of being, divorced from everyday experience. It is to posses qualities of life, love, compassion, acceptance, non-attachment that engage us *more* in life, but more sensitively, more aware. Soul and spirit are not false, unreal, separate realms but true in their own way and deeply embedded in the human experience.

What then is this Home of which I write, dear Unknown Friend? It has many names and many genders. Theologians have dissected it; philosophers pronounced upon it; mystics have immersed themselves in it; some scientists dismissed it. It is the One, the Absolute, The Friend, God – the Source of All from which we came and to which we will return. For some even the word or notion of God is itself an obstruction. We will look in detail about how to respond to our difficulty around the G word (itself a spiritual practice) and it is difficulties like these that are the ruts along the way Home.

Home is mirrored in some ways in the ordinary home we try to make for our everyday lives, a place of safety, security, individual expression, relating. It is reflected in the childhood household into which we are born and which, if we are so blessed, was a place of love and security, but from which all of us must depart if we are to emerge as fully human. Then perhaps long after the departure, when we have individuated, found the job or relationship or whatever other personal goals we had have now been met, or maybe whilst in the midst of the finding, there are moments of ripeness. Perhaps just one, perhaps many in one lifetime, but moments when we are ready to turn, to become more aware, to shift the way we are in the world and try to get a little closer to something that we had forgotten or pushed to one side for a while. Something for which we had been nonetheless quietly waiting in the right moment to command our attention. An adaptation from a website prayer[5] offers us some of the reference points for the map we will be exploring:-

Home is the cradle of life
Home gives the gift of self
Home is where we find one another
Home is the space of our intimacy
Home is the harbour of our security
Home is the shelter of our growth
Home is the sanctuary of our love
Home is the treasury of our memories
Home is the temple of God's presence
Home is the warm hearth of our love
Home is the heart of all our longings
Home is the hand of forgiveness
Home is the source of all healing

In this book I offer more explanation of what it is to seek and find Home, whilst being mindful that the journey there (and it feels like a journey for a while) is not without its cul-de-sacs, lost directions and even intersections of danger. In the pages that follow there are examples from real life, stories from wise teachers and suggestions for bringing ever greater depth, integrity and authenticity as we draw ever nearer to Home on the Way. Each of us will experience Home in our own unique way. I offer no prescription of what religion to follow, no image if any of God that is right or wrong. With over six billion of us on the planet we cannot all stand in precisely the same place as each other and see the Divine from exactly the same angle. The image will be unique even in some small way to each of us. I do not say, this is the Way and this is the only Way. In the spiritual supermarket we are spoilt for choice, but I may make some recommendations on the quality of the goods on offer, how to discern what is worth buying and what to leave on the shelves.

Four significant approaches to Soul Care, to nourishing ourselves in the search, are summarised. They are more, dear Unknown Friend, than spiritual exercises to solve life's problems or make us feel good. Their substance is in the way they encourage us to make a conscious participation in the search for God, the Friend, to get out of the way so that the Divine can speak to us. And see how I have already slipped again into using the G word quite readily! What is your response to that? Perhaps you are comfortable with it, perhaps curious, indifferent or hostile? Stay with me, we shall use that response to inform us in these pages. Your reaction may already be a way in which the Friend is speaking to you.

When we start to "listen", how we "hear" the Divine "speaking" to us is unlimited in its possibilities. From a hunch or intuition, to "hearing" a still, small voice within, from the advice of a soul friend to the inspiration of a beautiful day, from the dirt in the street to an inspiring piece of music, from a profound piece of scripture to a silly programme on the TV. We are surrounded by, in, the divine consciousness knowing itself. It floods relentlessly into our awareness at every level if we are open to it. The four soul paths outlined in this book help us to access that awareness, and to be the sources by which we discern the true from the false, the mystical from the psychotic.

We will explore, dear Unknown Friend, how we try to drown (sometimes literally in alcohol or suicide) a life without meaning, a life of essential separation, to fill up the hole in ourselves from which we have emptied God. But does it have to be God? Will not politics or social action or material gain satisfy? Yes to the first question and No to the second, as we shall explore.

All things must pass. In a life lived however fully engaged in the world, there is the undercurrent acknowledged or not that it will all pass away, we must pass away. No matter how we dress it up in confidence that "this is all there is" or "I am happy to live my life, I don't need a God or an afterlife." – somewhere beneath lurks the unconscious unyielding despair that denial of the numinous feeds on. The Absolute does not pass. In God there is no end (for us) and in the Divine we find the Life that is full, in this life and beyond. And if we do not seek flight from the world or resignation (masked as acceptance, but maybe really resignation that is saying yes to hopelessness), then the other way is to seek power in the world. If there is no God then we make ourselves God, and therein lies almost all the misery that has crashed upon humanity down the ages (including the perversion of God and religion, in the hands of those who are ignorant and have not done the deep inner work) in the pursuit of our own will to power.

This God, dear Unknown Friend, is not as we shall see some panacea, some trick of the mind to fill a hole in our consciousness, to wall out the despair of the world, of mortality, which might otherwise encroach upon us. This God, this Divine, this Absolute, this Friend is real. It is not the God of the atheist recently given much publicity, or interpreted from many scriptures, who damns and destroys upon a whim, not a fabrication of the unconscious making a honey pot to sweeten the bitterness of birth and death. For birth and death are of the body, held in the Divine, a life lived in space and time which dissolving in its own time frees the soul completely towards Home.

Many times in this book we will speak of God, and perhaps we will edge a little closer to knowing the One who, simply by picking up this book, may be calling you Home. That which radiates from God, that invisible, unconquerable magnetic pull, grace, the Holy Spirit, the divine energy, the source is already working its way in you. And what is God, dear Unknown Friend? For the one on whom this book focuses, on which our being and belonging have their Home, is the hidden guest behind this book. God is the ever present one at the party, the Friend of all, whom no one remembers inviting but is too polite to suggest otherwise. Nietzsche argued that "He who has a "why" to live can bear almost any "how""[6]. In being and belonging we find the answer to the "why" on which we can base our values for living. In coming Home we seek that answer, and perhaps find that it is also about seeing what life expects from us rather than what we expect from life. Perhaps we also learn along the way that it is not so much a matter of being a Christian, Jew, Moslem, Hindu, Sikh or whatever (for these too are ultimately just labels, useful identities to find our way in the world) as forever becoming one of these. In the endless becoming on the way Home, we are never a "this" or a "that" but always expanding into the infinity that is the Divine, of being "work in progress."

God is the one desire whom almost everyone avoids at some point, if not always, in our lives. He (sic) is the one whom you are sure is there in the mist of time but cannot see. He is not he, nor she, nor it, for God is beyond gender yet is in all genders, contained by none for all genders are held in Him, and yet, forgive me, I call Him He from time to time for after many years of cultural influence, theology, debate, dissonance, gender analysis, doubt, discussion I ended up at the same place. Call Him what pleases you dear Unknown Friend, it does not matter to me and it certainly does not matter to God. And I do not see him perched on a cloud, bearded, grey and English, firing spiteful thunderbolts at anyone as His fancy takes Him, anyone who dares to step out of line. He is not fixed in heaven, or standing outside of hell. He is in all things yet contained by none, for all things have their existence in Him; as do you and I, dear Unknown Friend. Heaven is not above nor hell below, in a geographical, astronomical sense, but in a conscious sense where the lower is a concept of density, darkness, (apparent) absence of God and the higher is the lighter, open, overt presence of God, but these are only perceptions. They are states of mind, labels, made by frantic minds demanding fixity that cannot deal with the numinous and nebulous, with paradox, with grey areas, with mystery, with the mystical truth of God. He is nothing, no-thing, although we seek to place Him, boxed and coxed, in an earthly landscape dressed and acting to plan (our plan).

The God I used to know was introduced to me at Church and school. He was remote, intimidating and seemed forever to be angry with the Jews or being nice to them according to his whim. He was not interested in the pain and suffering that, even as a child, I was witnessing in the world. He was constantly finding fault with you, meting out punishment and telling you how wrong you were. He sent his child into the world with the expressed intent of getting him killed, and set up Judas as the fall guy who didn't seem to stand a chance. He was there backing wars, the monarchy, the police, schoolteachers and every other part of the establishment I encountered, but seemed to not give a damn about the victims of war, or famine, or the unemployed or the homeless. He was a ruler hitting your hand or a cane across your bottom in class. He was a lonely room at home where you were sent because he didn't like what you had done. He owned lots of buildings that were empty most of the time. He expected you to give him money or whatever else you had although he owned everything anyway. He liked some people, especially ladies who wore hats and went to church on Sunday. He did not like young men with spots, those who had long hair and those who thought about what was underneath girls' sweaters. He disapproved of sex and come to that of anything that seemed fun, exciting, colourful or joyful. He liked white people best, and white men were his favourites especially if they were kings or policemen or headmasters. He liked men and women who married and lived together forever and had 2.3 children in semi-detached houses and had nice cars. He did not like single girls who got pregnant, anyone who enjoyed sex either solo or with someone else and especially a same sex someone else. He ignored anyone who was not English, people with old bangers or who lived in terraced houses with outside toilets. He was forever meting our judgements while wagging his finger and was waiting to give me hell (literally) when I died unless I pulled my socks up (also literally).

When this God died to me I came to know another. This God, my Friend (as the poet Rumi often calls him) I know is in this moment, with me now as I write these words, is the sitting, is the writing, is simply known and being known, the whole universe, every universe, is a mirror to God knowing God. He is neither he, nor she, nor it and all and none of these, yet I am stuck most times with "He" who smiles at my efforts and still loves me. This God I know is all and none, the single and the general, everywhere and nowhere. He has no face yet everywhere I turn I see his face. He is light containing all light; brilliant, impenetrable, and would blind me were my in-sight not veiled by Him, or me. He is also dark, darkness itself, unknowable, hidden; yet His darkness is luminous and here He reveals Himself as well. He is in all things yet possessed by none and contained by none; and all things are contained in Him, the creation is *panentheism*. This God I know is transcendent and beyond me, yet immanent and personal. He does not exist. Yes God does not exist, for created things have their own existence and to say that God exists in the sense that you and I exist is to make a creature of God. It is to place God in time and space and existence, but all time and space and existence are in God, the timeless. He is no-thing, shrouded in myth and mystery, yet accessible, reachable. He does not so much act and do or love, for this God I know is at once beyond loving, moving and doing, yet He *is* the loving, the moving and the doing. He is remote beyond my comprehension, yet closer to me than my own breath. He is father, mother, brother, sister, lover, friend, enemy; in the dance of my relationship with him he is that and not that. This God I know loves boundlessly, infinitely, wastefully all creation; none specially, all uniquely. This God I know loves unconditionally all things excluding no one and no thing, pouring out this love for all who wish to drink. This God I know is the source of all knowing and knows all, yet still I pray. This God I know requires nothing, not least worship, adoration or acknowledgment, yet still I offer them. This God I know loves believers and unbelievers in equal measure; known or not known, summoned or denied, He is always present. This God I know is the one in whose heart all is well, all that is right and wrong, saint and evildoer, good and bad, loving and fearful; all is gathered and made whole. This God I know loves with infinite, timeless patience, waiting in and out of time for all to open and awaken to love and come Home.

Perhaps, dear Unknown Friend, my brief foray in the previous two paragraphs about the God I knew and the God I know rings some bells for you. Perhaps there are similarities between my childhood experience and the God who sometimes dies when we grow up. In the end, they are all words, perceptions, struggling to make sense of something that is no thing. The Divine is incomprehensible to human thought except by metaphor and allusion, which is why only the poets and musicians seem to get close. Facts do not work for God, He is not fully found in literal truth, in reason or science for reason and science and facts are found in Him. But perhaps in mythology and the artist lies the secret, for while we cannot say what it is to know God, we can know what it "feels" with the eye of the heart, for He cannot be reified and objectified, even by naming Him God.

Facts seek to tell us what we know about the Divine, myth and art tell us what it feels like to know. With millions beyond numbering down the ages I seek Him. I do not assume Him to be there, or reason that he is there; I know him to be there. My eyes would burn out if turned upon Him, yet still I see Him with the only way left to me; to see, or rather to feel, His presence. Mirrored in the creation, I see His face no matter which way I turn; every face and no face, shimmering in all things yet invisible, tantalisingly close to focus yet lost the moment the eyes attempt to turn directly to Him. He is heard in the silent universe, this vast theophany, where each star and each molecule, each cell and beast, each grain and mountain when asked, "Who is God?" responds "I am". He is seen with the eye of my heart, where each moment breathed is full of that Presence which says only one thing, "I love you". He is the eternal I Love You, for that is His nature, the I Love You from which all creation pours and into which it returns. All the creation sings I Love You, for that is His song.

The God I know is big enough to embrace the possibility of his own non-existence and thus He is not offended by atheists or is a friend only to those who acknowledge Him. He "knows" but not in the way that you and I know and is beyond ego concepts like offence. God does not demand worship or power or anything else, indeed does not demand at all for He simply Is, what? Abundant love that pours from the heart of the Divine, radiating into every nook and cranny in the creation, so abundant it pours wastefully into where it is not recognised, for Love from the infinite is not wasted, for waste is to suggest limitation, ultimate shortage. There is no shortage in God. And He is no spiritual bully, does not force Himself where He is not wanted – we have that freedom, though perhaps an illusion of freedom. The soul longs for God, and seems to have ways of bypassing the ego and inviting God in. The unconcious can subvert ego power and lead us into situations where God breaks in. We may think that we are unwillingly "zapped", as seems to happen to some people, but the openness to intervention may be more subtle.

However, this is not to say conversely that God is some spiritually passive entity waiting for us all to eventually wake up by our own efforts. Grace, the Divine saving and strengthening influence, is radiating constantly into our lives. The Holy Spirit, God is spiritually acting in the creation, pouring in love to draw us Home. The heart and soul are not without attunement to this, for they are locked onto God, are of God, more certain than any "satnav", they know where Home is and someday they will go there. The ego, the personhood, the mind product, that collection of identities and drives that we call ourselves and which we may believe for a while has an existence of its own (ah, the seduction of power!) can do all in its power to hold back the inevitable, but give way it must. The spirit of God may even move in behind the ego's back, when the heart calls it in. In the purification from the power of the ego and the strengthening by spirit, the attunement of heart and soul to their source is ever more finely directed to the Source.

He is the one who loves us so greatly, for love is His nature, that we were let go so that we could leave Home. And He is the one in eternal waiting for each prodigal son and daughter to return, wealthy with all that we have been, impoverished of all we thought we were. He is the One who has manifested Himself in the earthly realm, as Himself, the One known in saints and holy men and women; and the broken and the disreputable. He is the One ever present but never seen, the invisible guide hidden in the fog of the life that is not life, until Life that is beyond life bursts through and we weep at the wonder of our immortality. And the soul is so safe, for the we who we think we are does not own it. What does not belong to us but is of God cannot be sold or destroyed. Your soul, dear Unknown Friend, is indeed of God, and God being infinite so the soul is a hologram of that infinity, imbued with boundless possibility.

Dear Unknown Friend, perhaps my words have provoked in you the question of how you see God. No two of us see Him in exactly the same way. To some he is she or it, almighty and unknowable, perhaps a little scary, to others intimate and the closest Friend. There is a Sufi story of a group of people blindfolded and taken to meet an elephant for the first time. The one who touches the trunk thinks the elephant is like a snake, the one who takes the tail thinks it is like a rope. One touches a leg and declares the elephant is like a tree. Likewise, no one of us can see or know all that is God, although perhaps the mystics come closest, in whose and in which experience they, and perhaps we, are dissolved in union with the Divine. However, after a while, experience suggests we may lose the desire to describe the whole of God anyway. Perhaps God is simply not to be known intellectually, but to be experienced.

Even as I write this it's quite possible that another universe has burst into being, and another and another, for He is so vast, His being unlimited. He is so tiny as to be in each cell of my skin, each breath, in the space between thought. In His remoteness is His profound intimacy, and thus He is not just the transcendent, unknowable, ground of being, he is also closer to me than myself, felt and held, if anywhere in my heart, where He is personal, knowable, feelable. He loves me and you dear Unknown friend, intimately and personally, for that is His nature, it could not be otherwise. He comes to us in whatever way we feel we can see Him, and enters only invited entering what is His own anyway. There is nowhere that He is not, and there is no one that is closed to Him. Nobody gets into heaven, Ram Dass once told me. Look at that phrase again dear Unknown Friend and let its teasing truth roll around for a while. For while we are busy being a somebody, full, literally of ourselves, our identities, then we remain in separation. To become no-body (Ah, to surrender so fully!) we find that Nobody does indeed get Home! And surrender to the Divine is either full or not; it cannot be conditional for that then is not full surrender.

When we are ready for Home we have let go of the desire to be a "me", have surrendered our will so completely that "somebody" is annihilated in God. All that we thought we were is surrendered and the soul completes its journey Home, being in Him, immortal, invisible, self and selfless. Soul work is not about going "up" to heaven but "down" into ourselves and strangely enough we find heaven is there. It is the *"kenosis"*, the emptying of the self in order to find the Self. In surrendering our identity to God we do not lose our freedom to be ourselves, we find it. It is the *fana' fi-l llah* of the Sufi's, the annihilation of everything into the beauty of the Divine, beyond limited concepts of existence. On the Way Home, the somebody that we have been with all its labels, man or woman, shopkeeper or surgeon, Christian or Hindu, all the legion faces of the person, all are surrendered. Wealthy in identity, we do not get through the eye of the needle. Refined and surrendered of identity, we re-find our true identity, free of substance like the One from which we came, the tiniest door of time is now open to us.

Nobody gets into heaven is not a council of despair but of joy! And thus the great paradox, in losing ourselves, we find our Self, at Home. Identities are useful to making our way in the world, but they are not who we are. When we discover our true identity in our Source, then we are set free. All names, all states, all experiences lead here.

Thus may this book be a guide and comforter dear Unknown Friend, as you follow the Way - Home.

Seek the One, seek Home, dear Unknown Friend. There's nothing else!

Yours in anticipation

A

Friend

...Sometimes the light was so close
So very close
That flesh seemed thin.
Sometimes high
Like the noontime over a summer lake.
Sometimes dim,
Like a waning moon behind a vapour trail.
Words slip out
And crack like paving stones
Under the tracks of Krishna's tanks.
Each thought broken
In the pointless shards exploring
The truth
That there is nothing to say.
And oh the perfection,
Whole in its partial wrong,
Whole in its partial right,
Made clear in the crucible of our despair
Burnished in the furnace of our hopes
And dreams,
Our dreams great and small
All dreams.
It was
And is
And shall be
all a dream.
Be reasonable Buddha,
The night is long
And the lamps we strap unto ourselves
Grow dim.
Is there no one with a light to help?
We cannot break the chain
The rust has set its links.
Surely it's time for tea?
If there is no God, is there no help?
No milk or sugar
Please.

He missed the point, I'm sure
He missed the point.
Suffering does not come from attachment
to possessions, relationships or events
Or even the gifts on the Christmas tree,
But detachment
From You.
We feed the million hungry ghosts
The compulsion
Of the blackbird
Stuffing the beaks of chicks
In the nest by the cherry tree.
She dies
Eroded by labour in the summer heat.
The soul starved of You
Waits
For the next season
Or the next.
And sometimes
When feeling lucky or
Maybe on a day when the police stop you for speeding or
Maybe when you miss your train or
During a treat when the chocolate tastes especially good
Sometimes
Just sometimes
We wake up...

Part 2

"Adam and Eve were driven from the Garden of Eden because the kind of knowledge they reached for – a knowledge that distrusted and excluded God. Their drive to know arose not from love but from curiosity and control, from their desire to posses powers belonging to God alone. They failed to honour the fact that God knew them first, knew them in their limits as well as their potential. In their refusal to know as they were known, they reached for a kind of knowledge that always leads to death" [7]

Leaving Home

The council estate of immaculate gardens and red brick houses that shone in the rain gave way to Cemetery Road. Here, as a small child, I felt I could breathe. Here the built area had not invaded. A small farm and open fields had somehow eluded the planners and developers and factory builders, leaving a green island bounded by the grey slate roofs and forests of mill chimneys which encircled it. Here were skylarks; I would watch them rise, singing, and sometimes even into my late teens I would lie for hours beneath them in wonder, hymns with wings on blue sky summer days. In this space it always seemed lighter, open, more free. There was a view, and the sound of wind in the trees and the mystery of long grass. Black and white cattle watched you watching them. On a summer's day the sky was endless, in grey wild winter it pressed down on the terraces and gunmetal streets far off. It was a place where somehow I could feel my own breath, as if some restraining corset had been removed and, unleashed, something inner seemed to soar and roll. Here I was happy, perhaps I was happy elsewhere, but here I knew I was.

I cannot offer a deprivation narrative. My family was poor, my mother a hard working coper and my father remote in job and booze and betting shop. It was not expressly loving, but it was good and warm enough. I was safe and well fed (on a diet so high in animal fat and carbohydrate it might in other times constitute child abuse!) and the first of that generation born into the reforming times after the Second World War that was to open up, for working class kids like me, horizons about which parents had never dared dream.

It was a time of transformation, for the culture and community that at once held and nurtured me also restricted and repressed me. For thousands of my generation and background, better fed, educated and housed than any before, the walls were about to give way; the sheltering walls, the imprisoning walls. Church was one of them; most people belonged to one church or another. English society at every level was wrapped up in it, it was almost obligatory. I arrived into a world where religion, as never before, was about to become an option, a personal choice, and not something you had to do because that was what you were supposed to do. This was the time that was to give birth to a movement, the post-modern, the desire to break free from old places and old bonds and old customs, some forever, but not necessarily for better, as John Lennon was to sing. Out of this milieu grew the revolutionary movements of the 1960s, the summer of love, the shaken and stirred cultural norms where old certainties of church and state, of social conventions from cradle to grave were never to be the same again. This was the era in which the "subjective turn"[8] was born, that time when an enormous cultural shift accelerated, long in the germinating, when who we were in the world was to be changed. Here the fermentation was under way where we were no longer to be defined by whatever way the law or the church or society or the community or the elite or whatever objective other cared to define us, which had been hitherto largely accepted, but by our own self, the subjective, the I, me, mine of self definition, on a scale unparalleled.

Thus the organised religions became increasingly sidelined, just one view among many. My generation and those that have followed it have grown up in this world of apparent self definition. It is a world of "believing without belonging"[9], the apparent freedom to pursue our own spirit without boundaries or rules. It is a reaction in the post-modern world to the totalitarianism of the modern; perceived as rational, systematic, logical, and progressive. This modern world view arguably reached its apogee in the cataclysm of the Second World War where totalitarian systems clashed and crashed in appalling destruction. The post-modern world set to liberate us from this "cold and cerebral" way of seeing humanity "by injecting a sense of choice and even playfulness"[10] Out of this grew the unwillingness to define moral absolutes, of holistic thinking, the ecology and many personal liberation movements, a wariness of logical thinking and "progress". But is this a real escape or a way of avoiding difficult questions? Is it a new way of action or a retreat into self indulgence? Is it freedom from totalitarian religion or unwillingness to take on the tough spiritual work of being in long term communion with and commitment to fellow travellers? Has religion really been abandoned, or have we created a whole new religion, the New Age?

While the New Age may not fit traditional patterns of religious governance and organisation it seems to have its own rules, moral codes, puritanical attitudes and approved behaviours that are nonetheless a religion by any other name. There may not be an Archbishop of Glastonbury, but there is a plethora of New Age teachers, writers and pundits whose courses, written and spoken words are followed with religious almost awe-like fervour. Yet they seem to possess no foundations that are firm, tested and rooted in spiritual truths that have taken millennia to grow. We may lay claim to individual freedom, but seem consciously or unconsciously willing to surrender that freedom to the latest fad, to style rather than substance, to the superficial rather than the deep, to the new rather than the tried and tested. In the flight from "meta-narratives", all embracing world views, spirituality and religion are split into endlessly competing camps of seemingly equally valid viewpoints. We may celebrate the choice and diversity, but this may come at a price of great spiritual confusion, lack of firm ground, and sloppy ethical systems. The open vista of freedom may in fact be a spiritual waste land (see Part 3) where we can pillage a bit from one faith, a bit from another, a bit from this or that currently trendy guru and construct something that keeps our personal, subjective inclinations happy. However, this may bring with it an atomised spiritual world, where "doing your own thing" overrides collective action, negates individual and collective responsibility, abandons rites of passage which hold families and communities together and give us a sure foothold, and reduces self definition to "I shop, therefore I am". Individualism is a blessing in that it helps to keep us safe from oppressive groups, a curse when it keeps us from connecting and working collectively with others.

But I return to a small boy, in grey flannel short trousers held up with braces. His shirt has a badly fitting collar, short ankle socks and brown crepe soled sandals; Brylcreem flattens his hair and a little quiff has been added at the front. Time for church, with mum and dad, yet I have no other memories of church with them but this one. It's Sunday and for some reason the memory is of Pentecost, although I was only maybe six or seven and cannot say the occasion fits with that word, for it was only decades later that I came to know what Pentecost is. It is also linked to Passover, and being passed over was about to take on new meaning for me. Wesley Methodist Church was full, as it always was in those days (sleepy then in its certainty, unaware of the mass evacuation to come by the next generation). The service progressed and I have no particular recollection of its content, except perhaps the same tedium I experienced in every childhood church service, expressed in kicking legs and "ants in your pants" wriggling with threateningly whispered "keep still" or "behave" from mum and dad.

The time for communion arrives and we shuffle forward to the altar rail. There's a man in a black suit and some sort of something going on but I can't make head or tail of it. The queue shrinks and I am kneeling down, mum to the left dad to the right. They kneel with hands cupped and raised. I do the same. I watch it all, head bowed, through screwed up eyelids, searching from side to side. The man in black drops a little cube of white bread in my dad's hands, says something about it being a bit of Jesus' body and I am confused – by what little I know about Jesus and the idea of somebody giving you a bit of a human body, which it patently wasn't but probably a bit of Warburton's white sliced. The man in black passes over me and offers the same to my mum. I am ignored. I feel profoundly confused, emotions run riot but I am not sure what they are – only later when fully grown do I make sense of them: lost, shamed, ignored, angry, sad, cut off...I do not think in my short years that I had ever been hit with such emotional turmoil. I wondered what I had done wrong, what was wrong with me, and it had to be my fault of course. The man in black returns, this time with a shiny silver cup which he holds to my dad's lips. He takes a sip, words about Jesus and this time blood. The image of Jesus' blood in that cup knocks me into deeper confusion. I can't see it, but there's a hint of red on the edge of dad's lips. I am passed over again. The same words, mum drinks too.

What set in then was panic that there must be something very bad about me, that I am being cut off because I am not good enough and my mind races to think of something I must have done to deserve this punishment. And it felt like punishment, like the time I was sent to bed without biscuits because I had been naughty. The reason escapes me, my mum telling me off for being bad always seemed confusing to me. Inside there is a kind of splitting feeling, like some part of me that feels at home in myself and the world, and some other part fierce and strong that has a power of its own. A power rooted and growing in something as yet quite inexplicable, never hitherto quite so deeply experienced, yet willing to break away, to go its own way for that way would lie power and safety and separateness, away, yes away on the deep and hurling wave that is fear, mighty enough to tear that childhood sense of OKness in the world and into a final sense that would be the seedbed of my experience of the world in my early adult life – that I was a thing of separateness. Pulled away from something in which I felt inherently at one, worthy, loved, in that moment was deep realisation of the cruelty of the world; the birth of suffering and disconnection. Some part of me had broken loose from the child I had been. It was that moment in the Garden of Eden repeated in every life down the millennia, the moment when we become aware of our sense of self, of our own essential isolation cut off from that idyllic place where the world seemed one and, despite the niggling events of childhood, from which I had until now not finally made the break. Feeding on the soil of fear, the polar opposite of the love that had hitherto bound me into a sense of oneness in the world, the "I" who I was to think I was for many a long year took root and grew into the man.

I did not know it at the time but this early experience, manifested in countless different guises but the same in its essence, is common to all human beings, for we all desire to be and to belong but must also separate. To not belong, to feel cast out, cut off, exiled, excommunicated, is one of our deepest fears. In fact the word fear (*d'hel*) in Aramaic (the common language of the people and which Jesus spoke)[11] has to do not with fear of death or pain or punishment, but with fear of being pushed out, driven away, and banished from home and family. In pre-modern cultures this was one of the greatest terrors, for there was no chance to hop on a train and go to another city. People largely lived and died locally in small family, tribal units. To be cast out from this meant the pain of living alone, a kind of death. In modern culture exclusion is still used as a means of control; some religious organisations (such as the Amish or Jehovah's Witnesses) and sects will "shun" people by ignoring them, cutting them off from normal social discourse or family and community connection if they have in some way transgressed the group's rules.

Each of us has our own unique breakpoint, sometimes sudden and shattering, sometimes slow to emerge, but the point is the same. A belief in a sense of on-your-own-ness out of which the individual is fashioned may be one of these. The sense of brokenness from an incomprehensible yet very real source can be so complete that our response to the world is to root ourselves ever more deeply in the fear from which it grows and go on the attack; pouring out our distress, quite unconsciously, on the rest of the world in our abuse of the creation, others, ourselves. The root of the violent response to the world lies here. Here also is the slow drip of the human condition, each drop falling into a bottomless chasm that never fills unless there is more − money, sex, booze; the pleasure principle filling the void, demanding ever more, relentless.

Thus was my earliest memory of the cruelty of separation, of being excluded from something; that first sense that, if I am here at all, I am here on my own. No matter what I might live or love, that undercurrent of loss would be ever present, and the fear of it drove countless joinings and separatings down the years all in search, consciously or unconsciously, of that oneness, that One. Was this just an illusion? Is there really no One, just a longing in a broken psyche for something lost, a substitute for love? Was the subsequent search an inevitable by-product of psychological maturation when we grow more deeply into our individuality? Was this merely a victimhood response, the realisation that I was no more than a random mass of atoms somehow and mysteriously formed in the world and cast out to find its way until at the end it dissipates and merges into the earth as if it had never been (except in the memory of those left behind)? "Is that all there is?"

Peggy Lee sang, and if "yes" is the answer, brings no response but to "break out the booze and just keep dancing"?[12] Or is that separation itself an illusion, that really Home is there all the time, a silent Presence nudging us back not into a place but into a state of awareness, sometimes imperceptibly, sometimes fiercely if we would but hear it. Does it pop into our lives down the years under countless guises? No bullying demands, no threats, just a patient invitation and waiting for us to come home, until the journey away has spun like some spiritual space probe, launching into the unknown until it reaches its apogee and the inevitable trajectory to base takes hold, returning with all that it has gathered along the way.

And almost fifty years later I am sitting in the abbey on Iona feeling like a circle, or at least an arm of a spiral, has been completed. I hung onto Christianity in my childhood and went through the motions of membership of the Methodist church, but my heart was never in it. Maybe I thought that if I said I believed and I belonged, with the latter arguably being the more important undercurrent, then I would eventually "get it" and feel safe and sound in my faith, in my family, my community, in the world – as everyone else seemed to be. (Later I learned that so many I met along the way were no more at Home than I; they had just learned to mask it better.) The teenage push and pull to break away accelerated me out of small-town England; at 18, leaving behind church and community, I set off. And after all it was the 60s and there was sex and drugs and rock and roll to discover. Yet in each encounter down the decades that followed, that empty place was yearning to be filled. Lovers, careers, material success, cars and clothes, all the usual hedonistic foods I consumed in abundance. Then when they did not satisfy and when the burnout crunch came, an overt spiritual search got under way with accelerating pace. The long buried hunger was now ravenous for satisfaction and I ate and drank long and deep in the quest to be full-filled. I passed through atheism and politics as solutions, soaked up the faith of the Hindus, Daoists and Buddhists. Wondered at Islam. Journeyed with shamans. Sat with Jews and Quakers, Zoroastrians, Alpha-coursers – every faith I can think of was picked up, chewed over, put down. I sat, too, at the feet of mighty teachers of spirit of world repute. I devoured every spiritual book I came across and supped every drop of the New Age brew in all its flavours. I stayed with some favourites; mixing and matching for a while. I tried drugs, dreams and deprivation in search of answers. I met people of great love and great evil, and walked into situations of great bliss and danger. I was blessed to have people along the way, especially one wise woman, to whom this book is dedicated, who stuck by me from the moment of the first painful awakening, to ease me, sometimes push me, along the path when it looked like I may veer off course into self-limitation or spiritual self-gratification.

I met a man of big love, Ram Dass, who came the closest I ever got to having a Guru. A woman, Mother Meera, teased for a while along the way with the remote unreachableness of her presence. I met a loving partner who kept me grounded on the earth. I encountered a woman who took me to the edge of reality. I had my personhood unpicked by a deft psychotherapist, my original intent uncovered by a loving astrologer, my awakenings questioned by a kindly "abba". In action, inaction and interaction with so many I learned the pleasures and pitfalls of the spiritual search.

When I was a kid that spiritual search was a one-stop shop with only one packet on sale – you could buy anything you wanted as long as it was Christian. Different flavours it was true, but much the same in essence. The explosion in world communications and travel within the lifetime of comfortably off westerners like me saw the old, safe corner shop put out of business. Mr. Thirkell's grocery on the corner of Ainsworth Road near my home in Radcliffe was but a short walk from my home for the essentials of life, with limited stock for limited people. The demise of his shop mirrored the demise of faith in my community, for by the 1960s he was to be swept away before the onslaught of the material supermarket, and the supermarket of the spirit which grew at the same time offered choices unheard of for those of my parents' generation. Now we can pick our religion like we can pick our pizza – a little bit of this and little bit of that according to personal taste. In the vast freedom to choose in the secular west, it is easier than it ever has been to seek out a faith, or none, that suits you. The trouble is (aye there's the rub) sometimes the freedom to choose is the freedom of the superficial. Spirituality becomes a dipping in to the bits we like, a dipping out of the bits we don't like when the going gets tough. Nobody ever said the spiritual search was easy, certainly not the great teachers on whose teachings the world's faiths are founded. Those who say it is easy peasy are probably the ones to walk away from. You can wander at leisure in the spiritual supermarket trying all the tastes on offer, but depth of spirit requires digging, discipline, dedication, direction – none of which are popular in a quick fix, celebrity obsessed, self-satisfying culture.

My dad would threaten to "beat the living daylights" out of me if I misbehaved. It was more threat than action, but let's look at that phrase. All of us experience things in life that beat, by fear and its various guises, the light out of us. Coming Home we dis-cover that light, that we are the light. Home? Our earthly home, if we are lucky, may be a place in childhood or adulthood where we feel safe, free from the challenges of the world, a place of respite where we can express ourselves, know intimacy, love, creativity. Home is the safe womb in which we rest, and from which we venture out into the world to do and to be. Safe and saved are closely related words. The earthly home of ordinary reality can be our sanctuary in the everyday world, and it's not surprising that we invest huge amounts of time, money and energy into seeking and maintaining a home. Freedom from want of a home is one of the foundation stones of human rights. But the earthly home must pass away; its nature is essentially transient. At any moment it can be taken from us. It may happen in the process of maturation as we leave home to establish our own place and relationships. It may happen through sudden financial crisis, ill health or disaster either natural or human made, that tears it away from us, perhaps forever. Our ordinary home is inherently temporary, no matter what securities we put in place to tell ourselves otherwise. Consciously or unconsciously this drives our search for ever more material security, for longevity, for perfect health, relationships, and finances. We can pour a lifetime's energy into meeting these goals only to find when we get there, that the goalposts are as far away as ever, that we can never have "enough", that safety, home, security are not absolutes no matter how hard we try. The home we make in ordinary reality is never permanent. At some level we know this however much we try to drown it out, and we expend so much of our lives trying to make it otherwise, all to no avail. Death and change are inevitable; indeed the Tibetan Buddhist Sogyal Rinpoche[13] wrote that these are the only certainties.

I think he is wrong. There is another certainty in which, when we look for and find another kind of Home even while we continue to participate in the world as usual, we discover something very special. And note it is to dis-cover, to remove the cover from something that by implication is already there. This is the Home all the great spiritual teachers offered us. It is to discover the "peace that surpasses all understanding" (Php. 4:7), the life that is the true life into which we have to be reborn, the life that does not pass away. This eternal, immortal Home is found when we realise that the life we live between womb and tomb is not the only life. The soul is of God, and being of God it is boundless and immortal as God is. And what is this God? It is love, not the mirror image of this love we have for persons or things, but a love that is the very source of the creation itself. When we fall into this love, or we work our way or are guided into it (if the approaches outlined in this book have any "goal" at all it is to help us get clear about these things) we come to know our Home that is not transient. It is here that we are "saved" as some traditions may term it, where we are "enlightened" – alight with awareness of reality, of the nature of the creation and our place in it, of the deep love that holds it all together. To be "saved" is to come to know that we are loved by God, the Divine, the Absolute, the One - no qualifications, no conditions, no limits, absolutely none. To know also that nothing, no thing, can separate us from that love. And we may literally feel and look "lighter" when we are thus saved – less careworn and anxious about the world as we come to live more in the moment and awareness.

There is a risk in the post-modern view that living "in the moment" or in the "power of now" is really a form of nihilism, of living without care for others, or the future or the past or the planet. For the "in the now" is just a perception, a facet of the eternal "now" that is contained like all time, in the Divine. Living in the moment of the love we find in eternity, yet grounded in our experience of space and time, the duality even as I have written it passes away where "all time is irredeemably present"[14]. In this "now" there is no escape from the ties of time and space, instead we come to live fully in them with love and compassion, for we have come to rest in that love.

Furthermore, it might be better to talk in terms not of "saved" or "enlightened" as complete states, as end goals, but as conditions of eternal becoming. If God is infinite and the soul is of God, then there is no end to our awakening, our enlightening, our knowing of love. Here we know the incomparable safety that comes of knowing in God that we are utterly and completely and unconditionally loved by the Friend as we are. To walk the world in this love is to know that no matter what we encounter, at some level though often immediately incomprehensible to us, we can be sure that "all shall be well and all manner of thing shall be well"[15] as Julian of Norwich said, an English mystic and woman who "saw" through the veil of this reality in her "shewings" her "revealings". Note the repeat word again, to re-veal – to take the veil of our perceptions away from something so that we dis-cover what is already there, waiting to be known.

The prophet wailed at the essential transitory emptiness of life. "Vanity of vanities! All is vanity" (Ecc. 1:2). Vanity in Hebrew is *hevel* - meaning vapour, wind and things transient and impermanent. The passing nature of ordinary reality has led many in all spiritual traditions into the quest for the possibility of a non-ordinary reality (arguably the "real" reality), the landscape of the soul, the absolute, God. The writer of Ecclesiastes seems to have been a mystic like Mother Julian; having looked through the doors of perception beyond material reality he too saw another, or rather beyond. Such shifts in boundaries, such spiritual emergence, from our established way of seeing the world can produce either gradually or suddenly a profound transformation in the way we live our lives. We can become more fully human, or we can crash into mental chaos, but going back again does not seem to be an option. Or rather, there is an option and that is to attempt to go back again and invest great energy in doing so, but this is not viable, the seeds have been sown. It's a bit like the old song "How you gonna keep 'em, down on the farm, after they've seen Paree." A glimpse of greater possibility stays with us and worms its way into our consciousness no matter how hard we try to deny it.

When Jesus said that unlike the creatures of the earth and the air, he had nowhere to lay his head, he was doing more than bewailing his inability to buy a nice semi'. He was offering us a vision that when we become fully and perfectly human (one interpretation of the concept of the Son of Man) we let go of our need for a permanent physical place which we own, for the place where we rest is deep within our own consciousness, in the love that knows us as we are known, the birthplace of our essence, the soul's origin. Here is Home, a place of utter safety, connection, oneness that allows us to be fully in the world yet not bound to it, to completely participate in the world with all its rich opportunities and challenges of every sort, yet to recognise their fundamental impermanence and be free of them at the same time. The Buddhist and Hindu traditions speak of this as non-attachment, so often distorted as detachment. In coming Home to love and being non-attached it does not mean that we love less. That would be detachment, and some of us study non-attachment (but really it is detachment we thus seek) because we think it will free us from the pain of being involved, from commitment, from responsibility. Non-attachment is still love, perhaps stronger and in some ways more painful than ever, but it is love without clinging. In being in Love, at Home in the Divine, we are able to love more not less.

Non-attachment is not about ignoring our responsibilities or our participation in the world. On the contrary we can approach them more compassionately, more meaningfully when we see the suffering that attachment can produce. Coming Home is not about not feeling the pain or the suffering of the world, but about accepting it and not being imprisoned by it by either feeling overwhelmed by it or striving to push it away. The struggle in us to keep it away evaporates. We are able to hold the light and dark of the world with equal compassion. Letting go does not mean ignoring our place in the world, rather it is to fulfil it but from a completely different place within ourselves, of equanimity, of knowing that fundamentally there is an OKness to the creation, that deep beneath and within and around the creation in which we live and move and have our being (Acts 17:21) there is a Love so vast and incomprehensible, yet knowable because we can feel it personally in our hearts, that holds and enfolds everything into itself.

It is taught in Buddhism that "suffering is" and that the cause of this suffering is attachment. The concept of Home offers us an additional perspective. It may be that the cause of attachment itself is rooted in the fear that we are separate, cut adrift from our Source, from God. Perhaps when we reconnect to that source then the need to attach falls away, for we are no longer afraid. At Home we rest in the perfect love that dissolves fear. The cause of suffering is not only in the endless desires of the ego to be powerful and safe in the world, or the realisation that it must die, but also in the struggle entailed in trying to become non-attached under our own steam, by the efforts of the mind.

The ego exists in a condition of constant incompleteness that is why its demands are legion and relentless. In Buddhism, the countless "hungry ghosts" of the ego are insatiable. The soul is in a condition of completeness. The soul is of God, of the Source, and therefore perfect of itself. It is on its journey Home both within and holding the personhood, the ego, the body. In fact in some schools of thought it has chosen to be so, to serve its divine source through its experience of the dense reality we know as ordinary life. The personhood, the ego, must die while we are alive, or at least its power must so that it can be wrested away from its quests and brought to serve the soul, God, instead of the ego self. The master must become the servant. Perhaps the cause of suffering is not so much attachment to things or to persons, but detachment from our Source, from Home, from the love of God. Re-turn to, re-call, re-collect this and we find the safe haven that we have longed for and from which, from this Home, we can move in the world and fully participate from a completely different place of knowing. Here we are "saved". "Behold", Jesus said so often, which means to wake up, to see anew (and great spiritual teachers like him urge us similarly). To see anew our Source is the beginning of freedom from the attachments, from the addictions that feed the hungry ghosts of the little self.

The flight into freedom, into God, into the welcoming arms of the Friend, and away from the straightjacket of who we think we are, sets us free from attachments to the illusions of this world. And in God, in this spiritual search there is an added dimension, perhaps one of the most significant of all in the spiritual search – the realisation that we are not on our own. We are not left entirely to our own devices in what can be a monumental climb (or descent) into freedom, Home. For those with a theocentric view of the world, there is the help of God, grace, the Holy Spirit, the energy of love, however we label and experience it.

And the search is universal, for everybody seeks meaning, purpose, direction and connection in life. We all at some point, perhaps continually, seek answers to all those great existential questions like "Who am I - why am I here -where am I going - how do I get there?" We all pursue love, joy, relationships, work and activities that nurture and feel "right" to us, which bring a sense of being and belonging. This pursuit may or may not be God-centred. This is spirituality and it lies at the very roots of what it is to be human. Religion can be seen as the ritual, liturgy, doctrines and practices that we may collectively enter in our spiritual life to codify and unify it with others, and which may provide answers to those existential questions. Thus, everybody is spiritual but not everybody is religious.

While spirituality for most people embraces some form of deity or transcendent realm, this is not a universal requirement. What seems to matter is that we believe in something and that we feel we belong to something, not least because there are direct health benefits.[16] On balance, those committed to some form of spiritual practice and/or religious connection are more likely to live longer, healthier and happier lives than those who do not. There is no evidence that one belief system is superior to any other and there may be downsides — for example some ill people can get worse because they think they have failed in their spiritual work or their faith, or that God has deserted or is punishing them.[17] Curiously the healthiest and happiest people in one study were not those getting support from their religious community, but those who felt they were giving most.[18] (Now, who was it who said that "it is better to give than to receive"?) What seems to be going on is that the spiritual-religious paradigm offers people a sense of centre, of focus, of meaning in an often meaningless and chaotic world,[19] without which we seem more prone to all manner of physical, mental and social ill effects.

One theologian, John Macquarrie, saw spirituality very simply as a "way of seeing",[20] not with our eyes but with our awareness. How, drawn from the reference points of our experiences and our beliefs, we "see" who we are in the world and how we relate to others, how we see our place in the creation and the meaning, purpose and connection in our lives. Religion can be seen as the conduit through which we channel and express our "way of seeing". This "seeing" can also change as we encounter beliefs and experiences that challenge our status quo - sudden insight, trauma or the presence and parables of great spiritual beings like the Prophet, the Buddha or Jesus, can change our way of seeing joyfully but can also leave us feeling chaotic and confused. Transformational experiences or intimations of the absolute can easily be dismissed as madness or delusion[21] [22] [23] [24] [25] and when linked to God can be dismissed as the need for an "opium" to dull the pain of an unjust world and an instrument to keep people under control (Marx), a sign of neurosis arising from the need for a father figure (Freud), or consolation in the sorrow of the world (Feuerbach). Others like Sartre put the desire for God down to our own desire to be God and find our own meaning in the world. Recent studies suggest our brains are "wired" for God,[26] or that we may be genetically programmed to connect with the Divine[27] — the outcome of an evolutionary process that advantaged a religious tendency because it helped people survive and find meaning in a distressing world. Physiologists place the mystic, ineffable experience as an effect of an outpouring of serotonin or endorphins, or a product of electrical discharges in temporal lobe epilepsy, while others have shown that it can be drug induced.[28] Is religiosity therefore just some kind of mental illness or deficiency which with the right treatment we can cure or with the right education grow out of? Is it just good health insurance evolved by some Darwinian process to assist our survival? Is God therefore merely a delusion, a product explainable by one or more of these catalysts?

Like millions of others, I experience God in my life, I know God at a different level of knowing (what the ancients called "gnosis") which transcends scientific analysis, easy description in words (although Poets like Rumi, Eliot or Whitman get close). When asked if he believed in God, Jung famously said, "I do not believe, I know".[29]

Evelyn Underhill's[30] classic text on mysticism describes five distinct stages, moving from the purgation of old ways of seeing to union with the Divine. Many people report such mystical union, and it is probably far more common than is generally believed as indicated by the work of the Alister Hardy Trust.[31] Recent research[32] is increasingly supporting what many spiritual traditions have always claimed – that consciousness is more than the product of the brain and that the absolute is not a delusion but a reality. Is the madman drowning in these boundless waters in which the mystic swims? Is our mental health system packed with people whose underlying distress is spiritual but not recognised as such?

The pain of the mystical/spiritual crisis or emergence can be confused with psychosis. But the former, as well as the slower work of more gradual spiritual awakening (if nurtured rightly) is transformative rather than destructive and as a result we become more present, more whole, more loving, more forgiving, more functional in the world and not less. Our compassion extends to ourselves and others, reducing the risks. We become more accepting, inclusive and embracing of others and ourselves, more discerning rather than judgemental. We are also more likely to be more trusting and able to work collaboratively with others, fostering a sense of humility and the possibility that we are not always right or always have to be in control or at the centre of things. Through all these "mores" which are all about "becoming", a spiritual experience ultimately enhances rather than diminishes our humanity. And mystics and spiritual seekers eventually learn who it is safe to talk to so that they do not get branded insane and locked up in hospitals!

Few people I have met have had the sudden, blinding, life changing awakening to Truth that Saul/Paul experienced on the road to Damascus. For most of us it's the steady plod up the mountain with many an apparent slip along the way. Sometimes there is indeed the urgent shake that comes in many different guises. It may be the earth shattering experience traumatic in its own way of falling in love, where the love is so intense and our egos are "thinned" by it that we come close to seeing the Beloved in the lover, the soul feels it has found its mate. Falling into love with someone in this way can be the ego shattering experience that projects us into a new way of seeing. It may happen also with the overwhelming love we may feel for the new born child. Shaken and stirred this way has its counterpoint in trauma – loss of a loved one, illness, burnout. A patient with cancer I recently met told me that she had learned to love (the terror of) her cancer because "without it I would have stayed asleep. My cancer was my spiritual awakening."

Thus plunged into spiritual crisis, our usual "way of seeing" is perturbed. I've written more detail on spiritual crisis elsewhere[33] [34] and will explore it further in Part 3. Suffice to say here that when we lurch into spiritual crisis, the often dramatic emergence of a new way of seeing, life that was once seen as normal, full of the usual ups and downs, now seems strange and alien before us, a new "waste land" that no longer seems our home. We have become strangers in a strange land, as Robert Heinlein[35] expressed it in his science fiction story. Indeed we not only may see the world as strange, others may see us as odd too. Yet paradoxically we may be feeling at the same time some sense of lightness of being as we feel the possibility of a new Home being present…but looking out on the old one? If where we used to be is no longer home, then where is it? Thus, whether we are rapidly shaken out of our way of seeing things, or whether the same shift emerged through gradual attention in spiritual work, we may hear some echo within that keeps calling us to the surface, through the shadow to find the light. Thus there is paradox in this struggle, for it is pregnant with the potential for transformation.

I mentioned being on Iona, that glorious isle where it is said the veil between the worlds is thinnest. This leads me into another aspect of where the spiritual search might take us – sometimes not to a different spiritual tradition, but to a familiar one. Back, in some senses, to where we started but with a new way of seeing. On Iona an ancient Christian site has been revived and renewed within the last century to produce a vibrant, open and inclusive Christian community that is spreading its message way beyond the boundaries of its tiny location. On my first visit, 20 years ago, I hovered around the edges, moving into the silent sacred space of the abbey, but only when no one else was there, late at night or early morning through its ever open door to sit in silent contemplation. However, by chance if chance it be, within the space of a few months I encountered people and situations that were to drag me out of my anti-Christian trench. And what follows is not a suggestion that we all have to return to or discover Christianity; I offer these words merely as an example of what can happen along the way. Each of us will have our own experience. It may be as in my case a call to return to something long abandoned, or we may voyage into a new faith, or none at all and we will explore the implications of all of these later on.

My hostility to Christianity, as I explored other faiths down the years, had grown not lessened. That early childhood lesson in exclusion was compounded in adulthood by the endless messages emerging from pretty much every branch of the church that there were some who were "in" and some who were "out". Doctrines and dogmas were all that seemed to matter and the public face of the faith appeared venal and contemptible marred by bickering, division and hatred of anything and everybody of one sort or another – women, gays, other religions, other Christians, anybody who didn't slot into a particular sect's beliefs. My opening of the gifts of other faiths had left the Christian parcel largely ignored. At the Interfaith Seminary[i] (a groundbreaking course training ministers and spiritual counsellors across faith boundaries) which I attended some years ago, a teacher for the Christianity module, Ray Gaston, entered a room full of arms-folded students, me included, and asked for our response to what Christianity meant to us. . He opened up the flipchart and asked us to call out our response when he said the word "Christian". I thought at first this man must be a fool – because for the next hour he, a man of the cloth, just stood there and took it; an outpouring of venom, suffering, anger and grief splattered onto the flipchart.

As the tide abated, he stood there very quietly and said something quite remarkable, three times. "I'm sorry, that is not the message of Christ, and you should not have been treated like that." Sorry – three times. There wasn't a dry eye in the room when he'd finished. Many of us saw and were able to let go of something that had affected us adversely in so many ways. Now Ray was not responsible for all that had happened to the group down the years, in fact he wasn't even born when (some) Christians were inflicting their distorted faith on us. So why did the apology have such a healing effect? Firstly his sincerity and humility were profoundly moving, secondly he stood there as a representative of a tradition. He was in communion with the Christian church, warts and all, past and present – that connection, that identification, not restricted by time and space is part of what being in community, in communion, is all about. Ray was not responsible for the past personally, but as an agent of that tradition whose mantle he had

---

[i] www.theinterfaithseminary.com

voluntarily donned, he now took part in its collective consciousness. His non-defensive, humble response, allowed many of us in that roomful of students to re-examine our hostility to the Christian faith. Something began to turn in me then, a growing realisation that despite all my spiritual work down the years and the heart openings and the deepening of my compassionate potential – I certainly wasn't willing to extend that to Christians and Christianity. Furthermore there came with that realisation that it was myself who was being harmed – when we close our hearts to another person or group, our hearts suffer from that closure.

Then a dear friend, who had found herself whilst at the Seminary returning to her Christian roots, poked and prodded me with difficult questions. Once on a long and glorious drive along the west coast of Scotland she just turned to me and said, "Have you ever thought of turning to Christ?" I was speechless and felt like a brick had just dropped into my guts, something I was neither willing nor able to then explore.

Then someone with whom I'd been friendly for years, a retired Canon from the Anglican church, became quite ill, and we would spend long evenings together exploring our favourite poem, the Four Quartets, and talking of matters of faith into the late hours lubricated by not a little fine port. This "abba", through loving and simple spiritual fathership, began to open doors in me, those old barriers of anger and exclusion that had long been locked.

It may have been just coincidence, but these three experiences converged before I took a holiday on Iona that year, determined to enjoy the time of spirit in the abbey but remain on the periphery of the community and its services. It was Sunday morning, communion was about to happen and for some reason I cannot explain to this day, I decided to go along. I sat at the back, on my own, aware that I had arrived armed to the teeth – with my guardedness, resentment, cynicism – waiting for what would surely come, some dogmatic statement about sin or damnation or hell or some other such unloving and excluding words. No doubt I would, as I had before when attending a service which I could not avoid (the compulsory birth, marriage and death rites of passage) in church, remain aloof to the whole hypocritical show. I was wrong-footed. No such words came; instead I heard only words that were loving, questioning, tentative, humble and inclusive. I remember being overcome by a profound sense of sadness and struggled to see where this might be coming from. I was hearing words from the warden in her sermon that were entirely welcoming and compassionate and something just didn't fit.

At that moment I had the strong feeling that my parents, long dead, were sitting either side of me. I could smell the tobacco haze that always hovered around my dad; the scent of the "Imperial Leather" soap my mother loved. Communion was under way and I was prepared to sit it out, when the abbey seemed suddenly silent and still even though people were moving and speaking. In this silence I heard a voice. It was a voice I had heard many times before, on the inside rather than in the ears, not so much words alone as wordsandfeelings combined. It just said "You are welcome at my table, everyone is welcome at my table, come eat and drink with me." I was struggling to hold back the tears and maybe to hold onto my sanity, but I had known this voice before, come to trust it. Three times I heard it. Then the moment passed, and I took communion. I knew it was time.

Inner voices? Intuitions? Spiritual journeys? Religions? Soul searches? Home? – what is all this about you may well be asking. I have been and am like millions of others, a seeker, a desirer of truth, a lover longing for the Beloved, the traveller heading Home. Such "experiences" are not uncommon and perhaps you too have had similar along the way. I offer my story here as an example, but it is just mine, and it could be any faith or none and each of us brings our own unique pattern to events like these. They illustrate the general principle of how numinous events can lead us deeper into truth along the Way, but they can also be seductive and side track us into blind alleys. In such experiences may lie madness or mysticism, deep irrationality or pure truth. How can we discern what is truth? Can those inner voices and other promptings be trusted? Do we dismiss them all as suggested above in much atheistic and scientific debate as mere phenomena of no value? After all, it is risky territory - some seekers go to the edge and fall over into insanity or disease or death, some get lost and give up - falling back into familiar ways that numb the hunger, some fall under the spell of cults and false prophets, dehumanising faiths or empty soullessness.

The way Home, even assuming there is such a thing, is fraught with pleasures and pitfalls. How can we walk the path with some degree of safety and equanimity? How can we sift out truth from untruth, the wise from the foolish, the false from the genuine? Often the boundaries are blurred, our faculties too limited. Was my Iona experience just another deluded moment, an old memory surfacing and nothing more, or an act of grace? Finding our way Home is not a solitary affair that can be pursued without guidance, and the risks of delusion and distortion are immense if we attempt to do so. The process is not helped by doubts we may have about the world's religions and their tendency to ossify and separate rather than nurture and set people free to come Home, to God. There can be doubts and prejudices too about the whole notion of God, the One, the Absolute whatever our thoughts on what he, she or it may be. But beyond these difficulties, perhaps we need to be wary of casting away the very real treasures to be found in the traditions that have emerged over thousands of years. Practices and approaches, common to many, that have been tried and tested down the years and designed to keep us safe and nurture the spirit in our awakenings and reduce the risks inherent in the individualist "me" search.

On our way Home we need map and compass, companions and guides if we are to walk the Way safely. It is to these that we turn next.

...And shadows fall here
Sometimes like a dark swallow
Skimming over an inverse lake.
Sometimes like the black fog of a burning oilfield,
Bitter,
Acrid,
Enveloping this our small infrequent world
In the terror of the uncreation.
The darkness unbound,
Beckons,
Come!
Come!
And some take off like flame bound moths,
And others plunge,
Reckless,
Into that black night.
None escape.
The shadow waits at the edge of the flame
The unknown shifting margin
Where light and dark, vying for authority,
Surrender in truce
To You,
You!
Who holds both light and dark in Your
Perfect undimmed
Thought...

Part 3

"The history of the world, with the material destruction of cities and nations and people, expresses the division that tyrannises the souls of all men"[36]

The Waste Land

In a Glasgow hotel you can go to the "Soul Therapies" room. Here a sign says you are welcome to "a peaceful haven within the heart of the city…switch off, kick back and enjoy the wide range of treatments and therapies on offer." And you can kick back into reiki, facial massage or a mineral salt scrub, then have a "fake bake" in the tanning machine and get a bikini wax or a manicure. In a popular newspaper, there's a section called "spirit" where there is advice on home décor and lifestyles. There's a company called "Spiritual High" selling drugs to the post-rave culture. A magazine column advertises "soul mates" – where specifications of personality traits and preferences invite the perfect partner. Just about every city has its alternative therapies free paper selling the wares of the healing armies. San Francisco has one called "Common Ground" with 150 pages and a thousand ads' and a menu of everything from hypnotherapy sessions to provide help with your "inner child processes" to "spiritual breakthroughs" via "intuitive coaching" to find your "soul mate" or find your "true spiritual self" (at $500 an hour). From London to Lisbon, from Berlin to Brisbane, from Moscow to Minneapolis, everywhere it seems offers the same fixes for the soul.

It's little wonder that assorted sceptics can have a field day of mockery about matters spiritual when our culture has so successfully dumbed down one of the most profound concepts that human beings have ever come up with – the possibility of soul. A meaning-lite, money making feeding frenzy has been engendered in the popular use of "soul" – usually referring to little more than the tickling of the ego's pleasure centres; the bathing of the personhood in sickly sweet comforts. Western capitalist civilisation has thus emptied our language and indeed our everyday consciousness of the depth and significance of the very essence of what it is to be human. Privatising spirituality has reduced it to a product ideally packaged for ready marketing to the consumer society. Reduced to our personhoods – "who I am" becomes the plaything of multiple attachments to countless roles and identities and functions. "I am" is what I do, what I earn, how I look…and all of these things can be bought. Privatised spirituality does not socially engage, it is about the self and all the comforts that the self demands, not about being a source of compassion in the world in service of others. Religions too can fall into this trap, reducing their work to commodity and control, which from time to time causes schism and fracture (e.g. Martin Luther and the early protestant movement or George Fox and the Quakers) when some individuals step forward to break free of these bonds. Neo-Pharisees tend easily it seems to gain the upper hand in all spiritual traditions from time to time, reducing the authentic religious experience to a commodity to be bought at a price (of rules, indulgences, trinkets) and thus controlled.

And growing in the same fertile ground of commodification are new therapies arising by the day, with old ones resold, restyled, repackaged – all planted and raised for the market hall of the personhood. In its endlessly shifting garb and restless hunger, the ego demands ever more food to keep it feeling good, more therapies to shore up its ever crumbling boundaries, more sweet, fluffy, feel-good junkets just to keep going.

Some of us live and die like this, some wake up spontaneously and know "it doesn't have to be like this". Some gradually awaken, prompted by an inner restlessness that seeks answers. Some like me, crash and burn when they can no longer take it. Sometimes the soul just punches through, or maybe the ego personhood power implodes to allow it to escape. Whichever, life can never be the same again for those thus transformed. Into this unknown landscape the soul now emerges, and sees clearly the waste land of the country it once inhabited. Our culture, now deeply rooted in the possibility that human beings can be happy and healthy with ever more scientific advances, material comforts and designer bodies and babies becomes a sweetshop of transient comforters where the language of soul and spirit and the depth and potential it offers, is lost in the superficial, the seductive and the short term. That people cannot ultimately be satisfied with these ephemera, that the insatiable desires of the personhood are exhausting is demonstrated in the filled waiting rooms of a million therapists, healers and counsellors. As the congregational religions, seemingly ever more stuck in dogma and decline[37] [38] fail to respond to this deep human urge they relinquish the territory of the soul to others who can bring heart and meaning to the search. But to find the true and the deep, we may pass through many distractions and false paths along the way. The genuine friend of the soul is rare in a market place filled with snake oil salesmen and women. It is perhaps an ironic example that one of Europe's most wanted alleged war criminals, Radovan Karadzic, was able to reinvent himself as a spiritual healer and teacher and hide safely among the unquestioning crowds. A few mysterious words, an enigmatic presence, some well chosen clothes and beads, and the right length of hair and beard fit the seductive image of the wise man. How easy it is to exploit the vulnerable seeker, and there are thousands like this. Sometimes to find the charming prince or princess, you have to kiss an awful lot of frogs.

The language of the soul has been proletarianised; the spiritual cat is now out of the religious bag. This can be at once liberating, but also has brought the attendant risks of pandering to the needs of the ego, in the mistake that keeping this happy is what it is all about. This loss of soul, this emptiness of so much of our culture is in part driving the search, consciously or unconsciously, for alternatives to satisfy the deep hunger which at some level every human being feels; that "God shaped hole"[39] that Sartre posited. The loss of care of the soul is perhaps the single biggest omission of modern culture, catalyzing the ever increasing unhappiness of so many despite material prosperity and freedoms undreamt of by our ancestors. Religions are often unable to respond to the need and the freedom of choice, stuck in beliefs that a "sticking-plaster" God is what people want to make everything all right. Most people in the post-modern world do not respond to externally provided solutions, the inner longing is more subtle and seeks the experience of the Divine. Some long for the absolute in varying degrees of inner spiritual pain, but many others do not feel in personal need and are seeking answers through a willingness to enquire and understand. In prosperous libertarian countries, we have more rights and opportunities than ever before to explore that inner need, yet poll after poll suggests that the congregational religions fail to meet it for many, that the New Age market lacks depth, and that no amount of designer clothes, homes, orgasms, babies, bodies or relationships can satisfy the longing for happiness. At every level of society we see the disaffection and disconnection that no amount of material gains or cultural distractions can fill. The environment, politics, relationships – every aspect of the human experience and the world we inhabit is diminished when attention to soul is left out.

In his poem, The Waste Land, Eliot[40] captures the disjointed conversations, the disconnected relationships, the sterility of language and the dark and dull existence of soulless community. Without soul, families, relationships, cultures, nations fracture and fragment. Purposelessness, nihilism and ennui ensue, the pain of which is drowned by the addictions to drink, or drugs, or sex, or TV or shopping – countless options for the countless holes in the psyche that can never otherwise be filled. The painkillers for the broken heart, the anaesthesias for the personhood lost in the meaningless.

As the soul has dropped off the map, psychobiological models have come to dominate, framing human beings as little more than the products of mental and bodily processes. We are nothing that cannot be measured, weighed and investigated in this form of scientific reductionism. Soul, if it is considered at all, is consigned to the realms of the religious or the therapy room and studiously kept there. Although there are signs of change, such as recognition by the business community that profits are linked to the wellbeing of the workers and their degree of spiritual support[41] [42] or the greater willingness of the political worlds to work with the religious, these are as yet drops in the ocean. A culture that has no sense of soul is a culture that is not whole, and a culture that is not whole is not holy. With no sense of the sacred, of the possibility that we are far more that what can be seen by the ordinary senses, then the one reality, the one self is all that in relentless despair we are left with. We may fall into nihilism, or to loving and living only for the moment, or to doing the best we can for ourselves and our children and hope for the best. Or maybe the world and its resources come to have no meaning or purpose but to make us feel good, and the pursuit of the feel-good is destroying our world, both internally and externally.

A couple of years ago I was asked to speak at a conference on brain death during Brain Awareness Week in the UK. It was my lot to follow a well known scientist who had done much work in the UK and internationally on brain death and coma, and his session was deeply appealing to all of the audience. He was so certain. We can feel very assured by certainty in others. The nub of his case was this: the function of the brain can be measured, "vegetative" (a horrid word for all it conjures up about brain-injured people) states can be assessed and given certain criteria, by which we can be assured the person is really "dead" and then life support machines be switched off.

The seductive simplicity of this argument left me feeling strangely nauseated. Needless to say, my subsequent session where I expressed serious doubts about this approach went down like a lead balloon in some quarters. Any suggestion of uncertainty, of humility in the face of human illness, of reverence for the possibility that we might be more than the sum total of our cerebral atoms and their functions was uncomfortable to many. And it can be seen why; it is after all so much easier if you are caught up in the difficult business of caring, and really tough decisions at the end of life, to feel, to need to feel, that our actions are rooted in reason and logic. Introduce the concept of soul, of the possibility of the real Self that is not the same as the personal self, and this steady ship of certainty is holed below the waterline.

The notion that we might have souls, that we are not so much human beings having a spiritual journey as spiritual beings having a human journey[43] runs against the grain of much of modern culture. One example springs to mind when I was involved recently in an enquiry where abuse of patients with Alzheimer's had been a prominent feature. While making the right noises about caring, some terrible things had been done to these patients, and a cardinal feature of the underlying problem was that a significant number of the staff – fairly conventional nurses and doctors – were not facing up to the underlying hopelessness they felt about their patients. Although much work was going on with "reality orientation", the only reality accepted was ordinary reality. The patients were seen as ultimately lost causes in their own form of (declining) vegetative state. This shadow in the unconscious was covered up by "chronic niceness"[44] but ultimately leaked out. Behind the mask of caring lay some deeply uncaring feelings and actions that were not being faced and which had led to these vulnerable old people being abused.

Health problems which diminish personal identity, like Alzheimer's, challenge our very notion of what it is to be human. Imagine a situation where first we forget our names, then whatever job we had, then how to dress, then how to eat, then who our family is and so on – eventually a point is reached either gradually through such diseases or suddenly as with severe brain damage where all identity is lost to us. Who we are or were resides only in the memory of those who know us. "Who am I?" becomes the key unanswered spiritual question, unanswerable by the ego self because it has been dissolved. This illustrates two other key points. Firstly that the ego tends to get a bad press, yet it is essential in the formation of identity and mind function; without an identity there is nothing to surrender. It is also the ego that develops an imagination, an ability to see itself, to reflect and thus it too plays its part in the dance between ego and soul in awakening. Both have a part to play but what has to change is the relationship between the two. The ego's mastery is destined to be turned into service of the soul. The ego is the individualiser, the identity creator, and it is a vital part of being in the world and in our coming Home.

Secondly, if the identity has passed away, then what is left? We still tend to treat the person's body with respect not least in recognition that it was once a person and out of respect for that person and his or her loved ones. We pay great attention to dead bodies, go to great lengths to "lay them to rest" and have fought wars over the bodily relics of saints or soldiers. But, and it's a big but, if the person has "gone" then really all we are dealing with is a bag of flesh and bone, so why not simply get rid of it – it's not a person any more? To some extent switching off ventilators or calls for euthanasia are rooted in this thinking. And yet most of us feel intuitively that there is "something there" even though there is no response any more. It may be our projections onto such persons, our memories or our inability to deal with our own mortality that keep us wanting to keep them on. But it may be that we are sensing, regardless of our religious beliefs, that there is indeed something "more" there, some presence, some witness - the soul - that is more than the mere identity that has gone.

Another example of what happens when we reduce people to their identities occurred when I got involved in the professional press about the nature of mental illness, something that is likely to touch one in three of us. I help to run a charity, the Sacred Space Foundation[ii], which was set up to support people in spiritual crisis, including that particular spiritual crisis known as burnout. A spiritual crisis throws our lives up in the air, all sense of certainty and security can be lost. Things that were once ordinary in our lives – work, relationships, sense of purpose - become meaningless, confusing and frightening. Often this gets diagnosed, unsurprisingly perhaps, as a mental illness, especially depression. Many mental health professionals responded with hostility to this debate, seeing no place for a spiritual perspective. Letters from patients and some other mental health practitioners were quite different. One, a doctor now working as a GP, described the devastating effect that a psychiatric diagnosis has had on her life and the stigma it has left behind, even though her problems have long since been resolved (after being made worse by psychiatric treatment). Another, also an ex patient but also a mental health nurse wrote of how "any public criticism of psychiatry often meets with an aggressive response." Another suggested that "there are still thousands of nurses not driven by wanting to really be with people". Two psychiatrists also felt critical of their own discipline, but curiously felt unwilling to speak out publicly because of pressure to conform to the status quo. One said he felt "like an alien at some of the case conferences when I feel my blood start to boil at some of the totally mechanistic ways people view our patients." Another wrote "we only think about the brain and refuse to acknowledge the possibility that there might be something else that makes us human."

However other calls for change are getting louder and not just from the health care sector. The current dominant paradigm which sees "mind", "consciousness" and "personhood" purely as products of the brain is being broken as suggested earlier. The reduction of human beings to biological processes where who we are is relegated to the outcome of a bunch of neurones and neurochemicals is being challenged more now than it has been in many decades. The idea that when we break down, we can be rectified if we can be tweaked with the right chemical or psychotherapeutic spanners, is increasingly being seen for the simplistic modernist notion that it is. Although I have focussed on mental health care here, because of my recent experiences, no part of our culture has escaped the consequences of

[ii] www.sacredspace.org.uk

soulless models. So what is this "soul" thing with which so many in the modern world seem to have a problem?

All spiritual traditions down the years have sought to define what "soul" is and it comes in many guises and explanations. Known as the real, true or highest Self, that "of God" in everyone, the essence – it suggests a quality of consciousness, presence and being that is in or holds but is not of the ordinary or "false" self as the Hindu tradition describes it. The personhood, or ego, that conglomeration of identities and thoughts in which we find our place in the world is a very useful thing to have for getting around, relating, separating, connecting but according to these world views (held by the great majority of people in the world) it is not all that we are. Influenced by the Sufi tradition (and in doing so his words could be applied to varying degrees in many faiths) Almaas sees the soul as "the true nature of everything. It is my nature, but it is also your nature. It is the nature of birds, cats, trees, rocks, everything. It is not the rocks, not the cat, not your body, not you, not me. It is the inner nature of these. It is what allows them to exist. That is the nature of Essence, the nature of everything, it is what is sometimes called God."[45] In the soul, in our essence which is both personal and transpersonal, found in all things yet contained by none, we not only find our individuality we also find unity with all that is.

Descartes famously pronounced that "I think therefore I am" (*Cogito ergo sum*). But thinking is the realm of the mind out of which grows, influenced by culture, experience, heredity and other factors that conglomeration of self will known as the ego, very useful in its own way in acting out our roles and functions in the world. The soul, the essence of all that is, is beyond language and thinking. It simply is. The ego believes in itself. The soul knows it is of God. The ego wants to live forever. The soul being of God knows its immortality. The ego is a created thing that wants to be God, the soul simply loves God. The ego desires to be, the soul is the "I AM". The ego selfhood, the person is the medium of being in the world, but it is not the true, absolute Self, no more than the part played by the actor on the stage is real.

The little self is the instrument by which we participate in the world, but we can spend a lot of time believing that the instrument is all that we are. However, without soul, without the knowing of our "essence",[46] we are caught up in the waste land where the barren interior landscape is bedevilled by a gnawing and ultimate despair, no matter how it is dressed up in worldly fun or liberation to "be who we want to be" (which usually means an inflated pursuit of the ego's agenda). And the interior waste land is mirrored in the exterior – the degradation of our cultures, indeed of the planet, and the murder and mayhem in the world are a mirror image of the interior degradation. People who are ensouled tend to find it easier to form loving relationships with themselves, with others, with the world and that which is beyond and within all these. The landscape of the ego, of personal selfishness, is ultimately a horizon of fear, for the ego knows at some level that its power is temporary. Thus rooted in fear, it holds these unconscious and sometimes not so unconscious fears at bay by an endless hunt for self gratification – more, more, more of everything. In Buddhism these are the "hungry ghosts" that haunt our consciousness, with bloated bodies but pinhole mouths; they can never suck in enough to satiate their needs. In contrast, when we act in the world from an ensouled place, from the Home of complete love which rests within, our response to the world is transformed. We no longer have to suck in everything to meet our desires – there is less exploitation, more compassion, less fear, more love.

The downgrading and destruction of our planet is one of the less attractive results of modernity and its denial of the sacred, the essential unity of and reverence for all things. A "significant part of human life is erased"[47] when external reality is treated as the plaything of our personhoods, removing the support of the human soul. The mediaeval Arthurian legend tells of certain holy wells or sanctuaries for the refreshment of the traveller, guarded by maidens who on request would proffer the water in golden bowls. But king Amagons abused this hospitality, raping one of the maidens and stealing her bowl. The result was that everything was instantly changed. The whole land went to waste, nothing would grow, human bonds broke down and vast suffering ensued. Arthur and his knights undertook to remedy this by prayer to heal the land and to rediscover the vanished holy site to restore its wholeness. But their task was useless, for at its roots the destruction was spiritual, only by the discovery of the Holy Grail, the renewal of essence, could the waste land be transformed back to its former nourishing harmony.

The "waste land comes when the spiritual is abandoned in favour of the material. Inner nature is rejected and eternal truths are forgotten." [48] The re-discovery of these eternal truths is a central task for the spiritual search. We cannot recreate what has been lost. We live in new times, new circumstances and hankering after the past is to pander in its own way to the agenda of the little self. If a tradition is lost, so may be the conditions that sustained it. The renewal of soul in the waste land of our culture is arising paradoxically from the very newness which helped to set it aside. The essence will be the same, but its form and manifestation will be different and unique to its time. We see it now in the shifting sands of the reordering of the religions, the movements in our understanding of the nature of consciousness, the ecology movement, and the rise of "integrated" or holistic health care. These and other indicators suggest that the waste land may also be the fertile ground for a renewal and reintegration of essence, of soul, into health and wellbeing. The alternatives are there, becoming more known and drawing greater allegiance.[49] [50]

Meanwhile there are more than a few timely reminders on a daily basis that the recovery of the soul for the world has a long way to go. Perhaps it is an ego pipedream that it might be otherwise, for at some other level the world is unfolding perfectly and the ordinary experience of the world is just a mirror image of the superficial experience of our egos. I was in London at the time of the July bombings in 2005. Looking at what had become of what moments before had been a reasonably ordered city going about its peaceful business, my friend said, "It makes you want to give up on humanity doesn't it?" In view of the carnage, the waste land made starkly real before our eyes, this might seem a reasonable response. But I watched most ordinary Londoners in the reports of this wonderful diverse city recognise that an attack on one is an attack on all. In fact looking at the victims – with so many faiths and races represented - an attack on London has now become an attack on the world. I watched the response of nurses, police, ambulance and fire officers and others who worked their hearts out to help and heal. I watched people of faith and none echo the words of Julian of Norwich that whatever confronts us now, a belief in God, humanity or some greater realm of being – of Love – through this "all shall be well and all manner of thing shall be well." In love and the expressions of love there is not despair but hope, for the fearful waste land ultimately cannot stand against a re-creation that emerges from the being of the soul.

The tension between these apparent two worlds, the one of bliss and the one of suffering, the one of the spirit and the one of the material, the one of life and the one of death is an unnecessary one and as we mature in our spirituality we come to see this more clearly. There is no "this world" and "the other world" (although it can certainly feel like that a lot of the time) for a truly spiritual, holistic way of seeing is able to embrace the paradox of opposites, the challenge of diversity. It does not have to be a case of Home or the world but Home in the world, seeing all of it in one, as part of all that is, unfolding exquisitely and elegantly in Divine consciousness in which the waste land too plays its part. The world is a spiritual waste land; but it is also a land that blooms and sings with beauty and possibility. Pundits often bemoan the neo-barbarism of post-modernity that is seemingly bereft of a moral compass, of a religious ethic, of a code of the soul. But it has always been thus and we need to see things in proportion. The waste land exists as it always has contemporaneously with the exquisite beauty of the face of the Divine. Our choices determine which prevails at any one moment.

The waste land lies all about us, but what lies about stems from within. "As above, so below" is an important spiritual principle; "above" or "below" not in a physical sense but in the sense of more or less evolved spirit and consciousness. The more expansive and loving, the more creation tends to mirror it, and vice versa. When we turn to our hearts, to love and the very roots of the soul, the waste land is transformed, not in some linear lurch from a lost paradise into hell and back again, but in the endless attentiveness to soul. The waste land is eternally becoming and fading in each conscious moment, with each breath. It is in a constant state of becoming and dissolving. Acknowledging, nourishing, choosing soul is the searching for and finding of the Holy Grail and thereby perhaps the world shall be changed because our way of seeing is changed. The waste land is what we encounter when we are exiled from Home, when the soul, trapped in the ego's relentless pursuits longs to be free. When freedom comes, we can embrace the waste land too as, like ourselves, part of all that is.

...What is God? Is not the question
The question is who asks the question?
Who?
Between the I and the not-I
Twin bridged by time and space
(Necessary for movement)
Lies the canyon of the unknown.
The bottomless.
Do not go here stranger alone,
Do not go here accompanied.
Come prepared,
Come naked in your unpreparedness
For here be the faultlines of your psyche,
The waiting earthquake of the soul.
Here, words and thoughts are broken
In the caverns of despair.
Dreams split like apples
Dropped from towers onto concrete pavements.
And hopes drown in oceans of tears.
Do not go here, stranger.
Do not go here
While you're a stranger.

We all stand on the bridges
Some retreat to try again
Some fall
Some rise.
Near or far all pass
All enter.
And stepping through the iron gates of the exit
Look back
(Do not look back – pillars of salt,
Pillars of salt!
Abraham wailing in the desert.)
Rabbit eyed with fear
We see the long road
Buried in the rubble of imagination
Bordered in fires

Stalked by other guards looting the rich pickings
Don't wait, go on, go on!
Beyond the gate
And up the rose climbed wide wall
Where the bell rings in an empty sky
A high hill sunless and moonless.
And there in the distance
No further than under our noses
A glimpse
Of something half remembered
Of something half forgotten
Set in the genes or tattooed on the underside of the skull
Embedded at birth, first birth
The eternal, internal compass home.
The immortal hand outstretched, to bring the bride stripped bare,
Waits to take us to
The seat by the lily pond
By the lake of dreams,
The waters of compassion,
whose droplets
Are Your substance.
Love,
When all has been said and done
Only Love...

Part 4

"Fate has flung me into the wastes of Memphis.
Go and tell fate: turn me round and hurl me again
Until I behold the wilderness of Judah
And reach the fair heights of the far north
and wrapped in majesty of Elohi's name
I'll don the splendour of his holiness, and whirl."[51]

Escaping Memphis: leaving the waste land and heading for home

My childhood in the 50s was poor by modern standards, but all my basic needs were met. I had food in my belly, shoes on my feet and clothes on my back. The state paid my schooling and my health care and provided a modest home. My dad had a poorly paid job, but it was steady money and with a little "overtime" he earned enough for a seaside holiday once a year for a week in a caravan and maybe for a bike at Christmas. My mum kept the house (and me) as clean as a new pin. Today I meditate with a mantra, a skill I learned easily because my mum began each day with them – "Have you washed behind your ears?", "Did you do the back of your neck?" "Have you put clean underwear on?" These rolled off her tongue daily before I left for school and her antiphon to my usual "Why?" was always the same, "Because what will people think if you have an accident?" It took me a long time to grasp the logic of my mother's thinking. If I'd had an accident (and I did once and ended up at the hospital and the first thing my mum did was to tick me off for being so stupid and the second was to check the back of my ears!) then surely the state of my cleanliness was the last thing she needed to worry about. But no. My childhood society was governed by one overriding thing – the fear of being "shown up" – shamed.

Nowadays, with all that went on in my family it would be called dysfunctional. Emotionally impoverished, we nevertheless had a kind of safety, and we were certainly clean. And there is not a moment of it that I do not cherish though much of it was not pleasant, for if not that, then not this and there is no part of my life now that is not full of blessings. I have in my time worked with many profoundly wounded people, and one thing I have noticed about their healing is the liberation that comes from a deep acceptance and, yes, love of their past. That level of forgiveness, where we go beyond perceptions of right or wrong, or "letting people off" for hurts done to us, sets us free to discover our true essence, to come Home. Healing our relationships with our primary authority figures, with the past, is invariably a prerequisite for healing our relationship with the ultimate authority figure – the Absolute, God, the Source of All. Those who undertake the spiritual work while bypassing the emotional work may find their relationship with that which they seek beyond the self incomplete.

Sometimes we avoid this work by becoming theologically sound, to be really knowledgeable about matters spiritual and religious, yet without the inner psychological work there is an inability to fully connect with ourselves and others. Even worse, without the grounding in the personal work which has produced the requisite humility and healing, we may apply these spiritual learnings in damaging and pathological ways. Thomas Merton writes of how "the most dangerous man in the world" can be the spiritual seeker "who is guided by nobody. He trusts his own visions. He obeys the attractions of an interior voice but will not listen to other men. He identifies the will of God with anything that makes him feel, within his own heart a big, warm, sweet interior glow. The sweeter and warmer the feeling is, the more he is convinced of his own infallibility. And if the sheer force of his own self-confidence communicates itself to other people and gives them the impression that he is really a saint, such a man can wreck a whole city, or a religious order or even a nation: and the world is covered by the scars that have been left in its flesh by visionaries like these." [52]

Healing, holiness and wholeness are closely related words. Holy work, soul work, is not just undertaken by immersion in holy books or religious rules in the hope that if we do so diligently, enough of them will rub off on us to cleanse us and produce enlightenment, bring us Home. I have met so many seekers who believe that a pharisaic approach to the spiritual search will make everything OK. The Pharisees it may be recalled were the ones who challenged Jesus and ultimately sought his death. They taught that the way to God was through complete obedience to the religious laws. Jesus said the first law was love (of God, neighbour and self) from which right behaviour and enlightenment would proceed. Following the rules was less important than the content of a persons heart, for it was and is through the heart that we find our way Home. Jesus' early followers it may be recalled were not known as Christians, that term was to come a generation or two later. The first were known as Followers of the Way, and it was the way of the heart that Jesus offered – revolutionary in its time.

Whenever this Way arises within a religion that has become ossified and rule bound, as without constant watchfulness religions often do, then we can be sure that the orthodox establishment will do all in its power to silence it. We can discern this pattern at work down through the ages as authority struggles to establish and maintain religious orthodoxy, while movements and schisms arise at intervals to fracture it. To some degree we can witness this at work in the Anglican church today as the old paradigm gives way but the new is not yet fully clear to us. It happened in the past between Protestantism and Roman Catholicism, and within Anglicanism with the Quakers and the Methodists. All other faiths bear witness to this pattern too. Once a religion gets hidebound by rules, we can guarantee that somewhere along the line a movement of the Way will arise to shift it or break away. The sand dune does not move from the centre but by the tiny grains in their countless numbers who, caught by the wind of the spirit blow over and across it, shifting it forward until one day that which was at the centre finds itself on the periphery, only to be caught by that same wind and moved itself. Forever.

I got into the rules myself at one stage – if I only could follow them properly, eat the right food, do the rituals – then I'd get to God and goodness. Of course, doing good does not necessarily mean than we are being good. If our heart is not truly in it, then what emerges is inauthentic and sometimes transparently so. Our capacity to be and become fully human for ourselves and others is thereby diminished. Jesus, the Buddha, the Prophet, Moses – all the great spiritual teachers had iconoclasm in common. As the age they lived in produced ossified faiths stuck in the assumption that the path to God or liberation was the path of the rules, they challenged (often at great price) such rigidity. They established certain rules for their followers, but these were inherently paradoxical – rules designed to break rules, rules that at some point must be left behind on the journey, to be transcended.

Spiritual searching without controls or discipline - without subjection voluntarily to rules designed to hold us while we seek rather than suppress us - this is not freedom. It is spiritual anarchy, self indulgence, irresponsibility, arrogance. It can be very difficult to know when rules are there to help or abuse, especially when we are vulnerable in our spiritual immaturity or crisis. We cannot always rely on our own discernment. That is why the practices in this book are essential. Not all rules are bad. A walk through any city would be chaotic and dangerous without the traffic lights and signs and the rules of the Highway Code to keep us safe and guide us on our way. Thus it is with surrender, where we agree to follow certain rules on a spiritual search, such as following those of a community retreat or the teachings of a true master. But in emptying our wills we do not have to empty our heads of the need to get help in discerning what is right and true, of knowing when a rule is there designed to help subvert our will into God or to have power over us so that we can be abused.

We have all kinds of modern psychological terms to understand why people slavishly follow the rules – co-dependency, projection and so on. Somewhere along the line we learned that we are not good, not whole, not loved, and shameful. The way to overcome this for some is to put the effort into doing good, doing the right thing and bottling up the underlying pain. Bound by these interior ties, reinforced by the suffocations of family and society, it is hard for the prisoner to break free. A kind of religious Brokeback Mountain emerges where conformity to collective norms locks us in an iron cage of repression. In this waste land of the spirit the suffering is endless. The exterior waste land of toxic disconnected relationships with everything - the land, society, other people - is a mirror of the interior waste land where we feel disconnected from our loving source, our essence, soul, within.

Yet the wasteland is not without hope, for in its mud there are seeds of joy, of freedom. Whilst it is full of suffering, it is also the place of spiritual awakening, of friendship and loyalty, of joy and creativity, of environmental and social activism. That is its paradox. It may be muddy, but it is a fertile mud. In the darkness the light of awareness is waiting to be re-membered, re-born, schooled into being. What we seek to make us free lies, literally, right under our noses, within the very existence we already have.   In the Shvetashvatara Upanishad, its location is charmingly specific; "The Self, small as the thumb, dwelling in the heart".[53] The Self within is inside, waiting to be stirred into life, and it is often the soil of the waste land that carries the stimulus for that awakening.

All the great spiritual teachers frequently exhorted their followers with words like, "Awake", "Behold", "Let him with ears to hear, hear", "See,". What were they asking them to see? The seeing was not so much a change of physical vision, but an interior seeing as we explored in John Macquarie's work in Part 2. It is a shift of consciousness, a *metanoia*, a transformation of understanding, an en-lightening to awaken to the nature of reality and to enter a new reality, the very source of peace itself and a new vision of life. Life that is not transitory but eternal. And this is already there; the invitation is to awaken to what is already present within. Indeed many of the words we use as I have suggested show that what is to be found is not new, but is waiting to be dis-covered, re-awakened, re-gained, re-cognised, re-membered and so on. The spiritual struggle is a kind of birthing of consciousness, of Divine consciousness, for that which we seek is already there waiting to come into the world.

What makes the vision crack? Why should the scales fall from the eyes so that we at last see clearly and can be re-born into a new way of being? Why should we be set free of the wasteland, yet full of compassion for it and willingness to stay in it not least so that others might be stirred to life too? As I suggested in Part 1, for some it is a plunge into the real pain of spiritual crisis while for others it is the steady drip into our consciousness of a new way of seeing, sometimes with sudden lurches in changed awareness where the prospect of Home on the horizon is a tantalising glimpse. A spiritual crisis is a tough place to be, and as yet much of our approach to it in a secular world is to either class it as a mental health problem, or ignore it or suggest a holiday. Indeed, many would argue that spiritual work without the crisis is just as tough, but spread more thinly over time! I recently searched the web and found over 8.5 million references to spiritual crisis/emergence. Numerous organisations and individuals are offering more imaginative approaches than a diagnosis of psychosis. Many of the websites of religious organisations seem more willing to acknowledge its existence – a territory which arguably has always been their own but sometimes lost to dogma and rigidity.[54] When the religions pull back from responding to spiritual crisis and emergence, either by ignoring them or inhibiting that direct experience of the Divine in favour of the rules, new priests colonise the vacant lot such as the still burgeoning army of gurus, therapists and healers of the New Age movement.

However, the religions have a rich tradition of know-how in relation to spiritual support. While psychiatrists like Grof and his colleagues[55] and organisations such as the Interfaith Seminary in London have very much pioneered the modern response, others have rooted their approach in age old traditions such as theologian Margaret Guenther's[56] concept of "spiritual midwifery" as the right role of the therapist/healer/counsellor in relation to the person in crisis or seeking spiritual maturity. To midwife is a different way of working with someone for the midwife does not see the person as wrong or diseased, but is there to help a perfectly natural process to occur. The soul is not sick; it is simply looking to emerge fully into being.

Anyone who has experienced spiritual crisis will know that it is arguably one of the most painful of human experiences. It is a heightened sense of the arid landscape of the waste land, yet in becoming more aware of it the pain is exacerbated because no way can be seen out of it. As the energy required to keep things stable increases, we become increasingly depleted, exhausted and heartsick with the effort. The greater the exhaustion the closer we get to a state of almost complete mental, physical, social and spiritual collapse. The deepest truth about our Self is seeking to be born, and like all births it can be a painful process. We may project the cause of the pain onto many things – a failing relationship, a difficult job, a financial worry – but the real cause lies deep in the soul, the essence of our Self seeking freedom and truth. Often the process is an unconscious one as we call to ourselves challenge after challenge that brings us closer to the edge, even though consciously we may think we do not want these things to be happening. Thus while we may feel like a victim of circumstance, that is a very egotistic view. What may be happening is a deep summoning up, from our unconscious, situations which will provoke us into another way of seeing. Others might see this as grace, the Holy Spirit at work, worming its way into our lives so that we may hear the call Home. Often at some point the awareness of our inherent helplessness sinks in. In that place of dread it is then we come to know that we cannot do this alone; that we need help, the help of grace, the Holy Spirit, the Divine energy, call it what we will for the soul to complete its journey Home.

The suffering is deep and at every level – physical, psychological, social, spiritual – when old ways of being in the world no longer work and disintegrate. We are like a frightened voyager, pushing out to sea in a storm. The safe harbour has been left (painfully) behind and is lost to sight beyond the horizon, but the new haven is not yet visible. Caught in the middle, there is only the terror of the unknown. Our normal ways of functioning in this state almost grind to a halt; disease (dis-ease) in many forms can occur in each of them. A few can become so distressed as the pressure mounts that severe physical or mental illness or even suicide can result. We can fall prey to the views of others who may exploit and abuse us in this vulnerable questing state (and not a few inauthentic gurus and religious leaders have capitalised on this down the years – and still do). The suffering is accentuated because the cause is not clear to us and our usual resources for dealing with it do not seem to work. The vision of how we might be without suffering eludes us, so we can stay stuck in the way we are, while exhausting ourselves trying to deal with the status quo. Nothing less than a complete transformation in our way of being in the world is called for and, whether we perceive it consciously or whether it is bubbling along in the unconscious, this too can be terrifying. The levels of fear, panic, pain and distress in our lives are often unprecedented.

Some respond by becoming a victim of circumstance - bad things happen and there is little or nothing we can do except give up, fight back or try to maintain the status quo. Struggling to keep going in the face of what seems like an attack can be immensely energy intensive, leading to the collapse known as burnout. Some things can be ruled out as unhelpful. "Job's comforters" – people telling us constantly that it will be all right, or making endless suggestions for change – just make us feel worse. Irina Tweedie, in her classic account of spiritual awakening (punctuated by periods of crisis) in the presence of a Sufi master, draws on a verse from the Ramayana and writes:-

"There are two ways Thou canst love me;
Either I should be so perfect that Thou hast to love me,
Or I will surrender before Thee, and Thou who Lovest thy Creation,
Thou willst love me for myself"[57]

At some point in the midst of spiritual awakening surrender is the only viable option. There is a certain inevitability about it, a sort of primordial interior programming to which we must all at some time (perhaps after many lifetimes, according to some traditions) respond and begin the journey Home. There is also a certain inevitability about the time it takes each of us to pass through and deepen that process. I have a hunch that somehow the soul has a pre-planned timetable of its own which can be neither held back nor accelerated. That we can either go with the flow or fall into forgetting and hold back, in which case the process embodies different levels of spiritual pain. The more we resist, the tougher it feels, the more we surrender into the process the less bumpy the ride. But to surrender is also a great challenge. The ego fights tooth and nail using every strategy in its deception toolbox to hold on to its power and the status quo. And in the secular West where individualism and the personal spiritual search are in the ascendant, concepts like surrender do not come easy.

Furthermore, some faiths disavow the possibility of interior exploration – keeping the shadow of the unconscious and the tricks of the ego firmly under wraps is preferred, because they are "evil". Better to adopt the approach of the Pharisees instead – ignore the internal process and just behave ourselves. But constraints like these cannot hold back the power of the soul within, punching to break through what has held it in place for so long. The ego has served its purpose. It has been in charge long enough, arguably keeping us safe as we have individuated and forged our path in this reality. But now it is time for it to give way, to move from being master to servant, and it rarely does so without a fight and a lot of pain and much risk. The apocalypse (from the Greek *apokalupsis* - meaning to reveal, to uncover) is not about a literal end of time destruction as it is sometimes interpreted. This derives from the egotistic perception of time and space and the dualistic battle between good and evil, fixing the Divine and the creation in time according to our own needs for certainty. The apocalypse happens in every moment of surrender as the ego gives way before the Divine, every collapse of the consciousness of the identity into the consciousness of the numinous.

Some might be put off from the spiritual search because they do not like the sound of this tough work, and especially the idea of surrender. However, the search is not about following our bliss, tempting as this is, but more a consciousness of "Not my will, but Thine". Yet, paradoxically in making that surrender we find the bliss. Bliss is not happiness, that is an ego mirror image of something far deeper; bliss is an expression of the soul, of union with the Divine. In surrender we become saturated in God, in the bliss that is beyond mere happiness.

However, surrender is not a condition that is complete, a static state; it is a process, forever unfolding and transforming. There is no endpoint, at least not until the soul completes its journey Home into that timeless place where "then" and "now" have no relevance. Meanwhile there is ongoing insight with all kinds of things emerging that could call us back into forgetfulness. Surrender includes a quality of watchfulness for such distractions, a prayerful humility without striving, that keeps us relaxed but ready and alert to the signs of those temptations that tug us away from the spiritual life.

In the meantime, if spiritual crisis is experienced, the immediate task is to get out of the situation, perhaps if possible away from the home and the workplace and retreat from the battle - as happens with the people who come into our retreat facilities at the Sacred Space Foundation in Cumbria. Inevitably here I am drawing on the many years of experience at the Foundation and the development of "what works". And what works is a formula tried and tested down the ages and found in many spiritual traditions. Spiritual crisis is not a time to try to make solutions happen – this is a time to come to stillness, to wait and see, to get out of the situation and find the space to allow the solutions that are waiting within to emerge. There are lots of possibilities, but getting at least temporarily out of the present environment and creating the space (the sacred space – where there is time for the soul to be heard) for the next steps is a priority. Resting, re-energising and recuperating – looking after our physical wellbeing by eating, exercising and sleeping better are part of the process, coupled with time to reflect on what is going on with us. This problem cannot be solved alone, so disconnection in retreat is not the answer, reconnection is what is called for, so the support of a wise counsellor who can guide us through the reflective process is essential.

Birthing within us what needs to come forth is arguably unsafe alone (look at the near death turmoil that even great spiritual masters like the Buddha or Jesus or the Prophet went through) – we need a "spiritual midwife" as suggested earlier, one or more, to accompany us through this phase. As we re-collect what has gone on, we can start a process of re-visioning our lives. Notice again how almost all the verbs in this process are "r" words – the journey is not so much to new lands, but a remembering of somewhere we already are. Using all kinds of reflective and awareness building processes, such as guided meditation, the Enneagram (a form of personality inventory which assists spiritual insight[58]), spiritual direction and so on, we can begin to return to that place in ourselves where we feel at Home – recovering a sense of meaning, purpose and connection in life – the very stuff of spirituality. Thus we learn to live our lives with what has heart and meaning for us with a deeper connection to our spiritual needs. Equally, we may find that the revisioning process enables us to stay in our ordinary lives more at ease, because something in ourselves has changed, some shift of consciousness or awareness that helps us to be with old roles and relationships in new and less harmful ways. The crisis of spiritual emergency does not mean that everything has to be demolished, rather, and perhaps more likely, we are able to stand more firmly and compassionately in our ordinary life because we now see it so differently.

On the other hand this can also be a time of often painful letting go. Whether this happens in the intense time of spiritual crisis if we experience it, or through the steady work of attending to our spiritual needs and awakening (gradual emergence rather than critical emergency) we may have to face up to changing some aspects of our lives that no longer nurture our souls. How we let go of or change relationships depends upon our awareness. We can terminate them in anger and bitterness. We can become resigned (a kind of passive disconnection) to them and their underlying inauthenticity. We can work with them to transform them into a new relationship. Or we can let them go as lovingly and consciously as we can.

The process of refinement leads us to (lovingly) let go of old habits, values, friendships and so on that are no longer nurturing or that we can no longer hold without feeling like we are sacrificing ourselves. This is high risk territory as we will explore in part 5 when we look further at discernment. Without careful support and discernment this can be a painful process for others as relationships or jobs or other interests are seen to be no longer part of our way Home. If we are not careful and our egos get a grip on this, we can find ourselves riding roughshod over many others in our driven spiritual search. There is a delicate balance here to know what it is right to let go of and what we must stay with.

The awakening of the spirit within and the journey Home can be and is a profoundly joyous and blissful experience, but as I have suggested it is also a high risk Way as our soul practices refine us ever more, harmonising our will with the Will. Like all journeys it needs careful planning perhaps taking into account that it will last years and cannot be hurried. Recognising this, the religious traditions down the years have evolved tried and tested means of helping this birthing process. For this reason alone we need to be wary of rejecting religions, for they have often had millennia of experience to find out what works and what does not. Because the religions have often failed in so many ways, tending to be containers of orthodoxy for the seeker rather than nurturing wombs to develop us and set us free, we need to be cautious about dismissing them out of hand, and later I will explore the value or otherwise of engaging with a religious tradition in our searching. Meanwhile, the rich lessons of experience they can bring offers four Soul Care key things that need to be in place, which have been commonly used in spiritual "midwifery" down the ages in all traditions:

1. Soul Friends – in the Celtic Christian tradition this is the *anam cara*. This is not a safe journey alone and what is needed is the support of one or more wise spiritual counsellors or mentors to whom we can turn for guidance. These gurus, teachers, mentors, guides are people who have walked the path before us and know how to support us in times of need. I have met a few in my life, who know how to challenge and guide lovingly. They exhibit a kind of fierce love, holding us with deep compassion and understanding, yet not letting us get away with our illusions and delusions.   In individualist Western secular cultures, one of the spiritual challenges is overcoming the resistance to surrendering to the authority of the guru, spiritual counsellor or soul friend,[59] [60] but without him or her we risk many dangers, not least psychosis, ego inflation or a messianic complex if our interior impressions go unchecked and unchallenged. The New Age tendency to say OK to everything, to allow us to avoid surrender into God and make Gods of ourselves is not the approach of the true soul friend, who may lovingly direct us quite firmly when he or she sees we are going astray or becoming aggrandised by our experiences. And our soul friend knows we are going astray for he or she has long since acquired map and compass of the soul's landscape. This knowledge (because they have also done the personal and emotional work themselves, freeing them from the risk of corrupting the work with ego agendas for power) is rooted in the humility of the true servant.

2. Soul Communities – groups of people with whom we feel at home and who lovingly nourish our ongoing spiritual awakening. It might be a fellow group of meditators, a church group and so on, there are many possibilities. It might be a permanent community, such as belonging to a church or temple or a temporary community, such as a course or retreat where we share and relate to others for a while. The community adds to the checks and balances that can keep us safe in the almost crazy time when one way of seeing is replaced by another. Such a paradigm shift can be full of joy but can also be cataclysmic. We can contrast the spiritual awakening that occurs in a spiritual community such as a monastery, convent or modern day, well run retreat centre, to that which takes place in

unbridled freedom – such as unsupported weekend courses without follow-up or in centres of New Age teaching where the attention to creating even temporary "holding" communities is limited or non existent. The holding quality enables us to pass through the crisis or the maturation work with greater likelihood of safety, integration and wholeness, rather than left to wander the streets or return home frightened or ego-inflated, disorientated, perplexed and alone.

3. Soul Foods – the inspiration of scripture, poetry, music, art, nature and so on that refresh, renew and revitalise us. And, literally, good food that nourishes our body e.g. many organisations offering spiritual support stress the need for a healthy diet and lifestyle. Things that "feed" us in every sense of the word can be included here, such as being in environments of peace and beauty, listening to words and music that have heart and meaning for us, having access to complementary therapies and healing approaches such as the laying on of hands and the deep relaxation that comes from bodywork such as massage.

4. Soul Works - developing spiritual practices which keep us on track and take care of us and foster deepening insight – meditation, prayer, yoga, retreat time, sacred dance, tai chi, exploring our Enneagram, labyrinth walking – there is an enormous range of possibilities. Soul works are the practical things we can do, some alone, some in groups with our soul communities, that help to keep us centred and at home in ourselves while we move ever deeper into awareness of Truth and our true Self on the journey Home.

These four elements together make for a safer and more fulfilling passage through spiritual exploration. They provide us with the structure for the next four parts of this book and we will explore each of them to see what can be expected.

Without them the insights can leave us buffeted by the interior storm, sometimes even bringing great personal danger to ourselves and others. People have been known in extremis to commit suicide, or desert their loved ones, or carry out terrible acts upon others. For example, a flurry of newspaper reports in the UK last year discussed several individuals who had committed murders because "God told me to". The line between madness and mysticism is a fine one. If we receive revelations in the midst of our spiritual awakening it can be hugely difficult to sort the wheat from the chaff unless our Soul Care principles are in place. When we are young (spiritually) we may not like it, but there can be a lot of sense in someone who checks that you have changed your underwear and washed behind your ears! Even without the extremes of spiritual crisis, these four Soul Care principles are essential to a healthy and maturing spirituality; they helped to prepare the ground so that the seeds of the soul can flourish, the Will of the Divine work fully in us. Our community, our practices, our directors and our sources of nourishment are there to encourage and guide us when we feel lost or discouraged, when we encounter challenging or arid times. If you have not already done so, it might be worthwhile taking stock right now and answering the questions:

In my spiritual quest who is my wise and trusted soul friend to guide me safely on the Way?
What are the spiritual practices, my soul works, to which I am committed?
Where is my soul community that nurtures my spirit and both challenges and encourages me?
What soul foods do I have in my life that nurture, challenge, encourage and inspire my search?

The care of the soul is needed in the alchemical process of its emergence and the transformation of who we think we are into who we truly are. With Soul Care in place the intense spiritual pain of spiritual crisis diminishes, or the struggle of the steady plod up the mountain can be less wearisome, but does it ever go away? If the soul is of the infinite, then there are infinite possibilities for its expansion, its awakening. To the cry "Where is there an end to it?" Eliot's response was unequivocal, "There is no end, but addition."[61]   Often (underpinned by fear) we seek to set goals for spiritual work, seeking that end point when we will be "there". We are not what we achieve. Our goals will not make us happy, only our being. All the hurts, challenges and obstructions are just the stuff emerging from our unconscious that gets in the way of our move into being. There are no goals, more a sense of transformed attention, a refinement of our attunement to the world, through and for Love. There is no "there". A Sufi wisdom story suggests that in spiritual awakening we may seek to set goals of avoiding suffering or seeking the blissful experience, but both are ego distortions and escape is an illusion:

Isa ibn Maryam (Jesus, son of Mary) saw some people sitting miserably on a wall by the roadside. "What's the matter?" He asked. "We have ended up like this because we have been afraid of hell" they said. Isa went on his way, and came across another group, also wailing and in pain. "What's the matter?" He asked. "We desired paradise and it has made us like this," they said. He continued his walk and came across a third group. They looked indeed like people who had suffered much and yet their faces seemed to shine with joy. "How is it that you are like this?" He asked again. "The Spirit of Truth," they answered, "and this has made us let go of lesser goals." Isa said, "These are the people who attain. On the day of accounting, these are they who will be in the Presence of God."[62]

When the seeker finds the "Spirit of Truth" there is a passing beyond pain. It is not that pain does not exist, rather that our consciousness around it and towards it has been transformed. It is not detachment, but non-attachment, an age-old truth found in all the great faiths, that to be free of desire, even desire for bliss or escape from suffering is freedom in Truth: "Without desire, we can plumb its depths; with desire, we can only see its externals."[63] There are certain eternal elements to this state of consciousness, this level of healing, and in my experience it is always the same – the process is one of forgiveness, the agent is grace and the outcome atonement. Through the way of forgiveness we come to accept and integrate all the parts of our being – our history, our personhood. This process is not sustained by the will of the ego; in fact the ego has no place in it at all except to get out of the way, to have its power broken. It is fed and watered by grace in surrender to the absolute however we experience it, the power that is of an indefinable, immeasurable source – it is spirit, energy, consciousness, call it what we will. It has many names in all belief systems, but it is the same agent of transformation that moves once our own will gets out of or is pushed out of the way. And that movement is towards union, wholeness (holiness), healing – the atonement – the at-one-ment, from which place of consciousness we may see Truth and the perfection of the path we have taken towards it. Towards Home.

...It is easy to know one.
It is easy to know two.
But to understand that one and one are two,
We have to learn the and.
Connection into disconnection
The breaking of the empty vessel
The holes in the net
The vacant room
The blank page
The incalculable value of the space contained.
In our hollowness is our fulfilling.
In our emptiness is our purpose.

Hold my hand and I yours
Let these roses cover the flesh and the fleshless
For what you see is not who I am
What you see is not who I am.

As we reach out for You
We fall through the door
Barring
One reality from the next
A door when pressed
Dissolving
In the resolution of my hand.
From the tea shop of memory to the
Wine bar of action,
Berobed in splendour
Beyond cloth or stitch.
Satiated in optimism
And the ground of our action,
Where doing and being
Slip
Into unity
Along the trajectory of dissolution, illumination, integration
Into the peace
Of service...

Part 5

"World crises multiply and everybody deplores the shortage, or even the total lack, of 'wise' men and women, unselfish leaders, trustworthy counsellors etc. It is hardly rational to expect such high qualities from people who have never done any inner work and who would not even understand what is meant by the words." [64]

Soul Friends: "God heals; I make the tea"

He'd been in retreat for a week and we'd worked together for many hours each day. His cancer diagnosis had thrown his whole life into uncertainty, and his response was to return to a search he had abandoned as a teenager. It wasn't that in his youth he had ignored questions about the meaning of life; it was just that the answers he got from his church did not fit with life as he was living it. And anyway it was the 60s and there were the Beatles and the Stones to enjoy, free love to pursue, drugs to play with. And so in his middle fifties facing death he was looking for hope, looking for God at last.

It was a humbling experience being in this man's presence as he groped his way toward something that he knew must be there. To watch him pass beyond thought and word and simply be, drowning himself in the Self. We didn't talk in much detail about what he saw or heard or felt, just exchanged knowing looks, understanding looks. No more was necessary in those shared moments of knowing; the kind of knowing that indeed requires no words or explanation. Through the oceans of tears he wept for himself, for his family, for the world, he began to see clearly that which he sought, not far off but right under his nose. And the tears of pain turned into tears of joy; water turned into wine.

The spiritual search is full of paradox. In going deep into ourselves we also are turned out of ourselves into the ecstasy – the *ex-stasis*, out of the static or usual perception of self – into new possibilities. Under the guidance of a spiritual director that process can be passed through safely and, in a culture where feelings are held in suspicion, the space is created for those feelings to be expressed. In ex-pressing, literally pressing or pushing out, we have the opportunity to see something from a different perspective, to find a new way of seeing, especially if there is someone around with the wisdom to help us do so and not simply express for its own sake.

When he left he said, "I don't know how you can do this day in and day out. How do you cope with all these people crying all over your floor all the time, all that anger and bitterness that comes out." I suppose I could have come out with all those off-pat counsellor clichés – about having good supervision, or taking care of myself, or knowing my limits and all that kind of stuff. But the only thing that popped out was – "It's easy, I'm not in charge."

One of the ways the soul is nourished is in the relationship between the person and their spiritual guide. The spiritual director (often used synonymously nowadays with the term spiritual counsellor) is found in all belief systems, from the 18-year apprenticeship of the novice druid to his/her master, the *murshid* (one who guides aright) in Sufism, the Socratic *iatros tes psuches* (soul healer), the *staretz* of the Russian Orthodox church, the Hindu guru, the roles of rabbis and priests – in many forms the essential elements of the soul friend, the Celtic *anam cara*, are found. (I use anam cara here in the sense of the wise spiritual guide, usually someone who is more spiritually mature than ourselves. In some schools of thought, the anam cara may simply be a companion along the Way with whom we mutually share our experience in order to learn. We can find many anam cara in this sense, not least in our soul communities [q.v.]).

Some spiritual directors work almost full time as such, accompanying and counselling the seeker along the Way. For others it is a part of a wider role, such as that of the parish priest. Personally, I prefer the term director, even though the concept of "direction" is often unwelcome in our western individualised culture. I look at it this way - if you get lost on the way home and you stop and ask for help, do you expect to be counselled or directed? At the same time direction is not a one way process from "higher" to "lower", there is mutual exchange at work in which both can deepen their capacity to relate, to know each other and themselves as human beings, to know the Divine more. I have never in all the countless sessions of spiritual direction I have offered ever left the session not feeling somehow closer to and known more deeply the other, myself, God.

A friend and fellow interfaith minister writes[65] how she came to the work with many questions about it, realised "Really it was a question about myself – am I good enough? Or do I know enough? Or who am I?" What she came to understand was that "the ground of being able to spiritually counsel another is deeply rooted in God, in knowing that who I am fundamentally is made by God and beloved of God. When I know this is true for me, I can hold this is deepest truth for another and within this truth we are one." She goes on to write that "I experience spiritual counselling as a journey, a relationship between two equal souls who are learning together that they really are deeply connected to and loved by their One Source. When I sit with another person in this way I experience a kind of deep stillness, a loving presence that seems to flow through me from the Source. As God looks through my eyes, feels through my heart, listens through my ears and speaks through my voice, that person before me is the most precious thing. Whatever is concerning them matters and holds the seeds of freedom. Being deeply attentive to whatever is unfolding in someone allows healing to happen."

My friend's summary encapsulates the essential qualities that we can expect of the spiritual director. The sense of not being in charge, of waiting upon God's guidance, of offering hospitality, mutuality and friendship, holding the safe sacred space that allows grace, the Holy Spirit, the divine energy to be manifest. To be so present with someone, the spiritual director must have done much healing and emotional work – on him or herself. Otherwise the helper who is not healed risks bringing all manner of unhelpful even dangerous personal shadows into the relationship. One of the hallmarks to look for in finding a soul friend is that they have done the work, they are themselves emotionally well rounded human beings and have been brought to a place of humble service free of ego agendas. The depth of humility that arises from this work allows us to come to know that we can be in control of very little, for as TS Eliot[66] put it, "humility is endless" and is of profound service to others. As my friend concludes "Does it really matter whether I feel God or not? Does it really matter what I know? I simply hold the space. God heals. I make the tea." The relationship with the spiritual director is essentially a God centred one with the intention of allowing the inbreaking of the grace/spirit of God into the relationship. It is the seeking of the *parousia* , the bursting of the kingdom into consciousness, into ordinary reality, the transformation of the way of seeing and being. God is not a spiritual bully, despite some scriptural assertions and interpretation. God does not break through uninvited (even though sometimes we think we did not do the inviting!)

This sense of effortless effort is reinforced in Guenther's remarkable study of spiritual direction. Likening it to midwifery (which is essentially a natural process of aiding the birthing of something, which already exists, into the world.) she writes "When in doubt, I always assume that God is at work, that is, the person is pregnant."[67] She writes further of the relationship between counsellor and counselled as fundamentally hierarchical, "not because the director is somehow "better" or "holier" than the directee, but because, in this covenanted relationship, the director has agreed to put himself aside so that his total attention can be focussed on the person sitting in the other chair" yet it is "a hierarchy which is a gentle and perhaps transitory one."

If there is a hierarchy at all, it is a hierarchy of wisdom, of expanded consciousness. In the transmission of that wisdom we cannot expect the spiritual director to give everything away to us at once. We mature spiritually at different paces, moving along a trajectory from what some see as a "conformist" stage, characterised by being orientated towards results and black and white thinking and dependence on a group, person or thing to sort it all out for us, to give us the right answers. Later we may move to a conscientious stage where we are more willing to see exceptions to rules, individual traits and roles; more commitment, dependence on ourselves is present. Thirdly there is the interindividual stage. Here there is greater toleration of self and others, of paradox and mystery in thinking, the embracing of development as a way of life rather than a fixed goal.[68]

We need to be wary when applying psychological models to spiritual processes, but these concepts do help us to understand that our degree of maturity will affect the kind of Soul Care approaches that will work for us and those that will not, which kinds of books we are ready to read and which will go over our heads. The spiritual director is able to discern what it is best to offer us, and is not contaminated, if they are spiritually healthy themselves, with holding things back from us because they seek power over us. Jesus was not being cruel when he spoke of not throwing pearls before swine (Matthew 7:6); he was stating a spiritual truth about not giving things away to people when they are not ready to receive them and perceive their value. Our spiritual director encourages that development in us that enables a free flowing transmission of wisdom, sometimes teasing or pressing us, lovingly, along the way to draw us into deeper maturity. He/She makes sure that we are not so confused that we cannot mature, but challenged enough so that we are encouraged to press on. It is a fine balancing act and hence the need for the effective soul friend (see checklist at the end of this Part).

Spiritual direction takes an unusual approach, some would argue unique, because it offers a loving, safe, non-denominational haven in which to find meaning, inner peace and wisdom. It incorporates deep listening, acceptance and spiritual practices (such as meditation, guided visualisations and prayer) within the framework of each person's beliefs. It helps people of any faith or none, to access the clarity needed to resolve inner conflicts and lead a joyous, meaningful life. It is specifically concerned with God, a Source, an Absolute. At the same time it is not about producing a state of spiritual passivity and acceptance of the status quo in our lives. Sometimes counselling and psychotherapy risk settling for enabling people to resolve their conflict and problems with the world and learn to live in it as it is. They may seek that which is "wrong" or "broken" about the person. Spiritual direction offers the reverse. It does not encourage passivity and acceptance of the way things are.

The spiritual director does not see the one before them as "wrong", but whole/holy and searching to express that wholeness. "Spiritual direction is concerned with healing and reconciliation, not with adaptation to current values, but with the transformation of consciousness."[69] In so doing, spiritual direction is not an instrument of the status quo (as some argue that religion and spirituality are) rather it is an instrument of revolution. For the transformation of consciousness brings a transformation in our way of being in the world. The fate of the soul and the fate of the world are intimately bound together.

A key feature of the work of the director is to help the person find truth by testing and discernment, for the path to spiritual awakening is littered with illusions and delusions. Stafford Whiteaker writes that "A spiritual director or guide is someone who helps you in your spiritual journey by being a good listener and soul companion, and by making suggestions for meditating, reading, study or prayer. Such directors and guides are often religious men or women, clergy or lay people who have had the special training and experience in helping people with spiritual matters. The important thing is that the person helps us with discernment and is someone with whom we can feel very comfortable and to whom we are able to entrust our confidences."[70] Finding that person with whom we feel comfortable is not always easy, although perhaps the cliché that "when the student is ready, the teacher turns up" may have a ring of truth in it. Meanwhile religious traditions, websites, counselling journals and retreat guides[iii] are among the sources of information. The search for and working with the right director are themselves rich opportunities for spiritual learning.

Spiritual direction is not about telling us the rules or one interpretation of the holy books. It is a companionship of mutual exploration and respect in the search for truth. Nowadays, spiritual direction has the benefits of the discoveries of psychology to draw upon and often a soul friend will explore our psychology as much as our spirituality. Many spiritual directors belong to a particular faith which influences their guidance while others seek to work in non-denominational ways. A lot of hostility and misunderstanding has emerged around spiritual direction as in many quarters it can be reduced to enforcing and reiterating dogma and doctrines rather than personal awakening. The best of spiritual directors of any background can hold a safe and loving space where we can explore our spirituality and all that has meaning and purpose for us in life and they are good at helping us see through and get past the various places in ourselves where we get stuck. Getting ego inflated, failing to see the unconscious at work, occasions of feeling disconnected from God, the tendency to turn interest in the Self into self interest –

[iii] See for example www.thegoodretreatguide.com, www.worldretreatguide.com, www.retreats.org.uk

these and other quagmires are familiar territory to the wisdom of the soul friend.

In the daily work of spiritual direction, it is noticeable how many people have psychological blockages that create spiritual blockages. Mike was an experienced meditator who came along because of difficulties in his marriage. His wife was following her Roman Catholic tradition and they had been getting into serious arguments about the existence or otherwise of God. We spent some time playfully with even applying the word "exist" to God (an idea explore in Part 1 of this book). This got us into an interesting debate in which he became more and more angry about the God word. When we explored this it was clear that his whole image of God was negative. He claimed to be an atheist, which was odd because he had very definite views about what God was like. Words like "bad tempered", "murderous", "unjust", "domineering", "inconsistent" and so forth fell from his lips. As our exploration unfolded it emerged that he had been brought up in a very hellfire protestant sect and was taught that unless he believed certain things and lived a certain way he was going to hell. He was neither able to believe nor live those things so abandoned his church in adulthood. It also emerged when we talked about his parenting, that his father in particular had been remote, domineering, punishing and shaming with him. Much the same qualities he applied to God in fact.

Mike is an example of a common phenomenon, our tendency to project onto God (arguably the ultimate authority figure) our early experiences of authority figures in our lives, such as parents. It is very common to find the main obstruction to God is our concept of God him/her/itself, exacerbated in the modern world from two broadsides, the domination of the secular agenda and the dreadful face of God conjured up by acts done in the name of God. Mike spent a lot of time revisiting his relationship with his parents and learning about forgiveness, but he also spent a lot of time, in visualisation, prayer and meditation revisiting God, getting past the images he was stuck with, and discovering a source of boundless love that opened his heart and brought him to tears. The image of God as the ego monster that Mike like so many of us had learned about turned out to be a false God. Psychology and spirituality here spiralled around each other, taking him to new levels of understanding. Thus his journey to God began by finding out that whatever we think God is, God is not. At some level, God is beyond definition, neither this nor that, *neti neti*, in Hindu thought. In the Old Testament, Moses (Ex. 3:4) presses God to identify himself so that he can give the people a clear image. I suspect Moses may have been somewhat frustrated by God's elliptical answer, "I am who I am". He may well have preferred something a little more definite to help control his restive followers. But God's mysterious "isness" may leave us frustrated by its lack of definition, while also liberating us into a boundless exploration of the infinite nature of God.

Spiritual direction allows a drawing upon the person's resources (spiritual) that counselling and psychotherapy often steer clear of and usually involves practices – such as joining in prayer and so on that tends to be outwith the counselling role. Spiritual direction is not about maintaining a professional distance, but a fluid merging of boundaries, a mutual participation in a unitary process whose outcome is always certain in the long or short term. It is indeed a high risk strategy in conventional terms of counselling, but with the learning and application of the skill of both getting out of the way and opening to God, it may be that the birthing of something miraculous and wonderful can be witnessed. Yet spiritual direction in being different from counselling and psychotherapy also has an ally in them for the fields are compatible and "frequently share raw material"[71]. Aronson emphasises the mutual territory and the limitations when he writes: "Meditation is beneficial and it may not solve one's psychological issues. Psychology is helpful, and it does not necessarily address spiritual concerns. For a balanced psychological and spiritual life, we in the West can benefit from both meditation and psychological assistance. One approach does not preclude the other. At their best they can mutually inform and enrich each other. In the end there are also some differences between the traditional and modern visions and these can be respectfully acknowledged."[72]

I've noticed that many people deepen their spiritual search after a period of counselling or psychotherapy. It is almost as if these approaches first help by clearing the ground of old problems, wounds and disappointments that then frees the soul to take flight on its search for Home. This was my own experience too, working with a fine psychotherapist at the time of my early crisis who gently and sometimes not so gently led me to face up to some things about myself, dig up some of the nastier skeletons in my unconscious cupboard, and begin a process of healing. It is still a source of curiosity that I ever turned up on her doorstep. To this day I have no memory of finding my way to her, or by what means I overcame my inherent resistance to inner exploration – I was fine thank you very much! Sometimes angels in our lives are real people who turn up when we need them, and some force, some divine possession, some spirit out of our conscious control seems to impel us towards them (or them towards us). Jones echoes the value of that preliminary cleansing when he writes "The therapist, the counsellor, the psychiatrist can help us on our way. They can rescue us from a particular block, get us back on our feet, can teach us to accept ourselves so that we can be on the move. But they cannot answer for us (nor would the best of them want to) those burning questions concerning the purpose and meaning for which we long. The spiritual guide cannot answer them either, but there is within the world of spiritual direction a conscious commitment to faith in God."[73]

Spiritual direction may therefore draw on elements sometimes considered outside the remit of the counsellor or therapist – grace, prayer, the invocation of the Other, sacraments, the laying on of hands and so on. God is very much at the centre of the spiritual direction relationship, where the seeker is becoming more sensitised to God and developing a relationship with God. All this is taking place within the human connection between director and seeker. This relationship may of itself be beneficial to some of us who find ourselves starved of others with whom we can have the level and depth of communication and conversation we seek.

Seeking insight can also happen to some degree in our relationships with friends. Is the soul friend that same kind of friend? The relationship tends to be transitory, for being a soul companion suggests a journey, where the companionship is shared while the journey lasts, but not beyond it. The spiritual direction friendship is different from social friendship, for "My director is my friend but I am not his. He knows an awful lot about me and I know very little about him...It's not an ordinary friendship. My spiritual director is friendly, open and human and shares stories. She's not someone I see at other times: so there is a specialness about it. It's a spiritual friendship in a liminal space...you put yourself in a liminal space so that things can happen which might not happen in a more fixed place or more fixed relationship. There is space for the Holy Spirit; a space which is there when we meet and doesn't exist anywhere else. It's a friendship dedicated to God; that's what makes it spiritual and something different."[74] And yet it seems possible that as the relationship evolves, ordinary friendship can emerge. However, it introduces where this happens, all sorts of personal dynamics that may limit or make more difficult the flow of the seeker towards that which they seek. Sometimes our time with a spiritual director may last a few sessions or be spread over a lifetime, and a unique form of mutually nourishing soul friendship may emerge. It is rooted in humility, hospitality, humour, respect, connection and service to God.

It can also be a tough relationship. For spiritual direction is not about telling us that whatever we are experiencing is OK. I have several people in my life from whom I have deliberately sought spiritual direction. This happens with Jeannie Sayre-Adams, with whom I have shared this spiritual search now for some 25 years. In our work together at the Sacred Space Foundation, in our co-authoring and teaching, and in our day-to-day relationship we have grown a relationship that is mutually supportive of each other's souls. Sometimes it is and has been challenging and stretching us in every sense, but always deepening in love. In the crucible of that human relationship, a drawing closer to God for both of us has been a profound result. That dance of love and soul friendship is a high wire act, but where it works, and my hunch is that it is rare, two persons can become a significant mutual foil for an unfolding consciousness of and relationship to God. In such a relationship, there is no end to the possibilities of that unfolding.

Others too have been with me along the Way, most significantly Ram Dass in the USA, who I guess would be the closest I ever got to having a guru (although he would eschew the title, for in India the guru is far more than a teacher of the Way, he or she *is* the Way). At home, a small group of wise friends, and sometimes fierce advisers, have been with me as soul friends down the years. There have been many others where the relationship was brief, perhaps no more than a chance meeting where some mutual spiritual exploration and illumination took place. It is important not to negate or overlook the possibility of spiritual direction arising in many possible encounters in which soul friendship is offered. At the same time, the consistent and continuous relationship with our spiritual director is the main aspect I encourage here; there is no substitute for it. Certainly this is the common pattern which has emerged in different faith traditions around the world. It was firmly a part of the monastic and pre-Christian druidic culture of the UK, it is enshrined in the teachings of Buddhism, Daoism, Hinduism, Sikhism and in the teachings of the desert fathers and mothers of early Christianity, and so forth. The central idea here is that subjecting oneself to the wisdom of the spiritual director is itself an aspect of spiritual work, and in that subjugation emerges the role of the spiritual director. As the barriers dissolve, the directed one finds their way Home through the direct transmission of wisdom, of the perennial philosophy in all its guises, from one person to another.

My early encounter with Ram Dass led me to hero worship him, to place him on a pedestal – common occurrence on the part of the seeker when we find our anam cara. That is unhealthy in the long term for soul friend and seeker alike. The soul friend is our effective guide precisely because they are fully human. When I noticed Ram Dass having everyday chatty conversations with others, sitting in his sports car or listening to 60s soul music, I learned about the importance of his ordinariness. In the human ordinariness of the soul friend is their specialness. The teachers need to use the loo (!) like the rest of us and we need to be wary of getting stuck in our projections onto them, making them models of some idealised semi-divine human. This neither liberates us nor the soul friend and it inhibits the full flowering of the spiritual direction relationship. We come to the soul friend because of the loving wisdom they can offer, and which they can reveal in ourselves, not to make idols of them. (If any soul friend suggests that we should do the latter with him/her then this is probably a relationship best terminated.) To hang on to them or to give way to the abuse of power is a kind of spiritual infidelity in which we betray the Divine, and ourselves. Some teachers say that "I am God". In a way there is truth in this, but the would-be guide who has not done the inner work distorts this. The ego gets a grip on it and thus shifts it into a power trip, where it leads the person to mistake being of God, with being God. For a person to say "I am God" is like a mirror saying "I am you". Furthermore, this inner work approach is distrusted in some faiths, which believe that accessing the Divine can only be mediated by a priestly caste. The soul friend is not such a gatekeeper. He or she may happen to belong to a holy order of one sort or another, but their actions are very clearly those of companion and guide not mediator. I suggest that no one stands between us and the Divine but ourselves and if there is a mediator, it is an aspect of that Divine itself.

And do not expect an easy relationship. The spiritual director, the soul friend works with us to turn up the heat on the fire of the soul longing for its source. I probably only met Ram Dass in person half a dozen times on a one-to-one basis, plus a few private phone calls and emails. Yet in each of those encounters (reinforced with the benefits of books and recordings) he would take no prisoners of my delusions! His is a deeply loving presence, but that love is sometimes fierce and burning, pushing me into taking stock of what was true and authentic and what were my ego driven distortions. We can expect the love of the spiritual director to be fierce love. In my first meeting with him I was taken aback that he was so directive, being quite clear about the risky place I was in and he gave quite specific instructions. He taught me something then about spiritual direction, that it is not always about soft and fluffy encouragement but sometimes about being quite direct and challengingly so. A spiritual director who does not challenge, test, push, question is not a spiritual director. Sometimes we can expect to be told we are doing fine, sometimes he or she can deliver a spiritual kick in the pants! Subjecting ourselves to the discernment and discipline process of spiritual direction does not fit comfortably in the individualist material culture where we expect to achieve only self gratification and congratulation. While, as I suggested above, the spiritual director is one with whom we should feel comfortable, it is important to recognise that discomfiture is part of the process too and that often we have to stick with the process of the relationship precisely because it is tough to do so, that is part of the discipline of spiritual work. It can be difficult sometimes to check out the authentic spiritual director when the relationship is challenging – is it thus because it is necessary for us to learn and therefore we must stick with it or is it an abuse of power from a false director? The modern spiritual supermarket can sometimes make it too easy to indulge in spiritual director-hopping simply because we don't like the tough stuff, yet it may be that hanging in there is exactly what we need to do when it gets difficult. A spiritual pick and mix approach means that we tend to just pillage the bits we like and avoid the rest, which while the latter may be immediately unpalatable, is just as much a part of spiritual work precisely because it stretches us.

To help is in our "way of seeing", and especially seeing differently, many individuals are available as there are organisations which offer retreat facilities either for quiet time alone or in groups and with or without access to a director. Likewise a spiritual director can be seen on a regular basis without going away on retreat – once one has been found it is wise to check out clearly what background he/she has, what style of working, costs and other arrangements – with the caveats I have listed below. Not all spiritual options or those who teach them are without risk. Sorting out the deep from the shallow, the flaky from the serious, the safe from the maybe even dangerous, of itself draws us into the spiritual practice of discernment. As yet there is no nationally recognised training or registration system for spiritual directors in the UK and there are strong arguments against this within the field through fears of "professionalizing" what is essentially a human skill and calling.

How to test out the good from the bad? Check out the person and the setting and be wary of those who:

Do not walk their talk – preaching brotherly love then damning to hell individuals and groups who differ from them.

Ask you to abandon all critical thought and follow them blindly – authentic directors ask you to follow the truth not them.

Say that their knowledge is secret and can only be given to an elect few who have been initiated to their standards (can you imagine Jesus or Mohammed or the Buddha saying that their wisdom was secret? They may have been cautious about to whom they revealed their wisdom, but they did not regard it as belonging only to them and to be denied to others).

Demand all your money, possessions, body – the real guide gives away freely to humanity not to acquire wealth or power over you, though he or she may set tough spiritual tasks to gain the knowledge.

Instruct you to get rid of all your relationships and activities not connected to the "faith".

Run an organisation that is really a big business rather than a service, unreasonably high fees for teaching/time are another warning sign.

Tell you your lack of enlightenment is all your fault because you're not giving enough money, obedience, sex etc.

Use bodyguards or minders to keep followers remote, indeed have troops of followers at all.

Have no tradition or field of expertise to draw upon – the good director is a repository of wisdom who helps you unravel that wisdom in yourself and they have the strength of spiritual tradition and discipline to draw on.

Have no ongoing direction/challenge themselves.

Are part of an organisation with pressure groups to make you conform rather than encouraging faith and trust.

Tell you their way is the only way – the director's work is to help you find the truth in you not impose his/hers on you.

Demand that you remain in their sphere of influence, and not take what you need from them and move on.

Leave you feeling controlled, intimidated, abused or exploited rather than loved, liberated, nurtured and encouraged.

Focus the attention on their teaching and themselves as opposed to the teachings and presence of the Divine.

Suggest that they be worshipped rather than what they point to.

Sometimes, even if we are astute enough to discern these factors, it can still be a hard decision to make alone, and thus other aspects of Soul Care as outlined in Parts 6, 7 and 8 provide us with checks and balances if we are unsure of our relationship with our spiritual director.

Meanwhile, it is worth remembering that just because someone has acquired deep wisdom in one thing, it does not necessarily mean they are wise in all things. A wise spiritual teacher knows their limits. The Dalai Lama at one meeting was asked a convoluted question about relationships by a young man, specifically the struggle he was experiencing in his marriage. The audience was hushed, expecting a profound response from a man who dedicates a large part of his life to spiritual practice. He thought for a while then said "Ask an expert!" I warm to teachers like that who have the humility to know the limits of their expertise! Wise spiritual beings are not necessarily wise in all things.

The Buddha is famous for his exhortation to his followers – "Be a lamp unto yourself." But he did not intend this as a license to go off and do our own thing in the spiritual search without restraint or guidance. He was encouraging his followers to be acutely aware of false prophets, gurus and teachers. A nurse friend of mine recently attended the much publicised Alpha course seeking to renew her Christian faith, but she left when it was made clear to her that homosexuality was a sin. Her son happened to be gay and she could not square the condemnation by the course facilitator, with the loving, responsible, wonderful human being that is her son. To keep people toeing the line in faith, it's a common approach for leaders to quote a holy book, chapter and verse, to justify a particular stance.

It's always struck me as odd that some religious people have had such a hang up about sex; it's a subject guaranteed to get the pages of the holy books rippling over to find a clause to support an absolute position. It strikes me as odd, not because of the view, but because of the way the book is elevated as a perfect document to be interpreted literally. In monotheistic faiths, this seems to be a kind of blasphemy, raising the book to the same level of perfection as the Divine. Most people of faith see their holy books as the spiritual material for reflection, interpretation and challenge in the search for truth. Likewise, those in ministry in healthy faiths are not held up to be beyond challenge. The absolutist position is horrified by both these aspects, and tends to view with dismay the interpretative approach and/or the challenging of authority that bringing our own lamp to the search suggests.

George Fox, the main driving force behind the establishment of the Quakers in the 17th century was motivated in part by the ossified state of the beliefs and practices of the established church. He was regularly and often angrily challenged (and imprisoned) when people would quote scripture at him in an attempt to dismiss his ideas. His response, when people would say "The Bible says this" would be "But what sayest thou?"[75] Like the Buddha, he saw it as wrong to follow any person or belief system blindly, but to bring the light of our own reason, our lamp, to shine upon them – to expose the truths and the deceptions. The words of Jesus have often been used to justify the repression of "sinners" in all manner of quite horrendous ways, yet there was no greater iconoclast than Jesus when confronted with the fundamentalism of his time.

The Sufi, mystical heart of Islam (often condemned by some Muslims for refusing to keep to orthodoxy) has an interesting tale to tell about the healthy approach to soul friends in particular, and religion in general. When faced with the certainty of an authority, the tale of the donkey and the Mullah is brought to mind. Mullah in Islam is a title of respect meaning teacher or scholar on religious matters. Mullah Nasrudin crops up in many Sufi stories, and is a figure associated with an unconventional approach to teach others about their uncritical attachments to persons or beliefs. Nasrudin borrowed a neighbour's donkey one day and the neighbour called at his home some time later to ask for it back. Nasrudin denied that he had the donkey, only at that moment for the sound if its braying to be heard at the back of the house. The neighbour heard it and demanded its return. Nasrudin faking a shocked expression asked indignantly "Would you take the word of a donkey over the word of a Mullah?"

A healthy spirituality is cautious about taking on board the advice of authority figures uncritically. But it can take courage to listen to advice of our own heart and trust our own knowledge and experience. In all faiths it is taught that we must not accept blindly but use reason and enquiry. St Paul, for example, in his many letters often advised followers to test; "Test everything" (Thessalonians 1.5:21) he says, echoing the Buddha. The moral of the Sufi tale is simple, be very wary of trusting authority figures, like the Buddha urging us to use our own lamp, believe the donkey not the Mullah! Beware of making Gods of people. All are of God and in some the veil of the ego has become so thin that they seem to shine with Divine light. But they are of God, not God. The One, the whole, the sacred unity within and around each of us is to be honoured and worshipped, not the aspect that bears it, no matter how wonderful our "guru" or any other person we happen to meet might be.

The intention in spiritual direction is to help us find our Home by inner exploration and guidance through the minefield of spiritual awakening. Through the process of testing and discernment, the spiritual director, the soul friend, helps us to see differently and ever more clearly. In many ways the relationship with the director can mirror our relationship with God, constantly calling us to go deeper. So often people have asked me how do I get to know God better? My response is, "How would you get to know me?" If we are forming a new relationship and wanted to get to know the person how do we do it? It's obvious, we talk to them, show up for dates, share a meal together, tell our story, talk about a book we have read. It's just the same to a degree with the spiritual director and more importantly with the Divine. We can read about God, talk about God, make time for God, talk to God, listen to God. Getting to know God requires many similar approaches as getting to know a person. Invite the Friend round for a meal now and again!

The hunger in all of us to deeply know ourselves and our place in the scheme of things, to be happy, to love, and that journey into knowing is not one to be undertaken lightly or alone. Knowing ourselves more deeply and our connection to that which is both part of and yet beyond the self, informs who we are in the world, what work nourishes us and how we should relate to others. Spiritual direction is one of the ways we can come to know and heal ourselves more deeply and heal our relationship to God. As such it is a pathway for us to become more integrated human beings. As we deepen our relationship to God under the sensitive and loving guidance of our spiritual director we find a wealth of love there to draw upon in our search. Indeed it is almost as if we may albeit temporarily leapfrog some aspects of our concerns in the world or with ourselves. We can spend a lifetime picking over the wounds of the ego. But it may be that by prioritising our relationship to God we can look afresh at ourselves, from a different perspective. While, as I have suggested, there is some strength in doing the psychological work first, the demands of the ego can be legion. While it is not possible to bypass the emotional work we can sometimes put it aside for a little while and dis-cover the Divine that has been waiting for us. Thus strengthened and renewed we find we have a far greater resource of love to draw upon to heal and to give a different perspective on those old wounds, or maybe even the wounds don't really seem like wounds any more anyway.

"I do nothing and nothing is left undone" Ram Dass once said to me. It has taken me some years to understand what he meant by this. Now, being with people whom I encounter for healing, in whatever forms it takes, I have learned that I do nothing. I may choose a word or use my hands in a particular way, but these are all outer gestures of something deeper taking place. The soul friend learns to let go of his or her agendas and other people's dramas, to get the ego out of the way and trust in God. Spiritual direction to me is simply prayer in action, my work, if it is work at all, is to stay connected to the Divine, to open myself to grace and just let it do its work – I am not the doer, simply the instrument of the doing, the friend of the Friend. And this is a kind of effortless effort. In this loving, prayerful, mindful state the soul friend does not get caught up in the effort of trying to fix us, does not become exhausted trying to heal the world's wounds. Director and seeker mingle mutually in the vast pool of friendship, the sacred waters of our becoming, but both ultimately flowing deeper into God.

The spiritual director offers us another safe milieu for our soul exploration in the landscape with which the director is familiar because they have walked the path already. It is a one-to-one demonstration of compassionate companionship along the Way. But that compassion and exploration takes place with others too, in community.

...Startled by the thunderclap of Your voice
In the 'ruhe sanfte'
During a silent meditation
Sitting there
Perfectly still
I move
We all move
A movement faster than the speed of light
Or chocolate biscuits disappearing
Off the plate at coffee break.
A time-lapsed sequence
As we shift from
Place
To place.
While remaining exactly where we are.
There is nowhere to go
Nowhere to be
But here, now, always.
In our blindness we see much,
In our deafness we hear all.
Opening doors to a new room
Only to find it the same one,
Redecorated
From chintz to new cool.
Moving in dreams from room to room
Only to find,
There is no door
And no room
And no walls.
We speak our truth
To discover its lies.
And the shaman
Masked in eagle feathers
Summons us to the party
Or the funeral.
We are all invited
But the invitation comes
Sometimes with a golden margin,

Sometimes like the black edged cards in the crematorium.
Some of us come dressed for dancing
And Hafiz
Bearing the stretchers, with Rumi in tow,
Calls "Help me here!"
But Rumi
Too busy dancing
Whirled and whirled
And is whirling still.
We laugh until we cry and cry until we laugh
And sometimes,
If you pay attention
Pay very close attention
You can see God handing round the tissues
Or making sure the kettle is full
Or putting someone's hand into the hand of another.
For the laughter and the crying are all the same thing.
That's why the Buddha smiles, knowingly.

And the Mona Lisa…

Part 6

"Wisdom sees everything not in separateness but in unity."[76]

Soul Communities: colonies of heaven

It's only a mile across, but the narrow stretch of jewel-like sea that separates Iona from the big island of Mull could be as wide as the ocean. As you cross the Sound it feels for all the world that you are leaving ordinary reality behind. In some respects you are, for this small island has few roads, none but a handful of cars, and only 120 or so souls are resident. Thousands of tourists flock there each day in the summer – taking short trips primarily to see the famous abbey and then most leave with equal speed. The rest of the island itself stays largely untouched by visitors who remain mainly within the short stretch from jetty to monument.

Loved by painters and poets for generations, rich in religious history, difficult to get to, gloriously wild and unpredictable in its climate; Iona has called people down the years, especially to touch something deep within. Little wonder that poet Kenneth Steven[77] writes:

"Is this place really nearer to God?
Is the wall thin between our whispers
And his listening? I only know
The world grows less and less –"

Thus Iona hosts a vibrant spiritual community[iv], founded by George MacLeod early in the last century, which is influencing religious thought and practice way beyond its remote island confines. Among the tourists are also pilgrims, some as day trippers seeking perhaps their Celtic Christian spiritual roots, others for longer periods to join in the spiritual life of the Abbey community and its many courses. The Christian community it offers is a world away from the fundamentalist, judgemental and sometimes vicious form that often gets the attention on the airwaves. Most Christians are not like this, and Iona represents a thread of Christianity that is deeply embracing, loving, non-judgemental and inclusive. It is one of those places where people in community are working to make the essence of divine love tangible. They work to create what some have called "colonies of heaven" (attributed to St Columba, the founder of the abbey and monastery in

---

[iv] www.iona.org.uk.

the 6th century, though probably the words of George MacLeod[78]) – a place on earth, in everyday reality, where the truths of "the Kingdom" are lived out.

Soul communities are gatherings of fellow seekers and can take many forms as we shall see. They are more than groups of people, neighbourhoods, townships and so on where such communities have economic and social purposes. The soul community, and we might be members of more than one, has the intention of expressly engaging in spiritual work and supporting others in the group in that work. The soul community may have other activities – providing health care, education, running a business and so on, but these are sidelines to the central aspect of spiritual support. A Buddhist community to the north of where I live (the Tibetan monastery at Samye Ling[v]) is an example. It has a shop, welcomes visitors, runs courses, maintains beautiful gardens, is engaged in social activism and so forth. But its central focus is teaching and holding a Buddhist community who meet in prayer and meditation, have access to spiritual directors and devote the bulk of their time to learning Buddhism. Communities like this are specifically set up to support seekers and are well defined, but there are other perhaps more loose affiliations as we shall see where spiritual support is also a possibility and which can act as our soul communities.

All religious traditions down the ages have sought to set up communities like Iona and Samye Ling (and I have visited scores down the years) in order to deepen their spiritual search. Sometimes this necessitates the community living by strict rules and cut off to a greater or lesser extent from the rest of society. For some this cutting off from worldly distractions is seen as essential in order to reduce temptation away from attention on God. Others saw their withdrawal as deepening their spiritual practice but to make it of service, for example in providing health care and hospitality.

I recently had a week's retreat among the brothers at Worth Abbey, a Benedictine monastery made famous by a TV series called "The Monastery" [vi]. From time to time, especially when my spiritual life seemed torn by other demands, or in arid periods when I had lost that connection to the Divine, I would imagine how much easier it would be to live in such a community away from all the tensions of ordinary life such as paying the bills, dealing with conflict, problems in relationships, meeting responsibilities. Retreats in places like the Findhorn[vii] and Iona Communities sound idyllic and indeed they are – for a while. After

---

[v]   www.samyeling.org

[vi] www.worthabbey.net

[vii] www..findhorn.org

experiencing these and others, I came to know that there is just as much struggle to stay focussed on God living in community as outside it. Living in community we still have to deal with interpersonal conflicts that arise (often!). Just because you are a saintly abbot or abbess does not mean you escape from the worries of the paying the bills or following the boss's orders. Enjoying the remoteness of Findhorn or Iona does not mean that we avoid getting annoyed when someone has not done their share of the kitchen chores or has eaten the last of the blackberry jam. It has been my experience that living in community intensifies rather than diminishes the tensions of living together. What communities seek to create are more healthy ways of dealing with them. Those that do not are unhealthy groups to be among, and just as risky, even dangerous as the unhealthy teacher or guide as outlined in Part 5. The relationships themselves and all the joy and challenges they bring to us, are thrown into sharp focus. How we respond to them is just as much a spiritual practice as chanting or meditation, for they offer us countless opportunities for deepening awareness and compassion, for walking our talk[79].

Living and working in community is like following a 12-steps Alcoholics Anonymous programme – the processes are there to keep you on track, to push and challenge as well as nurture and encourage. In our searching, our healing, our whole-ing there is a need for discipline, guidance, community support, inspiration. It goes further than an AA programme, beyond the courage to say "I am an alcoholic" and extends to embrace the possibility someday of graduating, of healing beyond it. To go beyond the need to say "I am a ..." and to rest quite simply in "I am."

The word "companion" has French roots and means sharing bread with others. Our companions on the Way are ones with whom we share the bread of our food, the sacraments and other rituals, and also our shared lives as food for each other. Working together, healthy community nurtures us out of our various egotistic addictions into mature, soul-centred adults. Or rather the process is one of continuous refinement in the fire of relationships into ever deeper connection to the Divine. Spiritual maturity on the Way Home is not about retreating from the world and having some sort of spiritual self pleasuring life, but about expanding and full-filling our humanity so that we can engage more fruitfully with the world, not less. There can indeed be times of retreat in solitude or in community as part of our spiritual work (see Part 8) but for most of us these are rarely lifetime commitments, more likely practices engaged in from time to time to deepen our connection to spirit. Joining a community to escape from the world and those aspects of ourselves that we don't like, anger, fear, shame, disgust and so on, is unwise, for whatever unresolved stuff we have we will bring with us, and cut off from the wider world in the closed world of community life it is magnified and intensified. Living in community is certainly not the idyllic escape that we might imagine it to be.

Sometimes we might seek a community because we feel that we must escape the fog of our ordinary lives just to "see" more clearly, and it may indeed have a quality of exile about it because we can feel like it is the rest of the world that has driven us away. But it is worth noting that living in "Memphis", in exile, is not always a negative, although it can feel like it sometimes. It can be a place of suffering, as the Jewish people experienced when captured and taken to Babylon, sometimes the suffering of being away from home is balanced when exile provides safety from persecution, as when Joseph and Mary escaped Herod with the child Jesus by heading for Egypt. For forty years I was in exile from Christianity. Coming home to that faith, in retrospect, was the easy part; the tough part has been and still is, staying there (a rich seam of spiritual work in itself!).

I refer not to the overarching faith rooted in the Christ and his message, but to staying with a tradition belonging to that faith such as (in my example) Anglicanism, which can leave you blossoming with wonder and joy whilst at the same time driving you crazy with its shadow side such as bigotry, rigidity and unlovingness. Like all faiths, all communities, all families, both light and dark are found in the same place. Healthy groups can handle difference and diversity, unhealthy ones can be full of threat and abuse. In exile we may have room to wander, to learn, to experiment, to see the bigger picture. We may return loaded with riches gathered along the way. Without the sorrow of separation, there is not the joy of reunion. I attended a Roman Catholic mass once in Dublin, and was profoundly moved by the simplicity and sincerity of the faith of the people I met, and yes indeed their certainty, although there was deep disagreement between us on many issues. I reflected that there was for me some envy there, some longing that I too could see the world so simply, so black and white. How much easier it must be, I wondered, to live in a world of absolutes, no grey areas.

A permanent residential commitment to a religious community is neither possible nor desirable for most of us, and perceiving it as an escape from the world is a negative unhealthy reason to enter it. A healthy approach is one where our intention is a clear move towards something as a positive firm foundation for successful religious life. If our intention is really to escape from the stress and struggle of ordinary life then it is likely that we will simply bring our fears with us into a more tightly knit group, often thus magnifying them.

Yet the monastic community life can be found in many ways in our ordinary lives. Attending a yoga group, a study session focussed on a particular religious or spiritual text, a meditation course, participating in our religious community – there are countless opportunities in which we can encounter others, some for short periods (perhaps the temporary community of a week's course) perhaps a permanent community with participation in our local mosque, synagogue, church or temple. And then of course there are the endless opportunities for sharing our spiritual life that can crop up with friends and family and work colleagues. Each of these encounters may expose moments of sharing and learning. It is also worth remembering that we can engage with a soul community in many different ways, and modern communications have opened up enormous possibilities for the "virtual" monastery. We can commit to prayer groups, support groups and other communities large and small across the globe through email, shared meditation times, distant healing sessions and so forth. I look now at my soul communities and where are they? They are my fellow ministers in the interfaith community, groups of friends and fellow seekers across the globe who I can meet through internet groups, emails and tele-conferences. There is a meditation group of people from very diverse backgrounds which meets locally, an Iona Community support group, my local church and the bible study group, the temporary communities I meet when I join residential or other courses from time to time. Each community offers scope for different levels of involvement but all serve to provide us with spiritual nourishment, and for us to contribute something in return.

As a general rule, and if we look at the examples set by all the great spiritual teachers, being on our own is not the way to get Home. Why? Because to deny the world and refuse to participate in it is to separate oneself off from the creation, and we are part of the creation, we are connected, all part of the One. To separate ourselves from each other and the creation is to separate ourselves from God. If the spiritual life is about anything it is about learning to become more loving, and loving takes place among people and the world, not cut off entirely from them. Few people are called to be hermits secluding themselves from the world (and even then, many in the hermit tradition made themselves available as sources of guidance and wisdom to their neighbours).

I recall Peter who was beset by the troubles of the world and wanted to focus on his spiritual work and nothing else. He said that he wanted to go and live in a tent on top of a hill and have nothing to do with anyone. We laughed a little when he realised that he would still need someone to make the tent, to provide the transport and the roads and the food. Few of us are called or able to live in complete isolation and indeed this may be just an excuse for avoiding the difficult work in the swampy lowlands of the human experience. We can retreat for a while as a healthy spiritual practice, which informs and transforms us in ways that we can bring back into the world as we re-engage with our community.

In our spiritual work to find Home, a community of fellow spiritual travellers is essential to the soul. First of all community is necessary because it provides us with the milieu to practice what we preach. Secondly because being among others we have the grist for the mill in our everyday contacts that refine us. Thirdly, because being in some form of community, temporary or permanent, offers the context for us to be helped ourselves. Fourthly, because in community we can be of service to others. Fifthly, being with others in community provides opportunities for shared spiritual practice which have quite a different effect than going solo – the impact of a "gathered" Quaker meeting or chanting in a group or dancing in a circle is very different from that of being alone. Indeed some forms of spiritual practice are impossible solo, such as circle dancing or choral music. The collective experience brings new dimensions to our spirituality. A sixth aspect of being in community is the opportunity to be of service to others beyond it - perhaps helping locally those who are ill or disabled or in undertaking collective social/political action as expressions of our values. Finally, our soul communities are also sources of friendship, fellowship and fun. Joy and pleasure are also part of the way home.

Of course, not all communities are healthy; they can be just as toxic and dysfunctional as any society or family. Cults which emphasise complete surrender to their doctrines or leadership are best avoided. Seeking out the healthy spiritual community is part of the process of discernment, for just because it is tough does not mean it is unhealthy. As with finding a spiritual director, we have to recognise that difficulty is itself a spiritual challenge and not necessarily something we must walk away from. But in general, communities in which we feel oppressed or threatened as opposed to challenged or stimulated are best avoided. If we look again at some of the pointers at the end of Part 5, about unhealthy directors, then these principles can also be applied to the soul community.

For the past couple of years I have been returning from exile and learning to participate once more in my local church. One of the reasons I felt able to do this was because I had been able to shed some delusions about community. Somewhere lurking in my consciousness was a dreamlike projection that someday I would find the ideal community where everybody agreed with everybody else, where we all believed the same things and where it would all be sweetness and light. And it was a dream. In my travels around many spiritual traditions and communities I have experienced each carrying just as much conflict, difference and diversity as any other – manifesting in different ways, but essentially the same. A soul community is just like a family in which all kinds of conflicts, resentments and difficulties can be simmering away beneath the surface, and sometimes not very much beneath. And yet like all families, at least reasonably healthy ones, even when we have our differences we can still share a meal together. There seems no point in doing all this spiritual work and professing deeper love and compassion if we cannot express them with our own nearest and dearest. If we are not at Home in ourselves then we cannot be at Home with others. In the soul community all these qualities are thoroughly tested.

A task along the Way is to find one or more communities that mirror our journey and offer explicit support. It might be useful at this point to pause and consider what soul communities, if any, exist in your own life right now. Just asking around a few friends, apart from the examples I gave from my own life above, I came across people who are involved in a meditation and support group for a Buddhist monastery, some active in Fair Trade or Make Poverty History groups rooted in their beliefs about justice and fairness, others meet to study sacred landscape, create gardens as sacred space, walk labyrinths together, enjoy sacred dance or sing in choirs dedicated to sacred music. The groups all have important social and enjoyable functions, but they are all directly and intentionally concerned with the spiritual life. Some are challenging, as people report the difficulties of disagreement and not always getting on together, but these are overcome, a spiritual practice in itself, as the groups have evolved healthy ways of dealing with these. Being in soul communities is not about just being among people and ideas that we always like.

Along the Way I had come to learn that my resentment of Christians and Christianity, because of my sense of woundedness and exclusion, was harming my own soul more than any others. If I could not embrace my fellow human beings, including those with whom I might profoundly disagree or who might be very hostile towards me, then I was doing to Christians, at least some of them, what I had perceived had been done to me. My exclusion of others was a mirror image of what I felt had happened to me and was equally harmful. Part of our spiritual maturity is to see that if we put even one person from our hearts, then we wound some aspect of that heart as well as excluding others. This does not mean of course that it is right to submit ourselves to any community as some kind of personal sacrifice and self abasement; we still have to be discerning and select communities which are healthy and nurturing to our souls. But it does mean that in not participating with one group we do not put them from our hearts, from our compassion. We can still be loving and respectful of people, even those who might behave towards us and others in quite horrible ways, while choosing not to hang around with them. It may be that at some stage we are called to work with unhealthy communities, but that calling is quite a different matter from seeking out one or more groups to nurture our souls, the former is the task of mature persons who are themselves healed before seeking to bring healing to others.

Being in a community aids the work of letting go of our attachments, encouraging us along the Way to more surrender of the self into the Self. There is indeed a sense of working at this sometimes, about discerning that we are making a commitment to saying "no" to something in the hope of saying "yes" to something grander, a bigger vision of who the uncluttered self might be, of Home. Discernment can get lost if we are falling into sacrifice, in the sense of striving, overworking, hurrying or pushing to make something happen, to reach a goal or to be pure. It is a subtle spiritual lesson to be learned - striving for a goal, yet giving up the goal; the energy in striving may be the very thing that keeps us from getting to where we want to be. We cannot "make" ourselves surrender, we can only slowly learn in the everyday to turn our attention to the Divine, settling more and more into a consciousness of "not my will but...". It is a cultivation of humility where the ego, the self-will gives way to the Will. We have explored much about humility and we will do so even more in later pages, but at this point a note of caution - beware of humility, at least false humility which is arrogance disguised. It is just as arrogant to decide our role and destiny before God as it is to say we are not worthy or good enough for such service.

A soul community is a milieu where we can check out how far the egotistic will has truly surrendered to the Divine will. It is the test bed to see if we can be truly as loving, inclusive and embracing of our fellow human beings as we seek to be of ourselves and of God. When Jesus offered his two consummate prime directives, to love God completely and to love our neighbours as ourselves, he was not asking us to disconnect from the world to do so, quite the reverse. Thus the soul community provides us with the opportunity to put into practice what we preach and have learned. It may be simply helping out with the soul community's work – preparing the meditation room, sorting the finances, helping with teaching, befriending and so on. And thus being connected into our own community of seekers, we may extend that compassion much wider.

If spirituality were only a private matter, then we would remain caught up in our private selves. When we are not drawn into relationship with others, then spirituality is just a kind of self-pleasuring, avoiding the hard work of transformation. Likewise the subjective relativism in post-modern culture and the New Age movement, "one truth for me and one truth for you" takes us away from the possibility of transformation yet again because it avoids relating and connecting. We can do the same with theology of whatever faith, studying it intensely yet not grounding it in relationship with others for that would pose too many difficult challenges. God is essentially unknowable, but through our spiritual work we can find a Home in the world that is knowable. Barth[80] wrote of the "prattle of theology". In the Lord's Prayer Christians say "hallowed be thy name" not "analysed be thy name". That is not to suggest that analysis and enquiry are contrary to faith or the spiritual search. But we are called to know the Divine ourselves not second hand and sometimes theological exploration is a way of staying in the intellect, avoiding the personal encounter with the Divine, with other people and also our innermost self; an unconscious drive to keep us from that encounter and all that it would entail.

I remember watching a grainy black and white TV programme about the run up to World War II. I was only maybe 10 or 11 years old and someone called Prime Minister Chamberlain was saying something about why Britain should not get involved in a war over a quarrel between peoples far away about whom we knew nothing (and by implication cared even less). I remember especially my dad's snorting reaction, and him saying something about trouble far away always coming home if you don't stop it. That moment must have impressed me as a child because it is with me still, and maybe my dad helped to pass on to me then some inkling that my responsibilities while I am here do not stop at my garden gate.

The Chamberlain excuse holds no water anymore. Modern communications bring instant reports of what is happening even in the most remote parts of the globe. We cannot say any longer that we do not know, and our awareness of suffering in the world demands a response. The fearful person looks at the world and is inclined to disconnect – "it's not my problem, there's nothing I can do, it's their fault anyway..." The loving person wants to help, but often feels powerless to do something about it. And pressing the guilt button that we should help is an unhealthy approach to the problem.

Few of us have the power of a Geldof or a Bono or a president or a prime minister to sway the opinions of governments and agencies into action. That sense of powerlessness can encourage us to switch off. Yet millions of people are inclined to the opposite – as the tremendous response to the "Make Poverty History" campaign has shown. The first lesson from this is that individually we may indeed be able to do very little, but collectively we can move mountains.

But why bother at all? Surely other people's poverty is not our problem? In a global market this no longer obtains. The food or clothing or electronics I buy are woven into a fabric of interdependency where these goods directly affect someone else's wage packet and conditions of work in a far off country. We can make choices to buy goods that are fairly traded, that are produced with respect for the workers and the environment. The choices are not always easy, but they can be made simply by checking that label and choosing not to buy something from countries and companies that exploit and impoverish their workforce.

There is a deeper level of consciousness at work here too. Every single major spiritual teacher down the ages drew the attention of their communities to poverty. All the various holy books that followed had something to say about the poor and what the responsibilities of the not-poor are. Their teachings offered a profound wisdom long before the modern science of quantum physics began to suggest it – that everything is connected to all that is; that we all bound to each other by an awesome intricacy and complexity in the creation. Try as we might to make the other's problem just that, there is in reality no "other", we are all one. The poets know it (Tennyson:"I am part of all that is..."). Scientists know it (Einstein:"A human being is part of the whole, called by us, the 'universe'...". The religious know it (Jesus:"Love your neighbour as yourself.")

The National Health Service (NHS) in the UK is an example of this principle. I was born into the newly formed NHS and my mother was very sick and nearly died. Access to heath care that was free at the point of delivery kept both myself and her alive, as it has for millions of others. The NHS system, indeed our taxation system too however flawed, is predicated on everyone giving something to lift people out of ignorance, ill health and poverty, with the expectation that some will take out more than they pay in. Why should we do that? Because poverty breeds violence and crime, so we all have an investment in getting rid of it. A child-free friend of mine once asked why she should pay taxes that go to parents with kids. Yet those kids grow up to be plumbers and shop assistants and doctors and nurses – all of which were essential to her. We are all interconnected. In giving we also receive. Our soul community, large or small, is a place of giving, and as I suggested earlier, there is some evidence that people who feel they are giving more to their community than they get out of it are happier and healthier.[81]

This is not to underestimate the power of the compassionate heart which lies in each of us, although sometimes buried deep, willing to help others in trouble. All sorts of genetic and psychological arguments can be put forward, but perhaps it is very simple. It is the very essence of what it is to be human to care for others and we can all do that in ways big or small. Individually it can sometimes feel hopeless, but collectively we can change things. Indeed, looking at the many recent studies on the non-locality of consciousness (e.g. those on prayer, distant healing etc.) then human consciousness transcends the body. Our intentions in themselves can influence wider reality. We might not be able to feed all the poor, but simple actions and healing intentions do have an impact.

Witnessing the monks at Worth Abbey, in their daily round of worship and prayer, I was reminded of a communist friend's dismissal of them as parasites. However, monks and nuns are not withdrawn from the world, rather by being in their communities and their own interior solitude at the same time, they engage more deeply with the human condition. Apart from the fact that the monks I came to know were offering a very useful service to the community (running a school, a church, various development programmes etc.) I felt they were doing something else, invisible but vital. The vital (*vita* – life) of soul communities, wherever they are, in their prayers and meditations while seemingly inactive are bringing life to the world, holding it in their consciousness. Where other parts of the world may have a warlike consciousness, perhaps by holding a peaceful one, those who apparently are "doing" nothing may in fact be offering a powerful counterpoint of consciousness that prevents our reality from a complete descent into darkness. Across the world, soul communities of all shapes and sizes are, I suspect, contributing along with individuals to a force of prayerful love that may be helping to hold the whole of the creation together.

And individual acts of soulfulness are of value too, for the one is part of the all. There is a story of a man walking along a beach after a storm; thousands of starfish had been stranded. He picked up one starfish after another and threw each back into the sea. His neighbour laughed at him "You're wasting your time, there's millions of them, nothing you are doing matters." "It matters to this one," he replied.

The soul community provides the context where we can walk our talk and in doing so it moves us into greater spiritual authenticity. It is also a place where we can get taken care of too. Not long ago I was quite ill and my consciousness was knocked sideways by a combination of pain, anxiety and medication which seriously disturbed my concentration. Spiritual practice such as simple prayer and meditation was not possible. I was touched that so many in the local meditation group, fellow interfaith ministers, friends in far off places in email contact, my local church – all these included me in their prayers (and it is worth remembering that there is compelling evidence for the power of non-local healing[82]). This is another example of the benefits if the soul community. The spiritual search can sometimes be a lonely and frightening place. The soul community can step in to help us in that distress when we need it. Jesus said to love our neighbours as ourselves and I am struck by how many people seem to miss the second part of that statement. We seem ever so willing to help others, unwilling to ask for it. Loving ourselves is part of the equation in the soul community, because we deserve it and because not least to do otherwise denies others the blessing of giving. It is just as important to ask for help and prayer as well as to offer it. When we cannot participate in this way it shows that we have much to learn about the mutuality of caring, our own self worth and humility.

Not long ago, whilst studying at the Interfaith Seminary, I was plunged into a place of deep distress within myself. Old hurts and patterns were surfacing that made me feel bewildered, lost and in much pain. My fellow students had gone to lunch. I walked out alone with a head like thunder. Falling into this dark place was a familiar pattern to me and in my youth I would drown such pain with drink or drugs or sex. Within 15 minutes of leaving the lecture room on an ordinary London street I was offered all three! What is going on here I wondered? I returned to the classroom to find some solitude, to try and get my head together, because I knew that if I didn't I was about to give up and leave the seminary. One of my friends on the course came back early from lunch. She said nothing. We were alone in the room together. But she went to the kettle, made me a cup of tea just the way I like it, though heaven knows how she knew, and placed the cup gently in my hands. With a slight touch upon my shoulders, she withdrew to sit silently in another corner of the room. My tears came shortly afterwards and something long waiting to be healed finally surfaced into the light of day.

My friend could have fussed around, chattered mindlessly, ignored me or sought to advise me. Yet she wordlessly and kindly offered hospitality, and withdrew as if knowing at some level that that was all that was needed. She offered me a profound service that day, although a casual observer might have seen little of obvious significance taking place. Superficially, one person made another a cup of tea without speaking. But go a little deeper beneath the surface of this vignette and we see captured within it the very essence of conscious service that comes with the blessing of the soul community. Hospitality is one dimension of this that can only be manifested in community, in sharing with others. Hospitality, welcoming and caring for the stranger or the excluded is an expression of love for the other which encourages the transformation of the other. To encourage – from the French *cœur*, heart – is to bring heart into something, someone. Hospitality with others is a spiritual practice where we extend our boundaries to embrace and include the other.

Being does not have boundaries. The Divine has no boundaries. Loving and caring in community, with others, we mirror that boundless love of God. When we cut people off, ex-communicate them, we exclude them from community with profound impact upon the other and ourselves. We wound ourselves when we are unloving to others. We wound others daily when we cut them off from us. That is not to say that we must engage with everyone, throw open our doors to every poor person or permit anyone into our soul community to do as they please. We still require socially grounded ways of organising our lives, there is still the need to hold the values and practices of our work. Community always challenges us to test out those boundaries of exclusion and inclusion, who is helped and who is not, how we stay focussed and yet embracing, hold off chaos and yet remain loving. The soul community is engaged collectively in "soul works". Our soul practices, as discussed in Part 8, in community take on new import. In creating our relationships, rituals and other ways of ordering our spiritual life in community we establish ones that work for us at many levels. But creating those rules will mean that not everyone can participate in the same way. We do what we must do, but in doing so we can make sure that we put no one from our hearts.

Ram Dass and Paul Gorman[83] write of how "At times, helping happens simply in the way of things. It's not something we really think about, merely the instinctive response of an open heart. Caring is a reflex. Someone slips, your arm goes out. A car is in a ditch, you join the others and push. A colleague at work has the blues, you let her know you care. It all seems natural and appropriate. You live, you help." This "naturalness" of helping, of being of service to others is a deeply affecting human response. It is not the sole province of professional helpers. Some have argued that it may be genetically determined – a Darwinian process where humans and their communities who helped each other were more likely to survive and therefore passed this trait on down the generations. Others see psychological processes at work, an extension of natural parenting or the result of patterns imprinted on us in childhood, where the child who helped the adult got rewarded with approval and satisfaction.

The major religious faiths have added their influence, for each in their own way espouses the duty of human beings to be of service to each other if we are to attain enlightenment, heaven or divine approval. Whatever the cause of our desire to be of service, it remains one of the most powerful forces binding human beings together. Mutual support is the essence of the soul community; without it relationships, communities, societies fall apart. It is not insignificant that some of the most powerful stories to emerge from any natural disaster are not just about the suffering, but about how people share what they have and help each other even in desperate and life threatening times.

Divine love by definition is superabundant and can never be exhausted. If God is infinite, and God is love, then the love is infinite. Spiritual work cultivates a consciousness of abundance. When we fall into being mean spirited, or afraid, or lacking in compassion it is usually because we have forgotten that abundance, perhaps because of a painful experience, or anxieties about health or money or other things. Our "prayer and fasting" (see Part 8) is our aide to drawing us out of that consciousness of lack and back into the essential abundance that is God. Our spiritual work teaches us that love is not the love of the ego, like a cake where if one person gets some another gets less. We come to know the true Love that has no limits, wherein we find we can live in the world with greater generosity because we know that we are not in lack, and never could be. Authentic spirituality mirrors in our relationships with others what we experience in God.

Ram Dass and Gorman add that "When we join together in this spirit, action comes more effortlessly, and everybody ends up nourished...We take pleasure not only in what we did but in the way we did it. On the one hand the effort was so natural it might seem pointless or self-conscious to make something of it. It was all what it was. Yet if we stop to consider why it all felt so good, we sense that some deeper process was at work. Expressing our innate generosity, we experience our 'kin'-ship, our 'kind'-ness. It was 'Us'. In service we taste unity." In community whether temporary, permanent or virtual, we find the opportunity to give and receive service. To be neighbours to each other, and this is service rooted in *agape*, compassionate love for one's fellow human beings and such communities are embedded in helping each other and not in seeking power or profits. Each caring relationship is also pregnant with spiritual potential. Countless opportunities to deepen our understanding of who we are and why we are here are presented to us; the soul work for expanding our consciousness and connection to Source, whatever we perceive that to be. In every helping relationship we may ask honestly of ourselves not only "how can I help?", but also "what is this doing to help me?"

I suggested that the soul community is also a place of testing and discernment, and a recent news report reinforces thus truth. A man felt he had been guided by God and told to kill his sister. Leaving aside the elements of possible psychosis here, this is an extreme example of what can happen when we have what we think are spiritual experiences but which are not questioned. The presence of a soul friend and a soul community might have asked that man some serious questions about the veracity of his calling. Reference to the soul food of scripture about killing, to the soul works of meditation or prayer before action might have added to the discernment of the truth of his "revelations". Another example comes to mind of Julia, who had just completed a series of workshops at a well known New Age retreat centre and reluctantly returned home, she was about to leave the country and had planned trips to pursue her spiritual goals, including a trek to India to Sai Baba, to see Mother Meera in Germany, to seek out the Dalai Lama and to work with a shaman in South America.

I felt uneasy about what was going on with her. While honouring the wonderful insights she had received on the course, which had been life transforming and the spur to get to God, I sought to query with her the implications of packing up and leaving. She became rather cross with me when I did not offer my wholehearted support for her journey. She was indeed distressed and struggling to make choices but the passion following her discoveries seemed to have quite knocked to one side awareness of her responsibilities. She could indeed set off, but she would be leaving behind three very young children, a husband, and two business partners to whom she was deeply financially and morally committed. Her personal journey, it seemed to me, included accepting some difficult lessons that included meeting responsibilities and not just abandoning them. Her desire for freedom was simply reckless and damaging for others. Perhaps her spiritual practice at this time might equally be found in dealing with her relationships and responsibilities as in jetting off and leaving them behind. Finding ourselves does not mean that we have to lose and wound others.

The history of religion and spiritual awakening is littered with stories of men and women who abused their calling, themselves and others when their convictions were not challenged. Soul friends and soul communities are prerequisites to guide us along the way, to test out whether what we are experiencing is the stuff of inspiration or delusion. Too many people have been wounded because they had no one or group alongside them offering spiritual accompaniment and, through discussion and prayer, providing checks and balances; opportunities to sort the wheat from the chaff, the authentic from the bogus.

In the soul community there is no "other"; we are all in this together, and in coming together we experience the ever present origin, the Presence that knows us as we are known. We do not exist in the world just as an "I" but as a "we", in community we express mutuality in the giving and taking between each other along the way to our personal and spiritual maturity. When we come together we may do more than meet as persons, for there is a transpersonal quality to it. Gathering to consciously and prayerfully care for one another mirrors, indeed invites the Divine to be among us. Then we may shift into recognition that it is not so much us but the very consciousness of the Divine working among us, doing the discerning, feeding the love, guiding the "way of seeing". Different faiths have different names and concepts, but it is essentially the same, the inbreaking of God into community. The soul community is the opening for God to pour into the world, for communities of heaven to be established, where that which is above is manifested below. The soul community is a community of companions, recognising that we each bring our unique struggles and our unique gifts, and many of them may be tough gifts – for there it might be argued that it's not much of a discipline where we only have to love people that we like or who love us. Those who are our "enemies" (including our own ego "enemies") also have something to teach us about love.

In this sharing we draw strength from each other and for ourselves where our spiritual search can find anchorage and the risks of spiritual waywardness minimised. New insights, ways of seeing, healings emerge. No community is perfect, in the sense that it is free of problems and conflicts, but in a way these imperfections are perfect, forming the grit for the oyster of the soul community. For no community is ever "there" it is in an endless process of becoming and each member and the whole is vital to that process. Each person's enlightenment contributes to the other, and until all are free none of us is fully free. The soul community is another milieu for our safe spiritual awakening on the Way Home.

...You can arrive at a hotel
One you have seen before
And sit in the same chair
With the same covers
With the same view from the window
And the same staff
And the same people from last year
Like Michael who remembers you
And you say, because you feel,
You feel,
"It's like we've never been away!"
And the space between now
And then
Was the frame for a work of art.
Like a dark room suddenly
And momentarily
Illumined by a camera flash.
And in between
Life sandwiched between life
Grown ever thinner.
God pours down the windowpane
In a summer storm and
Drips down to the cut grass
(Eyed by the corncrake
In the bushes) a holy libation,
God watching God falling against God.
And so we sit like children
Caught twixt cradle and coffin
Staring out at the window to the ocean
Feeling the repulse of the sea air
Rushing beneath the wings of disappointed terns
Diving again and again and again.
Into the fire, the remorseless fire
Taking flesh from flesh, flesh from bone
And wailing "I am, I am, I am!"
Stripped of change and chance
Ashes to ashes, dust to dust, dust to nothing
For there was nobody there.

Only the facing of the ocean
The endless watching.
Waves now fall and rise and retreat
And rise again
A momentary identity in eternal shuck and draw
Rising from the universe
Falling back into unfathomable unblemished depth.
You could hear this and hear nothing
Read it and read non-sense
Smudge your fingers in the ink to find
No word lives there.
For this you can only feel, and to feel must experience.
And going through it you know,
Know
Because you have gone through it.
There is the Way and
There is not the way.
My words slip and slide once more
Sucked into the vacuum of a receding wave
Broken like these shells on the rocks of time
Glistening in the memory when the wave has gone.
For there we have been which is every place
And no place.
There we have been where there is no have and no been
Only the now left floating in the ocean
Like a driftwood barge or a child's yacht lopsided in the surf.
In a moment, in the twinkling of an eye
All seas, all eyes, all words
Caught and held. Caught and held
Only to be lost again
Left behind in the corridors of memory, empty now and windblown through
The cracked plaster.
No memory
For no one was there...

Part 7

"In Nature's infinite book of secrecy
A little I can read."[84]

Soul Foods: inspiration and perspiration

Mother Meera draws thousands of people each year to meditate with her in silence and to step forward when ready to receive her blessing. She is one of the few New Age "gurus" in Anthony Storr's searing analysis not to be condemned for exploiting or abusing others.[85]   I went there many times down the years in the quest for truth. The evenings were devoted to silent time with her, but during the day I walked the dark forest south of Limburg or spent time in solitude in my hotel room. In these weeks I would dedicate my time just to the search, avoiding that temptation to bring the mobile phone or computer with me "just in case". There would be time to fast and pray, to reflect, maybe work with the tarot or the Enneagram (q.v.) and most of all to read. I would go with far more books than it was possible to read in a month, let alone a week. Yet in books of poetry, great literature, scripture from different faiths we can find inspiration. And to be inspired is, literally, to be in-filled with the spirit. When we read a book we enter into the thoughts of another person and perhaps in some way when truth that we read touches us deeply, we are entering into the mind of God. Sometimes I would read a passage, or go to a piece at random, and it seems to perfectly fit what I was seeking or experiencing at the time. Or the words and their meaning would be so wonderful as to make you want to take a deep breath. We breathe in, in-spire, books of truth and they feed our souls.

Then I might take a long walk in the forest, pausing often just to breathe deeply or meditate. Sometimes I was on a spiritual high after some profound insight, or still moved by the impact of Mother Meera's blessing. At other times it would be a real spiritual low as I struggled with some painful blockage, aridity or the sense of being in a void. Some people claim Mother Meera is an avatar, a divine being, a manifestation of the divine feminine in the world. They are devotees and worship her and ascribe great powers to her. I don't know if that is true, but I do know that those weeks in Germany were often deeply moving and replete with rich teachings. Was it her working some magic, was it me willing to bring my "stuff" there and work on it, was it simply the act of stepping aside from ordinary life that made the space for these things to happen spontaneously? Perhaps all or none of these. But these times also reinforced the need to take time out as a spiritual practice, a subject I will develop more in part 8, away from ordinary life. They gave me many lessons in the pitfalls of spiritual duality – I could return from Germany feeling blissed out and at one with the world, arrive in Manchester and begin the drive home only to have someone cut me up on the motorway and I would feel enraged! There can be times when we feel spiritual and times when we do not, times when we feel connected and at Home and times when we feel exactly the opposite. Spirituality here has become reduced to whether we feel good or bad. Part of the work is getting beyond the perception of "this is spiritual and this is not".

There is a story told of Guru Nanak – founder of the Sikh faith. Dismayed by the warfare in his country between Moslems and Hindus, he sought to find the common ground of truth to unite his people in God. He journeyed to Mecca, and rested in the street with legs outstretched. People remonstrated with him, for the soles of his feet were uncovered and by chance facing the direction of the holy city (an unpardonable insult). His response was to challenge his tormentors: "Show me where God is not and I will point my feet there."

If the Divine is all and everywhere, in all things yet contained by none and all things are contained in the Divine, then separation from or the possibility of God being in one place and not another are just thoughts, very powerful thoughts, but thoughts nonetheless. We may actually be Home all the time, we just have not yet realised it. The good witch of the north in the Wizard of Oz comforts Dorothy, who is weeping that she wants to go home, by reminding her "But you are home, all you have to do is wake up!"

Our true way Home is within us all the time, all we have to do is become aware of it. All our Soul Care is designed to cultivate that truth. Our path is not found outside us, in the light of some other spiritual career or some other person. As Jesus reminded us "You are the light of the world" (Matthew 5:14). That which we seek, and the way to it, is present in the here and now, ready and waiting in the depths of our own being. False teachers and practices lead us away from this into creating idols of themselves, becoming false gods. They become the object of reverence rather than what it is they point to, leading us into spiritual materialism, the adherence to or acquisition of (false) spiritual things and experiences, and dependency. Investing the power of wisdom in external things is a kind of idolatry, taking us away from hearing the whisper of the Divine within who is already calling us Home. Soul foods help us to hear that whisper.

The soul needs food along its journey Home, and we can find this in our soul friends, communities and practices, but it is also available to us in each moment, among friends or alone, for the books and other things of inspiration are all around us. Our soul works, friends and communities can only take us so far; at some point there is the time of the solitary quest too, alone in a book or in retreat. They are the books on our library shelves, the ones handed over to us which, by chance if chance it be, just seem to offer us the perfect words we need at the time. They might be the holy books of the great faiths. Books written by wise spiritual teachers, prophets and poets. But beyond them there is another holy book; it is the book of life, the book of creation. All around us life buzzes and blooms to a thousand songs with every moment pregnant with inspiration, food for the soul. It may be in the arts, music, sculpture, theatre and so on that we find new insights and ways of seeing that refresh and renew us.

It is perhaps no coincidence that the waste land of our culture has also witnessed a burgeoning interest in sacred music such as monastic chant or the arts in the form of icon painting. It may be in the beauties of nature and all that the creation has to teach us as it unfolds around us. It may be in things that are serious, but also in the lightness of a novel or the hilarity of a TV programme that new insight can arise as well. A limitless store of wisdom and truth is all about us, and which may provoke an awakening to the wisdom and truth within ourselves.

Great spiritual teachers down the ages used stories, parables to illuminate truth. Written or spoken they offer us insights into a deeper reality. Sometimes these soul foods can be troubling, disturbing, making us feel conflicted because they challenge our established way of seeing things. "Let him who seeks, not cease from seeking until he finds; and when he finds he will be turned around and when he is turned around he will marvel and he shall reign over all." – these words of Jesus in the Gospel of Thomas[86] suggest that being turned around, troubled, made to think again (in Greek *metanoia*) can be the catalyst of spiritual awakening.

Soul Foods are firstly those things which make our hearts sing. I have mentioned some above which I have in my own life, but there are many, many more. In a recent workshop with a group of hospice staff we looked at what our soul foods were. That feeling of being open hearted, full of life, in the moment or being "blown away" by some new insight or inspiration is what soul foods can provoke. We can experience these in our own individual ways in our everyday lives. The group mentioned things like being with grandchildren, gardening, diving, running, sitting by a lake, walking by the river, knitting, painting, mountaineering, having an aromatherapy massage, going to the theatre, friendship, preparing a meal, dancing, helping out at a community centre, visiting an ancient yew grove. These are all examples where we can feel that our soul is being fed and strengthened, full-filled and many as we shall see overlap into soul works (Part 8) and soul communities (Part 6).

One theme has been omitted from the list in the previous paragraph and that was the suggestion from one member of the group that drugs could be used to open us up to the Divine, a subject discussed at length elsewhere[87], and about which extreme caution is needed. People have been trying for millennia to get to God (arguably successfully) using what in modern usage have become known as the "entheogens" – substances which induce an altered state of consciousness associated with an experience of the Divine. Many drugs now readily available to us, from the legal (alcohol, caffeine, tobacco) to the illegal (cocaine, cannabis, mescaline) were once used by initiated individuals, rarely and sparingly, in tribal cultures. They were not the stuff of mass consumption and were regarded as possessing great spiritual power. These substances which induced altered states became sacred, the holy of holies for what they offered, and they were therefore relegated to special times, people and places.

Modern synthesised substances such as LSD and ecstasy are entheogens and are consumed on a massive scale for leisure and pleasure. Making available cheap agents of conscious change is fraught with dangers and one of the reasons for strict legal controls. Some might argue that, at last, access to the numinous is (more) available to all and might be of service in the world to wake us all up to a deeper reality so that we might appreciate and take care of the present one better than we currently do. Yet if we look at the way the early plant-based entheogens were used and controlled there are some important lessons to be learned, for the context matters. Taking ecstasy at a wild party, laced with alcohol, boosted by amphetamines and driven by rap, will have a hugely different impact (as some of the arrivals in any accident and emergency department amply demonstrate) than ingestion after fasting and ritual preparation, inclusion in a sacred ceremony and environment, and guided by a spiritual master.

Even so, a glimpse of enlightenment is not enlightenment itself and there seems to be no way of bypassing the long term hard discipline of spiritual practice even if there has been an initial opening of the doors of perception. There are no short cuts around the emotional work and the spiritual labour if we are ever to approach healthily, for ourselves and others, the true essence of our being. Furthermore the drug induced experience may leave the user wanting more to repeat it, or failing to trust it simply because it was chemically influenced, or it fades into the dusty and unused filing cabinets of memory.

So, to return to the non-drug soul foods, it may be that we approach these things without conscious effort, or it may be that we see the blessing they bring and set our intention to be open to what new offering might emerge from them each time. With soul foods, wherever we find them, there are added dimensions if we approach them consciously and in seeking thus we feel moved and inspired. By and large our soul foods are those sources where we seek, mostly as an individual interior experience, to draw closer to the Divine, and it is an explicit seeking. There are many pleasures in life and there is no reason why we should not enjoy these to the full, but a different conscious approach to them can reveal new dimensions if we are actively looking to connect with our Source.

All the Soul Care themes mentioned in this book can be approached joyfully and lightly, spiritual work is not all about suffering. In fact if we see the Way as one of pain, labour and sacrifice, then there is an attitude here that is itself worthy of exploration for example in our soul community or with our soul friends. However, as we have mentioned in the story of Isa, neither pushing away the difficult or pulling towards us only the enjoyable is advisable. Both such approaches, while understandable, are forms of attachment that obstruct us on the Way.

We are naturally drawn to places and things of beauty (*philokalia* – the love of spiritual beauty -which also happens to be the name of a wonderful collection of spiritual guidance[88]) to inspire us, but the *via negativa* also takes us into the dark places in ourselves and the world as well. We can find it easy to read a piece of scripture that does not conflict with our feelings or look at a beautiful landscape, and these are all part of soul food. But perhaps words and other things which we find difficult have something to teach us too. In being thus stretched we can go deeper by making the difficulty itself the stuff of spiritual practice, a soul food that might be indigestible at first but ultimately nourishes us as we learn to be more understanding and compassionate and at ease with conflict and diversity. Also once we get past obstructions, say in our interpretation of scripture, we may find jewels of wisdom there that we had not seen before. I once found bible reading, for reasons like these, very problematic. Years of work later, I can now find great depth of insight in, say, the psalms that I had not seen or felt before. Words in scripture can burst with new meaning that we had hitherto overlooked as we heal and mature. There are many scriptural exhortations to help the homeless and poor and those in prison. Seeing more depth we see that words like this take on new meaning than just the literal – are we not homeless who seek? Are we not in prison who are not free, because of our ego traps, to go Home? Are we not poor who do not know love? When scriptures write about driving away enemies, these can be seen not only literally as rather cruel exhortations, but also metaphors about driving off the power of the ego. Healing the old wounds that blinker our spiritual vision opens us up to new horizons of thought and insight. Things which we once saw as simplistic or unrealistic or unpleasant may still yield wisdom, especially when we see them from a *mythos* viewpoint (q.v.). This way of overcoming blockages and using everything available to come to know the Divine does not imprison, it sets us free in unfettered exuberance to full-fill the soul's intent.

There is the story of the Buddhist monk who received enlightenment by observing his own faeces flush down the toilet. Indeed it can be one of the toughest spiritual practices to contemplate something in the world which repels us and say that "this is of God too"? Florence Nightingale had a short phrase written on cards and placed in each room of her house "Be not afraid, it is I" (*Ego sum noli timere*). These words of Jesus (he tells people six times in the gospels not to be afraid) to his disciples amidst the storm as he comes to them across the water are perhaps in part a teaching that the storm and the miracles are of God too, the wonderful and the terrible are both sides of the same coin. It is easy to repeat those words of Jesus as we watch a beautiful sunset. Can we say the same when we watch a destructive flood wash over the land destroying all before it? Julian of Norwich, whom I cited in Part 1, offers us the deep insight of the mystic who moved beyond dualistic conceptions of the creation and saw God wonderfully and unfathomably in all things, even in things that most of us might see as evil or repellent. We will explore a little more about the concept of non-duality in Part 10.

Thus, in studying the words in soul foods, we learn how to read again, read differently, *mythos* rather than *logos*, that which may hitherto have been hidden to us because we tried to read the words only as facts. Interpretation can sometimes be a struggle. Some, especially those whose faith is under the surface rather brittle, can get stuck in literalist interpretation of holy books. Most people in most traditions see these as soul food to be chewed over and digested slowly, not swallowed quickly and uncritically. People whose faith is fear based, or lacking strength, and in whom there is difficulty dealing with paradox, controversy and grey areas will tend to stick to absolutist interpretation which does little to nourish the truth in our own souls. *Mythos* sees scripture as rich in metaphor and allusion in which truth rests, *logos* sees facts and literal interpretation as truth. Both can appear in the same holy text, but *mythos* offers us access to a deeper truth, it does not mean that the facts are necessarily wrong, rather it is what they mean that matters. I don't imagine that when Jesus told the parable of the sower and the seeds that people in the crowd interrupted to ask him the sower's name, or what sort of seed was being sown, or what time of year it was. Jesus, like all great teachers was telling a story, a *mythos*, but what mattered was the meaning, that is where the truth is found. Something can be truthful without being factual, for the story of the sower and the seed, for example, tells us a great truth about the outpouring of love from the Divine, broadcasting it to all, and how individuals may accept it or not. Symbolism helps because in many ways the teachings are hidden from or incomprehensible to the intellectual realm. In falling into relationship to God we look for an encounter with God. In symbolism, the language of *mythos*, of spiritual truth, of parable, we draw closer not just because we know it is right but because it also now feels right. We know the Divine differently thus.

I have encountered many who have difficulty even looking at a book or attending an act of worship that does not belong to their own faith. At a Christian meditation group recently, one parishioner reported that she had to attend in secret as her church saw meditation as a route for Satan. Deep and real faith has no fear, it is open to enquiry; scepticism does not undermine faith it strengthens it in the faith-full person for it permits questioning, uncertainty, exploration without fear that the underlying faith is under attack. A fear filled person will tend to unconsciously shore up their faith with absolutes. A faith-full person is not afraid, for faith is more than a belief, a hope in certain things; it is a deeper level of knowing. Several of the prominent and recently well publicised atheists I cited earlier tend to pooh-pooh faith as something foolish and irrational, the province of the stupid and venal. In their own way they are being as fundamentalist as the thing, religion, they condemn, for faith is not about a hope that something is true or hoping that something clung to is not a lie, faith is a knowing of something that transcends rational explanation, it is something deep in the soul, like Jung's quote in Part 2, about knowing God rather than believing in, that offers a different dimension to knowing.

It has been my experience that an interfaith dialogue and exploration can strengthen and deepen commitment to an existing faith rather than diminish it, not least by the discovery that Truth can be found in all faiths and that there is far more in common that unites us rather than divides us. The *mythos* space between the truths and guiding principles of the great faiths is really paper thin. In Part 5, I mentioned wariness of teachers who advocate uncritical use of scripture and it is wise to approach all soul foods with the same qualification. They can be subjects for rumination and contemplation, to challenge and motivate, and can be part of the material we take to our soul friend(s) and soul communities as a source of reflection and discernment.

The absolutist position sometimes arrives in food itself, literally. Extreme dietary requirements, sacrifice of pleasures (which I will touch on more in the next Part) often say more about the person than they do about a particular spiritual practice. There are, for example, very good reasons for being vegetarian, but it is possible to get caught up in a kind of fundamentalist, Pharisee approach where we convince ourselves that by making this sacrifice and following these rules we will get to God. I have never met a vegetarian or someone with some other dietary attachment who was any closer to God than anyone else. I have met some people whose diet and lifestyle choices left a lot to be desired by some standards yet they are holy and wise beings. There is no evidence that heaven is only full of abstainers from certain foods or those who dress or behave in a particular way. The desire to be good and to be pure can be the undercurrent that really drives the diet rules, which implies that the person has not really given them up in their hearts. The strict adherence can become a cover. Seeming to be "good" in something may mask the fundamental absence of our essential goodness within. Repression like this, which is another form of punishment, suggests more spiritual work is needed. Restraint, however, offers a more healthy approach for it suggests that we let go of certain foods or drinks because they affect our wellbeing and it helps our conscious attention to our spiritual work. Dietary restrictions such as vegetarianism may or may not be necessary, but what does appear to be necessary is eating and drinking with reverence and respect for all life and our own bodies. Other reasons include using restraint to help to break the will of the ego, or because we are genuinely seeking to adhere to part of a religious tradition that is dear to us, or as an offering to the Divine where by the virtue of saying "no" to some things we give space to say "yes" to God.

Paying attention to our diet and such things as smoking, drinking and exercise that affect our bodily health is itself a soul food. By eating and drinking wisely and healthily we honour our bodies and strengthen them in the service of our spiritual work and our way in the world. Surrendering some things to be spiritually healthy has quite a different consciousness than constantly sacrificing and depriving ourselves of things that really in our hearts we are not willing to do or let go of. What comes out of our mouths, how we speak authentically in the world, is as important as what goes into them.

I enjoy the role of being a trustee of Penny Brohn Cancer Care[viii] (formerly the Bristol Cancer Help Centre), a leading edge cancer charity in the UK. Participants in the cancer care and wellbeing programmes are encouraged to make significant changes to their diet that will improve their nourishment, based on the research

---

[viii] www.pennybrohncancercare.org

evidence for dietary connections with cancer. Freedom from alcohol, refined sugars, animal fats and an emphasis on organic vegetarian food is the norm. These dietary guidelines fit with national nutritional policies anyway; it's just that most of us eat far too much junk food, fat, sugar and so on. There's nothing wrong with having treats, but food and drink which make us feel unwell, limits our physical vitality or affect our state of consciousness are risky options if we are serious about our spiritual work, and part of our soul food's initiative may be to make some clear decisions about what we will or will not put into our bodies. Our selection of soul foods in terms of our diet may entail moral decisions, such as what is good for the workers who produce it or the environment. But we also need to beware of the neo-Pharisee, puritanical approach that suggests having these laws will of themselves save us. Only what is in our hearts will save us. A judgemental, holier-than-thou attitude about our diets is spiritually unhealthy. Being a vegan , tobacco and alcohol free, who gets plenty of fresh air and exercise (also soul foods) may be enriching for the spirit, but being smug or obsessed about it certainly is not and a sign of more inner work to be done!

Meanwhile, as the deepening of our spiritual seeking gets under way, it is right to take care of ourselves and to seek out the beautiful, the aesthetically pleasing to nourish all aspects of our lives – physical, emotional, mental and spiritual. Soul work is heart work and it is right to nourish our hearts in every sense. As Thomas Merton reminds us: "The concept of 'the heart' ...refers to the deepest psychological ground of one's personality, the inner sanctuary where self-awareness goes beyond analytical reflection and opens out into metaphysical and theological confrontation with the Abyss of the unknown yet present – one who is 'more intimate to us than we are to ourselves.' " [89] The spiritual work of opening the heart is that we transform now and it is necessary to sustain this work by honouring body, mind and spirit in all the ways we are able to encounter the unknown yet present. We cannot see God with our eyes; they would surely burn out in the face of such radiance. But we can "see" in our hearts, with our feelings, with that overwhelming sense of fullness and oneness that can arise in those moments when we feel inspired and connected. Anything that nourishes the heart, physical and metaphorical, is soul food for the way Home.

Nothing is sometimes a kind of soul food too. As I write the rain pours down on the green fields of Cumbria, there wouldn't be a Lake District without an overabundance of the wet stuff we so often complain about. It is hard to imagine anything less like a desert than this beautiful place where I am blessed to live. But the landscape of the fells evokes some of the qualities of the deserts I have traversed in my life – the sense of enormity and of massive indifference to our presence. The high hills, perhaps on a bleak winter's day or in summer very early in the morning before life stirs and the silence is so deep and solid you could almost touch it – they too have that sense of eternal brooding presence oblivious and uncaring of our existence. This place even though wet in abundance, can be its own kind of desert, any situation where we go inside, to an empty place, a place where we confront God.

The desert colours our cultural landscape, for the great faiths which have forged our history in Western Europe – Christianity, Islam and Judaism were born of desert peoples. We may not follow a particular faith, but, for example in our laws and conventions and ethical codes, we are profoundly influenced by desert-origin religions. The sociological evidence that I have cited points to an ongoing decline of religions in the UK. Fewer, and falling, numbers of people may be religiously Christian – that is accepting the core beliefs and participating in the life of a religious community, but huge numbers of us remain culturally Christian through the dominant influence this faith has had upon our individual and social mores.

Retreating to the desert was an early tradition of the Christian Church – to deepen our understanding of ourselves and our relationship to the Absolute, to the Friend, to God. I remember a song from the 70s – something about a long trek through the deserts of the US – and a line which says "In the desert you can remember your name." I sought out many deserts in my own spiritual awakening some years back – spending time in the bleakest of places such as the red desert of central Australia or the desolation of northern Arizona. In Death Valley, California, a night-time ride in a world of deep darkness and silence without the comfort of reference points brought me closer to death and my fear of it. Desert landscapes can open us to the wonder and majesty of the Divine. They can also strip us of our significance, summon the ghosts of our deepest fears to haunt us, face us with the terror of our essential nothingness – remembering our name only to lose it. Everett Ruess, an American explorer of deserts disappeared in Utah's Zion National Park in 1934. Later his boots were found but nothing else – and nearby in his handwriting was scratched on a rock "Nemo 1934". In Latin, *nemo* means no-one.[90]

Death Valley in the USA is a vast salt pan of a dried up lake deep in the desert and below sea level. I have a vague childhood memory of a black and white film of settlers in their wagon trains coming to grief and dying one by one as they attempted to cross this barren, waterless wilderness. However, an unusually heavy rainfall had caused the desert to bloom. My companion and I, with whom I had been exploring Egyptian mythology, paused in the mountains overlooking the white, baked salt valley. In the blasting heat of this fiery bowl, I said that it felt like the "womb of Isis", the great earth goddess, but my companion disputed this. The womb was a place of water not dry heat. But we descended to the valley bottom, to discover that the lake bed had acquired a thin film of water that had run off from the surrounding hills. The water was warm and salty like the waters of the womb. I walked half a mile out across the shimmering lake bed, just wanting to embrace the silence and the solitude and to tai chi in this wondrous place. As I returned a small knot of tourists had turned up and I noticed they were excitedly laughing and taking photographs of me. The water covering the salty lake bed was no more than a few millimetres deep, but it gave the impression on my return that I was walking on water. How deserts can stretch the spirit and the imagination, but also our sense of humour!

Deserts are not just the hot barren places. They can be anywhere, such as the wide moors where I live, that conjure up that same sense of diminution of self, of absence of the usual things that keep us orientated in space and time. The outer reflects the inner, that interior soul landscape where, stripped of its ego identifications our personhood is left bewildered – if not this, then who am I? The recent, excellent, BBC2 series The Monastery, showed what happened when five men entered the Benedictine Worth Abbey. Leaving behind all their usual sources of identification – jobs, relationships, mobile phones – these five entered their own kind of desert filled (or perhaps more accurately emptied) by long periods of silence, reflection and prayer. They arrived with names, but this particular desert soon left them wondering "Who am I?" – one of the core questions of the spiritual search.

Few of us have the time or inclination to subject ourselves to the soul work of a desert encounter. Yet the deserts are not only in remote places or the monastic retreats bereft of everyday identification. All of us, consciously or unconsciously are no strangers to the desert, for arguably the most terrifying of these are found on our own doorsteps, our day-to-day experience. There are the deserts of grief, loss and suffering of ourselves and others when all the securities and trappings of our ordinary lives and identities are carved away – such as when sudden and traumatic illness strikes. We encounter soulless workplaces and families where we are left wondering why we are there and made fragile by environments and situations that leave us feeling disturbed, barren, bereft. Often our deserts are familiar, more intimate, in which who we are, or who we think we are, is regularly, sometimes constantly, pushed to the limits. They are the arid places of the sick room or the heaving pub, the loveless home, the meaningless church service. They are the cracked plains of our communities where we encounter the drunk or drugged or deprived. They are baked canyons of our prisons and hospitals where fear, relentless, burns the psyches of those who must confront pain and loss.

The contemporary desert of our culture, the waste land, is as much a desert place of potential awakening as any retreat or sojourn in the desiccated Sahara – if we approach it consciously. It is the place where the assault on our humanity occurs at every level – physical, social, psychological, spiritual. It is the place where our personhood is forged, broken, and reforged. Joy and suffering, sometimes merged within moments of each other, are the undiminished scorching heat of our soul work. Deserts are also cold places, especially at night, where the chilly winds of solitude and the freezing air in the darkness of despair or desolation can push us to other extremes. The desert heat and cold, expands and contracts, splitting the ego just like frost shattered stone.

Sometimes we may retreat to our own form of desert and sometimes it comes to us and sometimes we may realise we are already living in one. But to retreat is yet another way to feed the soul, to enter solitude and stillness so that we may hear, what? – the still small voice within. It is the *hesychasm* - the way of uncluttered stillness and repose that we seek in deep contemplation into which prayer draws us. I've lost count of the number of people who have visited our retreat spaces in rural Cumbria who ask "But don't you get frightened and lonely?" or "Doesn't the silence freak you out?" Yet in the absence of other distractions, there is no better place to encourage the reflective turn into the interior realm and listen to that still small voice. Plato said that there is "More truth in silence" and this is no truer than when we attempt to speak of God. No matter what words we use, they never get even close. All we can do is try, and then give up and sit in silence before the wonder of the One who calls us back Home. The practice of listening draws us into being tuned in to God all the time.

There is a tradition in all faiths that to get to know what it's all about there is a need for times away from other people and ordinary life. Some might take to desert or mountain, some to monastic cloister or isolated Buddhist temple, some to solitude upon the sea – countless ways can be found to seek the space in the environment that enables us to escape the constant stimulus of ego-orientated daily life. It may be that we will do so for long periods, or it may be that we seek a brief retreat or respite by spending our break time in some quiet room or chapel. This is the sacred space[91] which I have.explored at length elsewhere, the seeking out/creating/opening to places that remind us of and hold a sense of the holy. Such places draw us to the interior *temenos*, the inner temple, the sacred space where we reconnect with the sacred within us and around us in each moment and which never leaves us.

We need moments of retreat, quietness, solitude to feed the soul and re-mind ourselves that God is present, has never been away and the thought that we are disconnected from God or that God has left us is just that, a thought. God, the ever present origin, never leaves, though we may often walk away and fall into forgetting so that it feels like it, but always it is we who wander not God. It's my experience also that God can feel withdrawn from us, perhaps to draw us into a more intense relationship, a stronger search. However, this is not abandonment, rather it feels like the temptation of the lover for the beloved, a kind of spiritual pulling away where the intent is not to wound us but to pull us closer in, into a deeper comm-union. This union, it may be noted, is not disconnection from the world into God but connection to God in the world.

Everything is sacred; everywhere we stand on sacred ground. Yet some places and things can seem more sacred to us, either because we have prepared ourselves to pilgrimage to them for worship, like praying in a great cathedral or stone circle, or because of what we project onto or draw from it, like a sacred icon. Or perhaps they simply feel so because so many people have prayed and worshipped there, maybe down many centuries so that we perceive an intense sense of the holy lingering there more than in other places.

Thus making pilgrimage consciously into retreat we can turn inwards, to explore the interior landscape and our relationship to God, which can itself be a forbidding desert for nothing seems to be there but ourselves – perhaps the most frightening thing in the world we can face. Some would find this temporary drop out from the busyness of ordinary life too much of a stretch. As well as bliss, we may also find fear there. For it is also the landscape of the shadowed and unreconciled, the broken and fearful, the wounded and unresolved. Beyond this may lie the nothingness, the loss of self or memory or identity and only what Dionysius the Areopagite called the "dazzling obscurity of the secret silence outshining all brilliance with the intensity of its darkness".[92] We will explore more about the "darkness" of God in Part 9.

Despite, or perhaps because of, the challenge that silence and solitude can bring, retreating from the daily grind for a while seems increasingly popular. Some do so intentionally as spiritual practice, some for temporary relief from the stress of ordinary life. Some in assuming they only seek the latter also find elements of spiritual awakening creeping in. One friend said, while on retreat in Greece, "I'm only here for a rest and to get me taken care of for a change." Two weeks later her whole life had been inverted, as she found herself questioning the very meaning of her existence. I said to her, "Sometimes the reason we come to a place like this is not the reason we think we come for!" The swirling realm of the unconscious, the movement of grace, call it what we will – has a knack of creeping up and mugging us and running off with us into the night, just when we thought we had it all sorted. "I didn't come here looking for God" another participant said, "and I don't expect him to be mentioned here." And I thought of the words of Jung's tombstone – *Vocatus atque non vocatus deus aderit* (Bidden or not bidden, God is present). The Absolute, the mystery, grace, however we think of it, seems to have a knack of hanging around whether we think it's there or not.

The "spirituality shopper" programme on Channel 4 recently could have been, and indeed was in some quarters, slated for its apparently superficial pick and mix approach. But there's no doubt that the participants were getting something out of it, if only a general feel good factor. There is nothing wrong with this per se, spirituality as stress reduction may have valid wellbeing benefits, but if it is spiritual depth we seek then such practices must be approached with a different intention. The series focused on how various spiritual practices like tai chi or meditation could enhance wellbeing and perhaps give a sense of the Divine. I wondered if eventually the health and wellbeing benefits would pass away without the consistent discipline of spiritual practice, rather than dipping briefly into something.

I discussed the programme with friends who had put themselves (or been put!) through many years of the fierce discipline of spiritual practice. I wondered if we were turning into grumpy old seekers having a bit of, what – spiritual envy? What does it feel like to someone who has put in many years of hard graft, commitment and discipline in spiritual awakening to see some fly-by-night person do a quick introduction to meditation and suddenly hit the spiritual jackpot? Of course, after all our years of spiritual "work" if we feel like that then there's more work to do! But perhaps more importantly, glimpses of enlightenment are not enlightenment. A session of meditation may put us on the first rung of the heavenly ladder, but in the long term there is no bypassing the tough commitment to spiritual work (which of course can also be light and joyful) if we are to climb higher.

In contrast, but not entirely unrelated, the exquisite "Monastery" programme which I mentioned above, illuminated what can happen at a deeper level when more serious commitment is made. For 40 days in retreat in a Benedictine monastery, five men put themselves in the hands of wise spiritual counsellors and long periods of silence, meditation, prayer and contemplation. Capturing spirituality on TV is extremely problematic. Whoever had the courage to broadcast the silent moments in the programme deserves an award. TV tends to avoid stillness and silence. One of the most powerful moments of spiritual awakening I have ever seen in the media took place when one of the participants, Tony, finally rolled his head back in the deep silence held so beautifully by his spiritual director. It was almost possible to see the lights coming on in a perfect example of deep listening. You could have cut the silence with a knife in that intuitive moment when Brother Francis, who was the spiritual director, knew that no words needed to be said. Sitting before Tony's dawning realisation; the sweeping grace of understanding that was flooding Tony's consciousness was almost palpable. I held my breath then, in anticipation, wonder and awe – and the joy of witnessing a magnificent demonstration of midwifery of the soul – you could sense something being born.

It also had something to say about the rigours of the monastic life, which the participants endured – and endured is not too strong a word. They were engaged in the community life of the monastery and none was left untouched by it. Discipline (a subject of Part 8) there was here aplenty. There was no swift ascent up the heavenly ladder, only a relentless climb, sometimes exhausting to witness. I do not know if these five men, having left the monastery, maintained their climb, but I trust that something of that fierce discipline informed and strengthened and encouraged them. They arrived in the retreat each heartsick in their own ways, and none left un-healed – a fine example of healthy spirituality being part of health as a whole. The wellbeing of each was transformed, perhaps for ever. This was no New Age fluffy retreat – these men went with loving guidance into the interior desert and all were burned, and fed, from a bottomless basket of soul food in the times of silence, stillness, ritual and so forth. And thus burned to varying degrees of their superficial selves, they found the communion, the brotherhood, of a deeper Self within – and with each other.

Retreat time seems to be calling more and more people, it is one of many soul foods that feed us on the onward search, and spiritual work needs the energy like any other work. Spiritual work can seem like the hardest work of all in fact when we really commit to it. I have been amused by those who say that God seekers are just looking for an easy time of it by bringing a sweet comforter, a panacea, an opium into their lives that helps them cope with the world. I have never yet met a serious spiritual seeker who has not found their work the hardest and most challenging (and most joyful) in their lives. Indeed it could be argued that those who do not seek have in some ways the easier time of it. This is not work for the faint hearted and good food is needed to sustain us.

...The darkest hour is not before dawn
It stands in the lonely moment
When all others appear to be in light.
Oh brothers.
Oh sisters.
Let the heart speak then.
It shall trustfully pray, even in sleep.
The angel comes
To sit upon your bed in the night,
Hold you with her eyes
Embrace you in her gilded wings.
We are not alone.
We are never alone.
The ocean forever reaches out for its own,
Waves found sent in search
Of waves lost.
This is not the lover who disappears down the long empty corridor of death
Or separation.
This beloved, the boundless ocean is faithful
Faith full.
Practice remembrance oh my brothers oh my sisters
Until we forget forgetfulness!
I asked the birch trees,
"Which way?"
And they pointed
Graciously,
To the west
Where the grey mountain drew the clouds around her,
Tucking herself in for the night
Under a pewter sky.
I turned indoors
Retreating from the impossibility of night
And watched a promise in the candlelight;
In the silence,
In the rhythmic recreating silence,
And the stillness
Disturbed only by the angel as her feet thudded
Upon the ridge tiles
(a bumpy landing).

And from time to time
I caught a glimpse of her feathers
Slipping across the windowpane.
I knew she was here to take care of me,
Though the demons pouring down the chimney stack
Had other ideas.
But I watched them, paying particular attention,
Very particular attention
To the flickering gleam in their eyes.
I couldn't help thinking of all those
Little figures trapped in celluloid
Like an overwrought Spielberg work
Or the gargoyles of Notre Dame.
You see, I was quite safe with them
Because this silent sacred space
Was an echo of the holy of holies,
Not the altar or
The tabernacle,
Curtained from the world,
But the global search for the perfect spot, found in the
Eternally present,
Between womb and tomb.
No,
As above,
So below.
When the search is complete,
When all the signs have been followed
(which always point the same way,
wherever you are)
the retreat into retreat
finds fullness in emptiness,
vacancy in occupation.
My mother would come home and throw off her hat,
With the shopping done,
And stick her hatpin in the waiting box,
"Put the kettle on, love.
Home is where the heart is."
Mothers always have the right answer,
Even if they do not know it at the time.

The angel swept her soft wings around the room
Wafting the demons.
My little pointy friends
Fell swiftly into the cracks in the floorboards
Dissolving into rust and dust.
She turned before she left and,
Winking,
Pointed to her heart
Offering a re-minder.
Whether here,
Or there,

I am at home...

Part 8

"When I gazed out, I found it beyond all that was outside me; when I looked in, it was further in than my most inward being." [93]

Soul Works: digging deep and digging long

Working with a soul friend, getting involved in a soul community and choosing our soul foods are full of all the fun and struggles of getting relationships right. They help us check ourselves and our motivations to ensure they are authentic and not excuses to avoid the difficult and demanding. Seekers of Home experience just about every feeling there is in the endless unfolding and discovery of our relationship in the Divine. The fear that "there is no end to it" is replaced by the excitement and joy of limitless possibility. As we look now at soul works, the spiritual practices we pursue, I am going to introduce some tough words – discipline, duty, devotion, and dedication – all words which those of an individualist turn of mind might find hard, not to say off-putting. What, in order to get Home, do you mean I actually have to work for it? OK I'm willing to do what my spiritual director tells me, yes I'll make an effort to stick with a bunch of people with whom I've got a lot of "issues" and I can just about apply myself to making sure my soul gets some decent meals, but now you say I've got to do some real work? Apply myself? Commit?

Yes! To some extent these four "d" words apply to all the subjects we have explored thus far and they apply no less to the hard labour and enjoyment of applying ourselves to spiritual practices. There are so many and I have explored some of them elsewhere in more detail.[94] Indeed it is not the scope of this text to give detailed guidance on different spiritual practices. Rather, what we will seek to do here is explore some of the key principles that need to be applied to our soul works if they are to aid us in the Way. It is not necessary to have a huge range of soul works, indeed sometimes less is more. Applying ourselves with greater depth and intensity to a few is of more benefit than spreading ourselves thin over many. Furthermore it may well be we already have some in our lives yet are not fully conscious of them. A switch of consciousness around them may help us to integrate them as soul works more fully. For example, I am often told that "I'm not like you Stephen, I don't do anything spiritual, I don't pray or meditate or anything like that". My response is sometimes to ask – "Do you have a job? Relationships? A health problem? A hobby?" All these and more, the stuff of our everyday lives, are rich seams of spiritual mining if we look at them differently.

The opportunities open to us are positively dizzying; we can spend probably several lifetimes trying them all in the modern spiritual supermarket. This has the advantage that we can select from a huge range, but the disadvantage of choice overload, of hopping from one to another, of abandoning one when it gets tough. A disciplined attention to a few seems to be what works best. In fact a friend, who runs a complementary care centre[ix] in Cumbria, once said to me, half joking, that we can reduce all soul work down to two things – "prayer and fasting". The first, prayer, is taken in its widest sense of simply turning to the Divine and fasting, not so much about food although that might be part of it, but fasting from distractions of all sorts that get in the way of that relationship.

Our soul works are the things we do, the spiritual practices that keep us grounded when we might otherwise go awry, reconnect us to God and to others when we might otherwise drift into separation, re-mind us when we fall into forgetting our route Home. They bring us deep pleasure too, in the fascinating and often exciting relationship of ourselves in the world and in the Divine. Spiritual practices help us integrate our spiritual life and diminish the sense of duality. They draw us closer to God, but they also provide us with ways of working for God. Soul works are not all about growth and getting something, but about being and becoming, giving rather than taking. They can engage every aspect of our being; body, heart and mind. Often they are pursued without really realising that they are soul works, because they are such an everyday part of our lives, yet their impact on our spiritual life can be deepened if we approach them more consciously. I have many soul works in my life, from those which might be seen as obvious spiritual practice, such as meditation and prayer, to even the mundane stuff, things I have to do around the house or things that are not particularly satisfying to earn a living. These can also be enlightened by approaching them prayerfully and consciously. In other words, just about every activity and relationship can become integrated with our spiritual life. Maybe after a while we may notice that there is indeed no spiritual life and other life, but simply life where it is rolled into one. The sacred and the secular are dualistic illusions, everything is in and comes from the same source, all separation is drawn together, in part aided by our soul works.

Our soul works lead us into a place of waiting, where we seek re-connection. All of us, even the most "expert" practitioners fall into forgetting and become self-indulgent or just plain silly. There is no problem with "feeding the beast" now and again; a treat to sweeten the ego and take some time out from the work for a while. The problem can be if such treats draw us back into old habits and addictions, keeping us from staying the course. In addition our soul works are

---

[ix] www.cccare.org

not all about hard labour. We can lighten up and indeed make fun and laughter spiritual practices in themselves, a subject I will return to later. The moments of forgetting, when they happen, are opportunities as we become aware of them to be led into more spiritual practice – of being in silence, of waiting. This waiting is not as in a queue, but being open to God and allowing God's presence to be revealed. It is a patient, if sometimes, difficult waiting which allows intimacy in a relationship to develop, a shift from ordinary time (our will) to God time (Your will). It is the cultivation of a different attitude that makes us aware of how much pushing we might be doing, relaxing out of this and evolving the quality of waiting without attachment to a goal. Yet there is also a quality of knowing, in the faith sense, that there is a goal of sorts, a different way of seeing. This knowing-not-knowing waiting is pregnant with possibility and not fixed in time or space or specific outcome. It is worth remembering that we should not expect an immediate response from our waiting, Divine timing is always perfect timing and is not the same as the ego's timing. Like a medicine, it may take quite a while to feel the effects.

The quality of non-attachment applies also to what we might experience in the pursuit of our soul works. Past lives, precognition, premonition, spirit guides and all the panoply of New Age, and not so New Age, speak are often grasped by the ego and made personal, puffing up our sense of power, pride and importance. I suspect all spirit "guides" are merely faces of God presenting to us in a way that is acceptable to us, or fakes, slivers of our unconscious moving in to bolster the ego. Past lives and other such things can be part of this ego agenda, psychic phenomena that, willed or not, bubble up before us along the Way, but they are not themselves the Way. As we expand our consciousness beyond ego power and liberate the soul from its tight corset, we may begin to experience the infinite. It is the world of quantum physics, the universal energy field,[95] the realm of the mystic of "all that is". When we come to know ourselves in this "all" then "all" is available to us, but our minds, in order to get a grip on it, may select out only parts of it (the parts that usually are attractive to us in some way and tap into our unconscious desires). If the soul is of God, and God is all, then we may have intimations of that all, past present and future. We may feel we "see" or "know" things that are beyond the ordinary and our egos can latch onto these things, attaching us to visions or spirit guides or endless past lives. (As an aside, and curiously, it's my experience that those who attach a great deal to "past lives" invariably report ones of power and status, rather than ones of impotence and the mundane.) We may personalise them, perhaps rooted in an ego need for identity or specialness. Or we may go crazy with them.

I have a hunch that lots of people in our mental health institutions have had intimations of the infinity of consciousness, but their minds being too fragile to cope with it, without the wherewithal to filter it and make sense of it, collapse into chaos. Our fragile minds are flooded with the consequences, like a million TV channels being received all at once, and they crash with the overload or get hooked on one bit of it to try and make sense of it. We might start believing that we are John the Baptist or that an ancient Egyptian priestess is talking to us, because in a sense this may be true; when we tap into the all that is, that place where time and space are meaningless, then the whole memory of the universe becomes available to us. It may be true that we are John the Baptist but that is because in the holistic realm of the vast connected and universal consciousness we are all John the Baptist. It is a mistake to pick up on one bit of it and make it our own; that is the path to ego inflation or madness. The universe is a manifestation of the Divine, but it is not the Divine itself. It is like a vast thought, an expression of the divine consciousness, and we can be transfixed by the thought, when what we really seek is the One beyond thought.

During a workshop with Michael Harner (a man who has done much to reintegrate shamanism into the modern world[96]) some years ago, he had some wry words to say about spirit beings, not least to remember that just because something is in the spirit world, do not assume it is any wiser than you are! In the ocean of consciousness, all of the water can become available to us, as it is available to every one who seeks, but it is important not to get sidetracked. When these psychic experiences happen, simply embrace them as interesting gifts of grace then let them go and move on, unless it is the Will that this should be part of our work in the world for the One we seek to serve – a subject for a process of deep discernment on the Way. In general it is best to treat these experiences, however wonderful, as phenomena offering insight and gifts to be worked with, but with great caution and then put down.

Psychic experiences along the way can lead us into spiritual materialism and ego inflation, they are seductive and we can become hugely attached to them, seeking more and more of these experiences because we believe they are spiritual and falling into disappointment when they are not repeated. As a general rule, no matter how wonderful the experience, for example a blissful vision in meditation, it is unwise to attempt to repeat it or to seek more. For here is the slipping back into attachment, of trying to get wonderful experiences which are actually distracting not nourishing us along the Way. Real spiritual experiences expand our consciousness, not our egos, they deepen us in love not in addiction to the "highs", they draw us closer to our souls rather than flying off into fantasy and they edge us closer to the Divine rather than have us wandering off into the temptation of shiny trinkets.

Interesting as these psychic phenomena might be they are therefore to be regarded with extreme caution and are best subjected to the guidance of our soul friends and communities, and used as material for testing and discernment in our spiritual work. (A little later in this Part we will visit a good abbot with some sound advice on this.) I could fill this book with my tales of fantastical, mystical times, but that would be pointless, for their point is not that they are tales to be told so that we or others think we are wonderful, but teachings to be integrated, accepted with humility. When we treat them as possessions rather than temporary gifts, then they possess us. What would you seek, the fullness of Home or a long rest in the cul-de-sac of an interesting and fascinating temporary accommodation? Remember the guidance of St. Paul (1 Corinthians 13:1), that when we become adult we must put away the things of childhood. The playthings of spirituality are such things if we are to integrate and mature beyond them. A spiritual identity is just another identity, we need to be ready to let that go as well, to become impoverished of spiritual possessions of whatever sort.

Poverty, chastity, obedience come to mind when we think of soul works, and these are more than simplistic interpretations of rules for sex and money. Poverty can mean reducing the clutter and distractions from our lives so that we can give more attention to the Divine, not just material poverty; we are not asked to live in penury and starvation. In fact in my experience God does not ask at all, not in the ordinary human sense, God is beyond asking, rather it is the nature of God to draw unto itself that which came from it, that attraction is part of the asking. Most creation stories, such as Genesis, begin with the creation, the material world, coming out of God, not out of nothing. It is a *theophany*, the intrinsic nature of the universe is of God and therefore good ("and God saw it was good" Gen: 1:12) – and the words God and good have the same linguistic root.

The creation itself, as we discussed in part 7, is a soul food, for God is not remote from us, but present in the very here and now, unfolding in all its possibilities right before us. That is not to reduce the nature of God to the created world, but rather to emphasise its essential goodness (again the mystics like Julian of Norwich reinforce this), its existence from and in God. When our reverence for the world changes because we see it as a face of God, an outpouring of God, our response to it also changes. We no longer see ourselves as separate from the creation, and therefore outside of it or lacking in some way, but immensely wealthy. We do not need to shore up our place in the world by the acquisition of material wealth and power but become more content with the requirements to meet our needs and to share abundantly with others. People who have become more spiritually awake are rarely in high profile political or social activist roles for they feel more at peace, that the world at some level is "well", whole, holy. And if they are thus active they tend to do so from a place that is egoless. They come to know that one way to change the world is to change their own response to it and to help others do likewise.

This is not to suggest that to become "spiritual" is to become passive or resigned to the condition of the world and its inhabitants, quite the reverse. We become more, not less, engaged with it but from a place of trust and non-attachment within ourselves. When Arjuna is faced with struggle in the world in the Bhagavad Gita[97], his divine mentor the Lord Krishna advises him that he cannot not participate, but to do so "with peace in your heart". He tells Arjuna also to keep his mind, his eye, turned to him ("prayer and fasting" as we shall discuss in Part 8) so that in being constantly reminded of the Divine he will not disconnect and lose that peace at the centre and become trapped by attachment. Keeping our eyes on God helps us to stay attentive to what matters and let go of the inconsequential.

If we approach the world thus the response both for ourselves and from others is very different than if we approach it with a desire to control or change it, even violently. The spirit is like a beautiful butterfly to be appreciated and accepted as it is – pin it down and we may still have the butterfly, but it is dead. And by controlling in this way we bring into the world the very thing we seek to condemn and change. When we have liberated ourselves, coming Home to a deep trust in God, in Love, then as part of the creation we affect it likewise. One person's shift in consciousness always affects the whole, as does the practical actions they may take from that place in themselves. Just as Buddhists may work to bring enlightenment to others, on the basis that no one is free until all are free, so Christians may work to bring Christ consciousness (and parallels can be drawn from all the great faiths) into the world as a manifestation of that same universal harmony that is the ground of the creation. Thus poverty as soul work is not about giving away all our material support and having nothing, for most of us living in the world and in community that is not possible or even desirable. Some people may feel called to the extremes of denying all worldly goods, but that is rare. Rather it is about letting go of attachment to them, about poverty in things that distract us from God, about sharing what we have with generosity of spirit.

Poverty includes silence, time away from indulgences like TV or chattering so that we can hear God speak to us. It includes living lightly on the earth so that we do not impoverish our earthly home or gain so many attachments that we cannot be free of them to connect more deeply to the Divine. It asks us to be more still when our lives are rich in movement. Poverty is saying "no" to some things in order to say "yes" to God. Waiting, silence, absence of things, staying power, solitude, time in the desert and so on - these and others are the soul works we practice when we embrace poverty. Some say "I do not have time", "I have children to raise" or a "sick relative to care for". Perhaps a better way is to change the way we think about these. Caring for another, if approached consciously can be just as much spiritual practice as any of the more obvious ones like prayer or attending a communal service. In fact, with attention to spiritual practice, we may find that we can approach our task with more time, more energy, more compassion, not less.

Being quiet, stopping movement in all senses may not just lead us into the peace or presence of the Divine. It can also become a blank space, a void, or a place filled with things that trouble us. This is not meditation or contemplation but one of the reasons why the soul guidance is suggested in this book. Emptiness might guide us to God, but it may also be a place where we encounter suffering, and the painful shadows lurking in the unconscious. Furthermore, teaching emptiness, which is part of many traditions on the Way without the support of soul foods, soul works, soul friends and soul communities, may just lead to nihilism, especially in the person who has not yet matured spiritually. I am very wary therefore of DIY meditation packs, for soul work like this can be full of states of consciousness where we need the help of a soul friend in person or a group of fellow travellers to support us.

We can experience a deep fear, a dread as we realise that an aspect of ourselves is deeply inimical to God. That this illusory, superficial, transient thing we have called ourselves is, at its core, antagonistic to God and we are left wondering perhaps fearfully, what the response of God might be to that enemy. In our dread we can withdraw, consciously or unconsciously, pulling back from the Way, disconnecting from God as we come to know deeply how part of our nature is false to life, false to God. Perhaps the magnitude, as it seems, of the task of surrender can overwhelm us. As our limited interpretation of the possible consequences sinks in we may retreat or rebel. We can struggle to bring back the false peace of our spiritual practice, those nice experiences of sweetness and light so that we can feel better again. We can see God as the enemy, projecting our fear outward, or we can become an enemy to ourselves, dragging ourselves off the Way in our fear. Paradoxically, it is not possible to seek emptiness even with the apparently "good" intention of wanting to be filled with God. Indeed in a sense we do not seek surrender, meditation or any other spiritual "state", for to target any of these with purpose is an oxymoron. To aim for emptiness for example suggests that we are already full – of the seeking, the ego desire to accomplish something, reach something, obtain something. All our works – of prayer and fasting – may contain the hope of something "more", but all of these at some point are to be put down, even the thought of the "more", even the hope of it. Arguably this is one of the most taxing of encounters along the way, to do the work yet let go of the work, to have concepts yet release them, to want something, yet allow the dissolution of that wanting.

The sense of loss, of being abandoned by God, of dereliction does not arise because God has left us. It is not the nature of the Divine to abandon that which love calls Home. The sense comes because at some level it is we who have abandoned our Essence. It may be that we have become full of expectation of rewards for the spiritual life, got hooked onto concepts of God, become presumptuous about the Way – all of these and more can subtly and sometimes not so subtly worm their way into our consciousness, building barriers between us and the One for whom we long.

All of these dread-full experiences are also hope-full, for they are signs that the work is going on, that the transformation is indeed under way, that in the suffering grace is at work. They are not punishment but purification. We are being turned inside out so that the surrender of the false self can be completed. This is the time to persist with prayer when all might seem lost, time to seek help when we might wish to go our own way, time to rest when we might feel panicked into action, time to embrace love when we might want to give way to fear.

If these are sometimes hard ideas to grasp, they are even harder to experience. They strengthen the case of the need for the four Soul Care approaches proposed in this book. Without them we may give way to despair and give up, or return to old habits, or harden our hearts so much that we become impenetrable to the spirit of the Divine itself.

Christine gives us an example of some of these concerns. She led a busy life. Sixty- or seventy-hour-weeks, meeting after meeting, papers to work on at home – and squeezing the family and a social life somewhere in between – the usual lot of many a high flying manager. As I listened to the long tale of her packed schedule, I was feeling exhausted just at the thought of it. It was not hard to see how someone could keep up that pace, because after all I'd been there myself, what seems now to be another lifetime ago. She was in that arid phase when something inside her knew her life was all out of synch, knew it had to change, but couldn't envisage how life might be otherwise. She was in a cage in part of her own making for the job paid for a lot of things – the big house, the flash car, the private schooling. All of which now kept her bound to the treadmill, or at least she thought they did, to keep the money coming in.

She was looking for something deeper, some way out of her current debilitating and disconnecting impasse but was trying to apply the same process to that search that she had learned to apply to her "successful", driven personal life. "How do I get "there"? She often asked. "How do I find that inner voice to guide me that I've heard about?" She wanted the check list, the action plan, the boxes to tick to "get in touch with my spirituality". In time she came to see that the busyness was also a way of avoiding being still, afraid that she might not like what she might feel and see within if she did so. Yet, some drive deep within her was pushing her in a direction that she was unsure of, but felt she must respond to, even at the expense of a break from work ('though strictly limited, and the mobile phone was constantly on hand, and the car was full of files "just in case"!)

She saw Eileen Caddy's book ("And God Spoke to Me") in the sanctuary at the Foundation's retreat house. "I've read bits of that," she said, and I wondered where she ever found the time, though the "bits" was the clue. Her brother had given her a copy and she'd treated the book to the rapid read techniques she used for executive meeting papers. "Lots of people tell me that God spoke to them" and she chatted away about how that never happens to her. In the brief silence as she gulped her tea I was able to add "I'm not surprised, I doubt if he can get a word in edgeways!" "Funnily enough" she said, "People at work have told me the same thing, and my mother says what a good job it is that my husband is such a quiet man." So we had a good laugh about our own ridiculousness and began to explore how a bit of stillness and silence might come into her life. Then she might be able to "hear" those messages from her deepest self. That which has been given all kinds of names down the aeons; the song of the heart that calls us to do what is right and meaningful for us in the world, even if it demands a shift great or small in the current way of living. When we do not pay attention, dis-ease and disease in one form or another inevitably ensue.

The Sufi mystic Hafiz says in one of his poems that everyone gets an invitation in one way or another, so that narrows down our choices to just two "to come dressed for dancing or be carried there on a stretcher!"[98] When we follow what has heart and meaning for us, life can feel joyful and fulfilling. When we do not, it's an accident waiting to happen. Of course that can be easier said than done if we have both time and money to make that search. And when we are young, time is spent rightly in defining ourselves – establishing roles and doing all those things like earning a living, making relationships, home, children. Indeed for many people these are what feels deeply right for us in our lives, at least for a while if not the whole of life, but sooner or later the voice of the call Home can get more insistent.

Christine found it tough to learn to be still, for paradoxically doing nothing and just learning to be can be hard work, at least at first. After a year, life was different. She changed jobs, downsized many aspects of her life, moved to a cheaper house, spent more time with the family, and with herself. She wrote "I don't have as much of what I used to have, but I and all the family have more of what we didn't have – happiness". She had a life that was materially wealthy, but in so doing she was impoverished in time, in human relationships, in happiness, in love. When she learned to let go of so many attachments and saw what poverty really meant, then she discovered the meaning of wealth.

Chastity is not just about giving up sexual relations. Chastity might mean being faithful to our chosen tradition, and sticking with it when times are tough. It means not being a spiritual dilettante and practicing our soul works superficially just to get them out of the way, or indulging in spiritual bed hopping in search of the next spiritual high. It means applying ourselves to the discipline of going deeper into few practices rather than many. The serious soul work cannot be undertaken without discipline, an unpopular concept in libertarian cultures where "doing your own thing" is seen as a hallmark of freedom. But it is worth remembering that the root meaning of discipline is the Latin *discere*, to learn. Discipline is about applying oneself to learning and not, as it has come to be interpreted, as subjection to rigid authority and loss of freedom. Freedom includes making the choice to learn from someone or something no matter what the cost and voluntarily giving up things – time, money and luxuries and so on in the hope of some greater reward.

It is not freedom but spiritual promiscuity when, in the spiritual supermarket with so much on offer, we continually try out different things and move on when going deeper is what is needed. We can dig a well to find the water of life, but give up when it gets difficult or rocky or muddy and the digging gets tough, then try and dig another well somewhere else.[99] So it can be with the spiritually unchaste, trying a bit of Buddhism and then a bit of Islam and so on, moving on each time usually when it gets difficult or boring rather than cultivating tenacity to faithfully reach the rich rewards of the water of life in its depths. Part of the discipline of working with any religion is having the insight to see that you have to keep digging even when it gets hard. No religious tradition is full of sweetness and light all the time or an idealised community of people without conflict. Sticking with a discipline, a community, a tradition is in part tested by our willingness to include the spiritual lows as wells at the highs, the nice people as well as the not so nice people. Chastity might mean honesty and integrity and discernment in relationships, of being faithful to God and to ourselves when other things might tempt us away. But since chastity is often assumed to be entirely about sexual propriety, let us explore a few things around sex and spirituality.

I grew up in the 60s on a council estate to the North of Manchester, and like most teenage lads of my age we bluffed a great deal more about sex than we actually knew about or practised. The mechanics, and little else, were explored with world-weary bluntness in two sessions in the science lab but beyond that the landscape of sexual awakening was largely without map or compass. I was 13, maybe 14, and wrapped in some daydream when I had my first sexual epiphany. It hit me like a flash - my mum and dad must have had sex. More than that, they must have had sex when they were old, I mean old! My mum was in her mid 40s when I was born – ancient!

At 15 I met Janet, my first serious girlfriend. School was about to finish and it was to be that last of devotion to my bike and my mates. I met the usual gang at the fair, but she was new in the crowd. I caught her eye momentarily and held it and had the feeling that I had never in all my life looked someone in the eye before. There weren't exactly violins in the background, but for a while all conversation around me became muffled, the fair disappeared, the bike no longer existed. There was just Janet and that lingering moment. I was lost for the first time. The second time occurred that night. Janet and I shed the gang and the rules, and were alone on a bench up Cemetery Road. Hesitant every step of the way, somehow her hand found its way into mine, then my hand across her belly, then our necks entwined, then our lips met. Like many of you, dear readers, that explosive first kiss shot me into another realm of consciousness, I imploded, exploded, dissolved into intimacy. It became the classic summer love and I was never the same again.

On a recent TV programme a participant was alleged to have sex in full public view. The head of factual entertainment for Channel 4 responsible for the programme, said "Sex is no different from property. Millions of people buy homes just as millions of people have sex." [100] I think he was wrong. My youthful awakening is common to many, and it tells us something about the power of intimacy. Yes, sex has a reproductive function, and yes it is powerfully pleasurable. But to reduce it to "property" is to desecrate it, to commodify it. To dumb it down to entertainment, and public entertainment or display is the antithesis of intimacy – the very essence of loving relationships. Loving relationships are one of our pathways to the Divine, for in loving the other we learn about and receive love, a mirror of loving God. Relationships are just as much a spiritual practice as any other if we approach them consciously as I have explored elsewhere.[101] Sexual promiscuity is proscribed in many faiths for reasons more than judgementalism or disapproval, but because it can be an abuse of love, an ego self gratification that boosts pleasure, power and desire but keeps us away from really connecting with another person and with the Divine. In fact sexual promiscuity can be a sign of our unconscious longing for God – endlessly searching for the perfect lover we are perhaps expressing the longing for the Beloved in whom that perfect eternal love exists.

The response to promiscuity does not require, and this book does not advocate, puritanical, oppressive rules around sexual expression, rather the encouragement to see sexual activity as more than self- gratification. Spiritual work is not about self-gratification, but about reducing the power of the self and the latter does not happen if we keep feeding it. There is another effect indeed of gratification and that is to increase the ego identity with sexuality. Sexuality is an incidental aspect of our personhood, an important one for sure, but it is not who we are. When we elevate it to a primary aspect of our identity, indeed make it our identity, then this too becomes just another ego trap. For example feminist, gay or manhood movements can only take us so far. They may free us from social oppression or a sense of lack of self worth, but at some point even these identities must go as well. For, in spiritual terms, the cultivation of an identity is only a partial journey, the whole journey leads us into the surrender of that identity, into the *fana' fi-l llah*, if we are willing.

Meanwhile, we rarely see in our media the alternative of deeper relationships. In a utilitarian culture, sex and relationships are for what we can get out of them, to be abandoned when no longer fun. Yet relationships, including their expression through our sexuality, can be a spiritual practice like any other. In the high wire act of joining and separating, balancing "my" with "your", learning to move beyond ego and see that what we can bring to the other rather that what we get from them is what matters – these are the very stuff of spiritual maturity. And our sexuality can be a glorious medium for intimacy, made the more glorious when two people choose to deepen it, practice it and explore all its dimensions perhaps down a lifetime of commitment.

127

Sometimes it's right to let go of a relationship. But there is also a case for persistence, patience and perseverance that can lead to an ever-deeper connection. Such is the spiritual discipline of love. Sexuality is part of spirituality, because it is part of our humanity. For some people the path to Truth may embrace celibacy. But it is not the only path. Loving, intimate sexual relationships where depth and maturation can be encountered are also a path to the same goal. Sexual union, that blissful state when all boundaries fall away is one of the means by which human beings can experience a sort of union that transcends the ordinary - a state like the mystics report in their relationship to God. It is one of the means by which we can fall in Love, from self into Self.

All faiths have histories of "issues" with sex, but none seem to have taken it to the level of some branches of Christianity. That sex in any form is "bad" or sinful. Pope Innocent III (1160-1216) stated that "the sexual act is so shameful that it is intrinsically evil" and another Christian theologian maintained that "the Holy Ghost is absent from the room shared by a wedded couple."[102] Few modern Christians, or come to that people of other faiths, would agree with these mediaeval perspectives – at least when it applies to straight sex, in wedlock. Step outside these parameters however, and the theological ground gets shakier. The waiting rooms of the modern priests – psychotherapists and counsellors – are replete with people who still bear the burden, straight or no, of repressed sexuality.

Few belief systems, whether theist or atheist, are free of problems with sex. It might be outright hostility (e.g. Roman Catholicism defines gayness as an "abomination", Islam in some countries condones stoning of female adulterers) or more subtle suggestions that sexuality and its expression inhibit enlightenment. I worked with a Hindu priest who was adamant celibacy was a prerequisite to a relationship with the Divine. "You cannot have ice cream and fire together", he told me, but I wondered; "In the heart of God, are not ice and fire one?" A Buddhist asserted it was not possible for women to become enlightened until they were reborn as men. It's little wonder that we live in a world of sexual hang-ups when the signals from so many sources of authority are negative. No religion, Old Age or New Age, has escaped the distortion of sexuality through power and fear leading to abuse especially of women, children and those it picks out as "other". A classic psychological script when we are fearful and brittle in our faith or ourselves is to find some other to condemn in order to feel more secure. Religions and people that exclude people from their love are not whole, and a religion that is not whole is not holy. Sexuality divorced from spirituality is unhealthy and is trapped in the old paradigm that sex or the worldly creation is inherently evil. Our sexuality is part of the sacred; spirituality is in the physical too.

We turn now to obedience, which is not just about blind surrender to rules or to persons. There is a process of discernment at work here too, it does not mean that we must obey everyone and everything if, for example, the one we obey abuses their power over us, as in the case of sexual abuse by a false and unhealthy soul friend or community. Obedience is rooted in the Latin word *oboedire*[103] which means to listen as well as to obey, to incline one's ear towards someone and attend to their guidance. "Listen to me" is a phrase commonly used by great spiritual teachers, which carries with it a call to pay close attention, understand and act or change accordingly. It is more than hearing the words, rather it is the kind of hearing that touches us deeply producing transformation in our way of seeing.

The discipline of obedience tends to fall foul of the individualist cult that is wary of letting others have authority over us, yet we all live by rules, even ones we create for ourselves. Obedience as a spiritual discipline (discipline and disciple are closely related words suggesting a willingness to take notice or follow in order to learn) urges us to pay close attention, to understand and integrate something deeply and transform the way we are in the world. Thus we might be a disciple of a particular religious leader or school of thought, there is a quality of discipline/ discipleship/obedience in our relationship with our soul friend (not least when he/she challenges us), in our application to our soul works when we might feel tired, bored or disheartened or in the call to a particular religion. We stick with it not as a form of self punishment or abuse by others but because we are committed to going deeper. Knowing, perhaps in faith, that it is necessary to keep digging deeper if we are to reach the water, the water of life, at the bottom of the well.

Paradoxically, obedience is not a labour or loss of choice, for at some level of course we have freely chosen to obey. This discipline face of obedience also has a loving quality to it because of our love for the Divine and a desire to get closer. Thus there is a degree of willingness to surrender things which would distract us e.g. forego a lot of alcohol in order to remain clear headed to commune, to fast (not just food as suggested, but that can be one way) in order to pay closer attention to our relationship to God, to give way to a regular practice or to our soul friend because of the spiritual authority imbued in them. Discipline implies self control, the diminution of ego desires and trivial comforts that distract us from God, that rein in the thoughts, impulses etc. that take us away from what is True, our heart's desire. The discipline of love has an essentially gentle and loving quality to it, even though it can be incredibly tough at times, but that is not because the discipline is tough, it is because the ego is tough – seeking to heave us back from the Self's love of us, that draws us magnetically to itSelf. As awareness of the love of God in/of/for us deepens, the battle like quality diminishes once the ego begins to accept who is in charge (although it will always search often more subtly for ways to be the boss again).

One of these subtle ways, incidentally, is the ego trick of returning us to old patterns and engendering hopelessness - that we will never be free. I am reminded of Geoff, who in his struggle to heal his relationship with his father would regularly sink back into blaming himself. "It's my fault again - It's always me that's wrong", was his default position. We can probably do very little to change the ego and its scripts, the pattern of this aspect of our personhood may well be pretty well set, but what we can do is learn to witness it and its power tricks and respond differently.

Geoff was like a man who would leave home every day and fall into a hole in the road. He kept on doing this every day until one day he was more aware of the hole, and learned to walk around it. Thus it is with some of our personality traits. They are there, they have become part of our identity and our inner landscape, but they are not who we truly are. We are not our scripts and histories. We can catch ourselves before we fall into such traps by disciplined attention to soul work that raises our awareness of them. Thus aware, we are less likely to be trapped by them once more. The holes have not necessarily gone away, we have simply learned how to respond to them differently, to not allow ourselves to be dragged into them. Geoff's self blaming was a form of self discipline , but it was a punishing ego discipline trick to keep him stuck in his old way of being. It was a means of keeping him from God, from the very awareness he needed that would subvert the power of the little, egotistic, false self.

The discipline that is not discipline, whose real name is punishment, comes from the ego - the desire to hurt ourselves because we feel bad, the need for pain or suffering because we feel we are not worthy of God. Or we have projected our unworthiness onto God and made him a demon who demands pain otherwise we don't love Him enough or He will not love us enough. It is a chthonic force seeking to keep us from God by keeping us locked into suffering; an inverse discipline that keeps us thinking we can only be enlightened by suffering. It's a trick of the mind/ego that keeps us from asking the question, is there love in this? Are we involved in spiritual discipline in order to get closer to God, even though some of the tasks are hard e.g. by reading difficult books or fixing a prayer time when we'd really rather sleep? If the motivation for the latter is to wrestle control from the ego so that we can be free, beneath that tough reality we know there is a hope worthy of it and will persist, and in time the opposition diminishes. The discipline that is really punishment on the other hand is the discipline of sacrifice not surrender; it is the discipline of fear not love. The discipline of fear is relentless and interminable - for we are never good enough in this approach to get to God. The discipline of love permits closeness to God, that is the reward in a sense, the goal.

The discipline of love is the foundation of the contemplative way. Contemplation is found in all faiths, one author from a Roman Catholic background sees it as "The heart of the Christian mystical element since its beginning is contemplatio, that is, the contemplation of the soul on the presence of God through the inspiration of the scriptures. The Desert Fathers and Mothers of the first Christian centuries saw in *contemplatio* the vision of the 'pure in heart' mentioned in the Beatitudes (Mt 5:8) and tried to live this through their solitary contemplation."[104] Analysis breaks things down into parts in our efforts to understand things. Approaches like prayer and contemplation help us to see the elements as part of a whole, to see the relatedness in things, of all things. The contemplative has to concentrate first, to pay attention to preparing themselves and then may be drawn into a prayerful state which may involve the approaching of God with our list of requests. But this too passes as we move into a meditative awareness where the mind settles and the heart begins to open to the Divine beyond which the contemplative state awaits, the state that is no state, the "condition of complete simplicity costing not less than everything."[105] In contemplation, we move beyond our methods, our soul works, our mental constructs, definitions or efforts and enter a deep and simple form of receptivity, a Sabbath for the soul when the "work" of prayer and meditation is let go and we simply are in the Presence.

Is this what all our soul works bring us to? Once we get past or set aside our "method", it seems a commons strand in all these practices that they draw us closer to the Divine, to a point where all our agendas, thoughts, constructs and expectations fall away. The mind and all its works are relinquished for what it stands before is ultimately incomprehensible to it in the conventional sense of knowing. Here there just "is". It is a movement beyond prayer, a stillness attitude or posture of consciousness where faced with the God who knows all 'Prayer is really a waste of time. The incarnate form of our prayer may be concerned with getting something done, forwarding our plans, and the generosity of God is such that he will let himself be incarnate even in these ways. But the very heart of prayer is not getting anything done. It is a waste of time, an even greater waste of time than play... For a real absolute waste of time you have to go to prayer."[106]

If prayer is really only asking God for things, entreaty, then arguably it really is a waste of time before the Divine all knowing. However, there are other aspects to prayer - bringing ourselves into a space of intimacy with God where we might be transformed. It is the sacred space where we draw close to the Divine and our various methods of soul work are transcended as we shift our consciousness into the unknowable, indescribable Presence. Furthermore, the scientific studies on prayer are also revealing some intriguing results that cannot be explained by conventional science.[107] An increasing body of research into prayer and non-local healing, points to the possibility of physical reality, not least health and wellbeing of those prayed for, being changed by our prayerful intentions.

Prayer may therefore not be a waste of time even before an all knowing God. It is a means by which we are drawn into a deeper relationship with each other and the Divine. Prayer may thus be just one more method, the point of which is not the method itself but what it leads us to. As Thomas Merton again says: "We should not look for a 'method' or 'system', but cultivate an 'attitude', an 'outlook': faith, openness, attention, reverence, expectation, supplication, trust, joy. All these finally permeate our being with love in so far as our living faith tells us we are in the presence of God, that we live in Christ, that in the Spirit of God we 'see' God our Father without 'seeing'. We know him in 'unknowing'."[108] This "knowing in unknowing" is found in all religious traditions. Though the words used to describe it may differ, the experience is essentially the same. Whether we rest in deep silence or whirl like a Sufi, whether we surrender into the moving meditation that is tai chi or pray at sunrise, the practice at some level is not important, it is merely the opening of the gate to something more, a glimpse of Home. Thus what our method takes us to is not an "add on" which we fit in now and then in order to "achieve" something, bliss, communion with the Divine, insight or relaxation but a purpose which becomes purposeless, where we let go of expectation of whatever sort and sink into the Divine Presence itself, which is already there, waiting.

It is the waiting on our part without hope or love or faith[109] where all agendas are set aside. The kind of serious faith "of breathing when you're drowning" [110] for "Once we recognise our nothingness and helplessness before God then we can begin to pray. From such a perspective, even a coldness or impossibility to begin prayer is in itself a sign of this helplessness before God – a sign of His grace towards us and the necessity for our dependence upon His grace. For, as McCabe and Merton remind us in their own ways, ultimately there can only ever be one teacher of prayer – and that is the Holy Spirit. Such a prayer, such a *contemplatio*, is not a *fugit mundi*, a flight from the world, but leads us back into life, into the arms of the world."[111] Back into life in which we step into the unknowing in every encounter from a restful place of being in the moment, for we have been fed by the unknowing of God, where we know that we know very little. No expertise in work, no professional management of relationships, is ultimately possible in every human encounter. This contemplation as the embodiment of all soul works is not a flight from the world but *eros*, a willingness to engage with it at every level, body, mind, heart and soul, but from a completely different place within ourselves. Here is Krishna's advice to Arjuna fulfilled. Here we discover the peace that passes understanding. Here we discover the sacred interior place of enlightened consciousness from which we can fully participate in the world.

Spirituality is thereby no longer disembodied from our "ordinary life" in this dualistic way, for there is no spiritual life and ordinary life, just life lived completely and fully integrated. It is not a matter of God or the world but God in the world. In such a life we do not "burn out", in whatever social activism engages us[112] for we have abandoned the idols, the addictions, of our own gaols, our (often unacknowledged) pride in them, our desire to make everything perfect and just. Instead we relax into serving the One from whom all these emanate and in whom they and we exist.

A spirituality engaged with the world does not deny political power; rather it knows its limits. Power rooted in the will of the ego, no matter how benevolently masked, always leads to corruption and abuse. The spiritually aware person is alive to the tricks and deceptions of this kind of power which is incapable of humility, although it can try, Uriah Heep like, and appear humble in order to gain power more subtly. Spiritually based political power is power set in *power under*, in service of others, of God, not *power over* others, which seeks to dominate for its own ends. Dictatorship in all its forms is always about power over. Power under is not rooted in our will but the Will. The Jesus story of the towel and the bowl (q.v.) is an example of this. Politics like science or any other human endeavour, without heart and surrendered to the Will is inevitably oppressive, even deadly.

As spirited social activists, however great or small, in whatever arena of life, we are in the "war" but with peace in our hearts, the peace that passes all understanding. Being indifferent to the world and throwing ourselves into making it all perfect according to our standards are different sides of the same coin; both hold a kind of energy of fighting (either the struggle not to or the struggle to participate). The contemplative has spotted this trap and "Therefore, merely abstaining from affairs which we are unable to accomplish or complete, even if we wanted to, certainly does not prove that the disease of worldly ambition does not dwell in our minds. The same is true of despising those things, which, if we affected them, would make us look important among both spiritual and worldly persons. It is rather a matter of our also rejecting with unwavering strictness of mind those things which cater to our power and which have the appearance of a kind of goodness."[113] Looking for the 'true action' behind the appearance of goodness is rooted in our capacity for discernment in ourselves and with others.

When Jesus washed the feet of his disciples (John 13: 3-10) he offered a profound teaching on the nature of obedience, service and spiritual awakening – that the way up is the way down. We do not become more spiritually mature by worshipping delusions of grandeur and status, but by the humility of recognising our own lack of self-importance (the opposite of many New Age teachings). In washing the feet, a taboo part of the body in those days, he lowered himself to the ground. He used a bowl and towel - the kinds of things that only slaves would carry, not "important" people. In fact it could be argued that the bowl and the towel make an interesting symbol of an important aspect of Christianity, and for that matter for any faith that seeks to get to the core of what it is to be enlightened. In what others dismiss as dirty or low level work, is often found the highest element of service and in many traditions the path of service is the path to God.

To accept the burden of the towel and the bowl (which with deep appreciation we come to see is light) is no burden at all; if the source is from God not ourselves then it is no effort. The burden, if any, is staying with that consciousness and putting aside ego desires for power and status. Our culture floods us with images and rewards which reinforce a set of values that to be materially wealthy, famous, in control and powerful are the main goals of life. Happiness can be found in designer clothes, homes, food, bodies, babies. A life of style is for winners, a life of service is for losers. Yet every spiritual teacher down the ages has offered a counter argument to this. We are not called to live in material poverty if we are to mature spiritually. However, the calling does ask us to divest ourselves of attachments to the superficial including the power trips of the ego, which distract us from getting to the truth of our own essential nature, and that which respects that nature and the rest of the creation.

In lowering himself to the ground, to the earth, Jesus humbled himself before his disciples (and *humus* – the earth, and humility are closely related words, so too is humour). He demonstrated his lack of ego attachment to a position of power. In doing so he offered a supreme model of the leader as the servant and the deep spiritual teaching of the nature of enlightenment. For the way up (to greater awareness, expanded consciousness, enlightenment, God) is paradoxically the way down – away from attachment to material gain, power and prestige. This is the opposite of the ego's agenda where that which is "high" is prestige, fame, wealth, power over others. It regards soul power, power under, as no power at all, indeed abhors it.

Humility symbolised by the towel and the bowl changes our approach to the world. We do not encounter people and situations from our own perspective but from the perspective of the other. From a built up ego to a demolished one, that old power is broken and placed under the authority of the soul so that we may draw closer to Home, to worship, to service, to right living. No other God, be it of money or status or self aggrandisement can be worshipped on this altar if we truly wish to come home - to God. The "jealous" God (Ex 34:14) is not jealous in the human ego sense of desiring what another has, rather in the sense of not being approached, loved or worshipped as anything but a unity with no false distractions or idols getting in the way.

As if to illuminate this further, towards the end of Jesus' life, the towel and the bowl make another appearance. This time (Matthew 27:24) Pontius Pilate, in an effort to prevent a riot, gives the crowd baying for Jesus' execution what it wants (and neatly absolves himself and Rome of responsibility) he calls for the bowl of water and famously washes his hands. Signifying that he thus took no responsibility for Jesus' crucifixion, he used the towel and the bowl as symbols of power – they were probably brought to him by a slave, there is no indication that he lowered himself either physically or otherwise. He had the power over life and death as an ambassador of Roman governance. The towel and the bowl here are about power over others, not power under others in service, that is living in the world in such a way that we remain aware of our own essential transience and powerlessness and that real power, when we are empty of such precepts both flows through us and in us. That power is one of love, for oneself, for others and for God. Liberated from such ego attachments we are set free to be full-filled in the world to pursue whatever destiny, perhaps written in our hearts at birth, awaits us on the journey Home.

Strength, power and freedom are found in surrender to the will of the Divine, of moving from our will to the Will, from doing our work to the Work. Individualist society does not like this and the ego doesn't either. That is one of the great paradoxes of the spiritual search, by surrendering our power and our desire for power, we lose ourselves, in losing ourselves we find our true Self in the Divine, in service, in the power of humility.

Whatever soul works we engage in, and there are many, they are not ends in themselves. They are ways of opening to the Divine, of mining for Truth, of stimulating the imagination so that we re-imagine what is true, God. They engage all our senses – the intellect, the body, the emotions. Space does not permit a full exploration of them here, but a discussion with a small group of eleven seekers shows the enormous range that is available to us, and this just in one small group. More information can be found elsewhere[114] and in the suggested reading after the reference section :

Pilgrimage – making a visit to a holy shrine or sacred place. The discipline of planning it, carrying it through, the encounters judged good or bad we have along the way, the willingness to surrender to the vagaries of travel, the reverence with which we approach the place - all these are full of potential for deeper spiritual awakening. Pilgrimage is not spiritual tourism, where we visit a place to be entertained, or take pictures or in search of a spiritual high. There can be a pilgrimage quality too in our daily practice, for example in the way we spend time preparing for it and carrying it through.

Silence – making time in life to be quiet, perhaps going to a place reserved for it or bringing it into daily life e.g. having a silent meal or reserving a place in the home for quiet. In silence, when the world around us and our inner world is quiet we may truly "hear".

Meditation – quietening the mind, often with a repeated phrase or mantra which may or may not have a particular meaning. This is closely related to –

Contemplation – we may concentrate first to pay attention and plan our time for a session, then meditate to quieten the mind, there may be included a degree of prayer moving beyond entreaty to where prayer is then (and this process cannot be controlled, for to make it a goal is to create an obstacle – the goal gets in the way) we may enter a consciousness of waiting, as discussed above, where we simply sit utterly in the moment, before in the Divine. Words cannot describe it for to use words is to fix the unfixable and name the unnameable. Contemplation is often regarded as one of the highest of the spiritual arts.

Lectio divina – Literature focussed on the spirit, the Divine. This is one of the soul foods mentioned earlier, developed here as a practice to stir up spiritual awareness, and to draw us deeper into contemplation. For example a short piece of scripture or other inspiring words may be read and we then sit with it, reflect upon it, use a phrase as meditation, let the words and meaning of it roll around and shift our consciousness and understanding to draw us closer to knowing God, what God is "saying" to us.

Tai chi – a Chinese discipline of body movements which are carried through like a moving meditation.

Yoga – both for the joy of being in a group, for the sense of bodily wellbeing and for the meditative quality that brings a sense of peace and being in the moment.

Body prayer – a series of movements associated with certain prayer words with the body moving in rhythm and depiction of the words.

Prayer – coming before God, making time for God, and offering our hopes and fears, asking for help. Letting God see us inside. Paradoxically God knows us completely so why pray? Because prayer is a form of being intimate with God, in prayer we draw close and may pass beyond words into contemplation. Intimacy with God is perhaps the essence of prayer. All prayer is the creation rising up to the Divine.

Retreats – time for the practice of community or in solitude to be alone with God and to be free of distractions for inner exploration.

Enneagram – an advanced form of personality assessment that is much deeper than other types and embraces aspects of spirituality and guidance on healthy spirituality. It is a useful guide to discovering our essence. It can be regularly revisited and studied in depth alone or in groups to deepen our understanding of the soul and of God.

Labyrinth work – there are many forms of labyrinth, with probably the most refined being that in Chartres cathedral, now replicated and available in many places and often offered at courses and conferences. It is possible to make one in home or garden. It is a pathway with one way in and one way out, not a maze with blind alleys, designed to permit walking meditation and prayer.

Work and relationships – conscious exploration of these on a day-to-day basis to enrich our capacity for being more loving in the world, healing old wounds, practising walking our talk and so on. God is not relegated to the place of worship. A maturing spirituality is engaged with every aspect of our lives.

Working with dreams, tarot and astrology – seeking meaning and understanding by the use of symbolism.

Sacraments – participating in worship and holy rituals alone or in our soul community.

The practice of generosity/compassion – actually doing things that involve sharing and giving, for example tithing part of our income to our religious community, becoming active in social enterprises that work for the wellbeing of others, fundraising and making donations, giving rather than receiving. Being involved in peace and justice movements. The practice of virtue is as much a spiritual practice as any other, being a truth speaker, and authentic agent of love in humility at work in the world to aid others.

Sacred song and dance – such as circle dancing, hymns and chants.

Creating "sacred space" – helping at church, mosque or temple and perhaps creating a special space in the home dedicated to spiritual practice. The physical space becomes "holy" and helps connect us to the sacred space in our relationship to God which is not visible.

Journaling and reflective diaries – Keeping notes about our spiritual unfolding, and re-reading them to discover new insights, perhaps taking them to the soul friend as food for discussion.

Icon painting – as a devotional practice in itself and to work with the rich, sacred, mystical symbolism that icons contain. There has been a great revival of interest in icons in recent years. The painting of and/or the prayerful reflection upon one stills the mind and draws us into contemplation of the Divine.

Sabbath time – maintaining a day of the week (not necessarily a Saturday or Sunday) dedicated to our soul work, relaxing, being attentive to spirit, putting aside the distractions of labour or chores. Being in the moment and relating and connecting as fully as we can to our Source.

Writing poetry, haikus, painting, composing – as prayer acts focussing on the Divine and the inner creative experience.

Fasting at regular intervals – a common practice in many traditions, to put aside bodily needs for a while as a preparation for approaching God and as a discipline to rein in the power of the ego.

The work is not done alone and we can only do so much ourselves. By our commitment, our practices, we show up, present ourselves, the rest is the grace, the Holy Spirit, the divine consciousness shifting in us. The former makes space for the latter.

The list is a long one and we could go on a good deal longer, and even such a small group has thrown up a diverse range of options. Staying focussed on a few and giving them time seems to be the important feature. As the practice grows we may find ourselves ever more yoked to love where what was once seen as spiritual and non-spiritual becomes more at one. Being part of a religious tradition can mean that we embrace many of these as part of a coherent whole. Our soul work of choice, with practice and discipline can become as natural and everyday so that eventually we may begin to realise that we are always on pilgrimage, always in meditation or prayer. Our practice provides the milieu for us to get to this place where remembering has become part of our lives, we have started forgetting to forget. This is the principle of "as you sow, so shall you reap" – the fruits of the work when applied diligently are the thing we seek, Home.

Sometimes, perhaps often, we can feel hopeless or stuck, that is why the four key elements in this book offer us the context that will bring us out of such an arid place. The spiritual practice of *contraria contrariis senantur* is an intriguing one to pursue when we are feeling stuck. This suggests we do the opposite of what we are feeling at the time to shift out of the stuckness. Feeling mean? Give some money to charity. Feeling sad? Go for a walk and seek the joy in nature's beauty. Feeling without time or inclination to meditate? Stick to the routine anyway. "Sticking with it" even though we might be feeling hopeless can of itself lead us out of that stuck place, and as we move out of it we can feel encouraged, simply because we feel we have succeeded in doing so. In the Aeneid, Virgil noted how success encourages success; "Success nourished them; they seemed to be able, so they were able."[115] But beyond approaches like this are the gifts for the soul of remembering our soul friends, foods and communities as well as our works and of course grace itself are there to nourish us. We are never alone and need never stay stuck for long.

Soul work does not rule out the gift of grace, of the inflowing of the Divine directly into our lives, awakening us to the presence that is already there, helping us to see who we truly are, not fuelling the search for a new "me". The treasure we seek is where the heart is, right under our own noses. What soul works do is prepare the ground that encourages this re-turn, this re-awakening fired by the gift of the spirit, of the Divine energy to pouring into our lives. Like a dam slowly undermined, it must eventually give way to the water that has built up behind it. And in between times, what happens? Moments of joy, moments of sorrow. Arid times when we feel God has left us, blissful times when we can see that which we seek and it almost overwhelms us. The abandonment when it happens is not real, no matter how harsh and long it seems. Theresa of Avila spoke of having arid years when she could not feel the presence of God. Yet often this darkness of God is a prelude, a refining, to being drawn closer.

Sometimes we can feel we are in an empty place, a void where there is neither up nor down, absence of feeling. This ego trick, an attempt to dishearten, it too must pass and is often a state that follows a period of illumination. It is something we can move through by "prayer and fasting", to bring to our soul friends and community for guidance and support. It can be changed positively to a waiting time of integration and settling. Sometimes we can feel blocked or stuck because we have got caught up in goals, or hurrying, or because a period of rest and integration or renewal is needed (not least of physical energy). If we find we are in such spiritual inertia we can take heart, for it is a sign that the spiritual refinement process is working, not the reverse. Sometimes this is mistaken for the dark night of the soul but that, entering the unknowable mystery of the Divine, is quite different from the spiritual ache of feeling stuck or in spiritual pain because there is something we are not seeing.

Eventually we evolve an attitude of equanimity, but in the meantime spiritual highs and lows are a common feature. There are rich spiritual practices here too – learning not to seek just the highs and to push away the lows, for the highs can seduce us into a relentless addiction and the shadow too, as we shall see, has purpose in teaching us. The teaching of Isa bin Maryam in Part 4 is worth recalling here. Both spiritual highs and spiritual lows (*consolatio* and *desolatio* in the spirituality of Ignatius of Loyola[116]) are places of surrender into a closer relationship with the Divine, they are to be neither pushed away nor pulled towards us.

Sometimes we can feel hopeless that we are "never going to make it", sometimes fall into grandiosity that we are "there". Patience, persistence and perseverance in "Prayer and fasting" is a response to free us from being captured by either. It may also be a time to set soul work down for a little while, to reflect upon and celebrate how we have transformed and relax into life's simple pleasure – fresh air, the company of good friends, sleep, a good meal, giving ourselves a pat on the back. Whilst we may feel that we are stuck or have made progress on the journey, all of these - stuckness, progress and journey - are themselves illusions, for none of them is permanent. Being stuck is always temporary in which we sometimes just need to take a break from spiritual work and lighten up or work with our soul friend, foods, community or in prayer to discern the right response. "Progress" too is a false premise. While we see ourselves as getting "better", or making "advances", "growing" we need to recall that these are all ego concepts of judgement. Spirituality is not about growth in the egotistic sense and getting something like power or aggrandisement, rather it concerns lessening, surrendering, merging, losing the self until we find the Self. Our religiosity, our spirituality is not something we create to make the sacred; rather it is a response to something that is already there.

Perhaps it is better to see progress not in the linear sense of moving from A to B, but as an expansion of awareness. In mediaeval times the King's "progress" around his kingdom meant travelling around with his court from place to place returning to where he started but knowing his realm more. The progress here was a procession, a circular ambulation of knowing, not of attaining a distant goal. And the "journey" whilst being a helpful metaphor to some degree, does not capture the essence of what is going on. And this "progress" is not smooth, it often lurches between *consolatio* and *desolatio*, between moments of bliss and moments of feeling stuck and cut off. Yet even disappointment contains the seeds of hope, although in a culture that is not a culture of hope we are perhaps conditioned to remain more in despair than see that it will come to an end. For all things must pass.

As Meister Eckhart succinctly notes, it is a journey that is "only an inch long but a mile deep".[117]. We are not really going anywhere but here and now, that is where the journey brings us, right back to where we started and yet we know it more fully, perhaps for the first time.[118] Are there distinct stages of spiritual development or is it a flowing process, back and forth? Can we say along the path that there is some sense of "progress", some measure of movement from A to B? Some authors as suggested in the discussion under soul friends[119] intimate that the latter is indeed the case. But perhaps it is better to see these as phases rather than as checklists to monitor our maturing. Arguably the desire to monitor maturity is itself a sign of immaturity! As our consciousness expands, rises and deepens towards God, then there do indeed seem to be some "mores" as suggested below. But there are some caveats here too. Firstly, just because we feel we have "advanced" or "expanded", does not mean that we cannot fall back, fall into forgetting, even corrupting all that we have learned. The latter is especially easy when spiritual knowledge outstrips inner transformation and the person has not acquired the accompanying humility, for example in doing the emotional work and submitting to the checks and balances described in this book. Secondly, just because we fall into forgetting, does not mean that we cannot remember as in the use of "prayer and fasting". Thirdly there is another paradox, that in becoming more we also become less, more soul-aware is less ego-full.

Getting lots of spiritual highs is not the goal, indeed there is no goal at all. Goals are the labels of the ego. To meditate with a goal is a spiritual oxymoron. I recall a story told in a class by Jack Kornfield. Two monks approach the abbot, excited to tell him of their meditations. "Master," said one, "today in my meditation it was amazing. I saw lights of many colours, felt surrounded by love and felt at one with the whole of creation." "Hmmmm," murmured the master, but said no more. The other monk said, "Oh master it was so ecstatic, so beautiful. I saw the entire universe unfolding around me and felt drawn into the very presence of God himself." "Hmmmm," the master eyed them both again, paused for a while with his eyes closed. The monks were puzzled; they had expected his praise and approval. After a moment the master opened his eyes and smiled, saying, "How interesting, but maybe tomorrow your meditations will be better!" Surrender not acquisition is what we are about. The goals have to be got out of the way so that God can be revealed in us. Intensity of our sense of connection ebbs and flows and wanting the highs and avoiding the lows are both ego temptations to be dissolved. As striving declines we learn to be more docile, more receptive rather than trying to make things happen, emptying and opening to all that is.

A few years ago I spent a couple of weeks teaching on a gloriously seductive Greek island where holidays[x] are organised with a focus on personal growth and awareness (with a bit of Ouzo and sunshine thrown in!). As with so many "growth" experiences I wondered what is being grown. The agenda of the ego is legion and we can spend our whole lives in endless processing of experiences, relationship problems, co-listening, group sharings, having spiritual highs and so on. Is this just another neat trick to get surrounded by the personal comforters of unlimited exploration and attention, keeping us in that cycle forever? Does the modern day dance of so much counselling and psychotherapy succour that relentless appetite for self-exploration – thus avoiding the deep soul work, and the loss of ego power this would entail? For in all spiritual traditions, the ego is not to be grown, it is to be rendered powerless. "Personal growth" holidays and retreats seem to have the potential to keep us stuck in ego exploration and gratification, but they also have the potential (q.v.) to open doors and invite us into deeper work.

A trick of the ego can be to trap us in the endless search for who we are, for one identity or another. In seeking answers to the question "Who am I?" we can spend a lifetime in analysis, group processes, courses and one practice upon another. This cycle of self-interest can look on the surface like spiritually seeking, but in reality it is just another ego trip. Authentic spirituality breaks free of this cycle, dives deeper and deeper into God, realises that the search for identity is just another trap and surrenders into the Divine Will where identity is no longer

---

[x] www.skyros.co.uk

a goal. Paradoxically, it is in this state of consciousness of humility that our true nature is revealed to us, and all identities used in the world become useful tools for functioning, for service. Our true identity and purpose in the Divine is revealed to us. Had this occurred while we were still attached to our ego, then our ego would have grasped it and corrupted it. The answer to the question "Who am I?" is that we realise the pointlessness of the question. The question played its part in spurring us to seek, but its relevance dies in the face of the annihilation, the *fana*, in God.

However it is disguised, the ego lusts for power – to be special, to be attractive, to be invincible, to be immortal. If we do spiritual work but without the emotional work to understand our ego desires, unconscious tricks and wiles, whatever spiritual insights we receive will become distorted. We can even fool ourselves that we are seeking to surrender into God so that we can serve God, but ego shadows of seeking to possess God, or be like God lurk in the background, ready and waiting to mug the soul of its birthright. Surrender into the Divine is just that, surrender, there are no half measures, and that includes surrendering the notion that we are in charge of this process in any way at all. For a while we may think that we are contributing and with the best of intentions doing the work, indeed we must, but at some point we come to know that it was not we who took the Way, but the Way who took us.

Our egos, our personhoods, have "being in charge" as their raison d'être. Does it, do we, unconsciously keep picking over the wounds and seek out new questions only to maintain the distraction and avoid the surrender, the extinction, the annihilation of the self before the Self? Is there a point where enough is enough of ego exploration, a time to break free of its seductive power and engage with the discipline of various spiritual practices, which eases, sometimes pushes, it out of the way so that the soul can be set free? Spiritual work is not about self actualisation, but about self immolation; once we have found the self then we can see it for what it is and dissolve its power until it serves the soul and no longer masters it. Meditation is one good trick, among many, to keep the ego occupied while the soul sneaks in. Like some computer seduced into an unwinnable noughts and crosses game, all its energy gets distracted into it, leaving the soul free to sneak round the back and pull out the plug! On the other hand egos are useful things for paying the bills – they just have to learn who is really in charge. And of course, in order to surrender, there has to be an ego to surrender in the first place.

A recent Channel 4 series I mentioned earlier (the tellingly titled "The Spirituality Shopper") highlighted some of these issues. Could people really be steered to deeper spiritual insights through a seemingly superficial pick and mix approach, a sampling of spirituality without the discipline and hard work that all the great spiritual teachers have advocated if we are really serious about spiritual awakening? I suspected the programme would sacrifice the serious to the televisually superficial, but a friend watching with me pointed out that while the participants' experiences may have lacked depth, they were still getting something. Doors were being opened for people who might otherwise not even knock. My initial reservations were misplaced. The participants certainly got a feel good stress-reduction factor - worthy in itself. But who is to say that a peep through the crack of the door of perception may not lead to a full walk through later on? How can we know for sure when the desire to be whole, to come Home in each of us works in such mysterious ways? The ladder that connects heaven and earth is everywhere present – we may simply not always see it, but once we step on that first rung, who knows what might happen next. Much of the New Age fluff we see around us may yet be the ground for seeds to grow in some circumstances – "you never know" as we shall explore in Part 9.

"Know yourself" (Greek. γνῶθι σεαυτόν or *gnothi seauton*) was inscribed in the forecourt of the temple at Delphi. To know ourselves we must plunge deep into the unknown realms of our interior castle, as Theresa of Avila called it. And it seems we have two choices. We can go there willingly, that is consciously, to explore and become more whole, or we can bumble along through life hoping and trusting that somehow we will get it all together and learn to be a better person. Our conscious application to our soul work helps to inform and understand, to clarify and to heal (and none of us is unwounded) so that we may know the self and that in which the self has its being. Our soul practices draw us into an expanded way of being – more whole, more loving, more aware, more compassionate, more at ease with the world with more equanimity. These "mores" and others like them are the very stuff of becoming a more fulfilled fully conscious human being, the fruits of the spirit. We become suffused with the Divine light in more and more of our being; the Divine consciousness becomes embedded in us. To ascend to a higher consciousness we also descend lower, to unpick the ties that bind and restrict us, our fears and angers and resentments and hatreds, many of which are lurking away in our unconscious, limiting us from being more at ease with the world, catching us in ping-pong reactions over which we seem to have no control and which hurt ourselves and others.

In summary, the fruits of our spiritual work help us to:

1. Be expansive rather than contracting – the experience leads us to be more present, more available, more functional in the world.
2. Be entirely loving, increasing our capacity to love and be compassionate to others, without the desire to harm ourselves or others.
3. Be more forgiving, accepting, inclusive and embracing of others, not judgmental, shaming, punishing or excluding.
4. Deepen our capacity for discernment rather than judgementalism – being less inclined to judge others or things or situations as good or bad, right or wrong and more able to sort out the true from the false, the nurturing from the diminishing, the harmful from the harmless, the important from the trivial, the whole from the unholy, the will of God rather than that of the ego.
5. Encourage a sense of trust that enables us to work collaboratively with others.
6. Foster humility and the possibility that we are not always right, that we do not always have to be in control, that having our beliefs tested and challenged need not be threatening.
7. Draw ever more closely Home into relationship with God.
8. Experience a sense of having balance, harmony and equanimity in daily life including being comfortable with the particular individual personality that we are.

Our soul practices are also to be enjoyed, but we need to beware of satisfaction becoming self satisfaction and falling into forgetting (of the Divine). Again this reinforces that being spiritual is not just allocated to certain times of the day, but a constant turning towards God, a checking with/prayer towards God at every opportunity and, no matter what is coming up, handing it over to God. Religions such as Islam, with injunctions for regular prayer recognise the need for a certain routine, a certain rhythm and commitment. This helps us inhibit disconnection and to pull us back when this happens. Building a rhythm of soul works such as prayer is part of the soul's journey until there is no longer any separation between the secular and the sacred, for both then mirror the truth that all is One.

One aspect of this discipline, of regularising spirituality is about becoming authentic. All the great spiritual teachers homed in on hypocrisy wherever they found it. And hypocrisy, not living authentically, not walking our talk, can creep into our spiritual life ever so easily. The checks and balances that soul friends, communities, foods and works provide, help keep us in the way of authenticity, which is also the Way Home. The way we live our lives through our soul works is a demonstration of its authentic fruiting. Please consider these two passages:

"Love is patient; love is kind; love is not envious or boastful or arrogant or rude. It does not exist on its own way; it is not irritable or resentful; it does not rejoice in wrongdoing, but rejoices in truth. It bears all things, believes all things, hopes all things, endures all things." (Corinthians 1:13,4-7)

Try replacing the words "Love is" with "I am" and the word "It" with "I" amending the verb tense accordingly and read the passage again. Consider: just how loving, patient, kind, willing to bear all things and so on are we really? Now try a similar approach with this passage from the Jewish prophet Micah:

"....and what does the Lord require of you, but to do justice, and to love kindness, and to walk humbly with your God?" (Micah 6:8)

Sitting with these simple words, we can also let their meaning roll around in our consciousness. Again, can we say that we always act justly, love kindness and walk humbly with God?

These two passages offer some benchmarks for our authenticity. If by engaging with all our Soul Care and spiritual work our consciousness really is expanding, what are the fruits by which this is known? Have we really become more loving and just? Have we really grounded our interesting spiritual work in the world by being more sincerely engaged with it and not less? If there is any test by which we can measure the fruits of our soul work, it is to set them against values like these. Thus, in humility, we can see where we might fall short and recognise that we are forever "work in progress". The fruits of the spirit are not so much fixed states or goals reached, but integrated into our being in ways that are constantly being renewed. That is why our four Soul Care themes are so essential to support us in our spiritual awakening, our constant becoming of the true Self in the world.

...Spaceless and timeless
We come to serve You
We all come to serve You
In welcoming our birth
In revelling in our death
As each little birth slips into the next
Little death into the next new life
Into ......
There is no end to it
Our endless becoming
Then unbecoming
Rising and falling
Waves crashing identity and oblivion
Filling and emptying
For when all is said and done
All said
All done
And the slip into knowing
Nothing was said
Nothing was done
Beyond the stagger of the new born lambs
And the collapse of the aged ewe
Only You
And the restless waves
Upon waves
The bedrock of being
Everywhere and nowhere
Always and never.
The clock ticks and the
Universe continues its silent prayer.
For You are the prayed for, the prayer, and the pray-er.
We set aside fear of the emptiness of God
And find the fullness of God.
The tectonic plates binding the soul in place
Crack.
The slow drip on stone completes its inevitable history
Extinction of self in Self
We become
Light
Extinguished by light...

Part 9

"I said to my soul, be still, and let the dark come upon you which shall be the darkness of God."[120]

And let the darkness...

The rich, spicy smells hit us as we walked into the restaurant, and the head waiter rushed to meet us to offer us a table. We were expected, my distinguished friend and I, and all the waiters seemed in a flurry to help out. My friend was wallowing in the special attention, for he had been here many times before and loved to have the staff acknowledge him and treat him as someone important. I recognised this feeling, I had felt it myself before, and recognised also that I now noticed it and no longer wanted that feeling, finding it now only vaguely amusing and discomfiting simultaneously. We sat down to talk and the waiters hurried back and forth seeming to compete to be each more obsequious than the other.

I spotted one waiter who was a little different, hovering around as if desiring to speak rather than serve. He seemed overly nervous. Eventually he plucked up courage as he hung back with a few empty dishes, and turned around to speak. "Excuse me sirs, professors, may I ask you a personal question?" he said almost bowing. My friend looked annoyed and across the room for the head waiter, to summon help I thought. "Of course," I replied and I saw the look of consternation on my friend's face. "Please can you tell me," he pressed on, swallowed and said "if you believe in God?" The look of sheer panic on my companions face was one to treasure, I had never seen him speechless before. "Of course," I replied, "though I think the word know rather than believe is what I would use." The waiter seemed relieved, scurried off and brought the next dish while my friend looked sour and apologised, saying he would complain to the head waiter. I stopped him before he could do so and our questioner returned with the next dish and promptly asked a whole stream of questions but I noticed he focussed a lot on the subject of hell. He was clearly agitated and deeply troubled by something, but for the rest of the evening he scurried back and forth with various dishes, coming back with new questions and listening attentively to my response. My friend became strangely quiet and I could tell it was with me that he was now getting grumpy.

The head waiter had by this time spotted our own waiter's unusual attention to our table and asked if all was well. I interrupted my friend who sought to complain to say that I was more than happy to converse and was enjoying the excellent service and did not wish him to be admonished. The conversation continued, our waiter spent longer and longer each time hanging around. When he asked, "Do you believe in hell?" I replied, "Yes of course in a way, because are you not in it now?" his face changed and his agitation subsided. "Hell, to me can be here and now, it is feeling separate from God, fearing punishment from God, that is hell enough is it not? The fire and brimstone stuff is not real to me. Heaven and hell can be here in each moment." The conversation rolled on, and we had the most interesting philosophical discussions about the loving nature of God which seem to lighten his spirits. In contrast to my friend's sullen gloom, he was positively radiant by the time we left. As we did so I asked our waiter a question. "Do you mind if I give you some advice?" He beamed and said he would love it, and I sensed he was expecting some profound and wise statement to be uttered. But I just said "Please remember, my friend, that just because people have fancy titles like professor, it doesn't mean that we have an inch of wisdom more than you do. The very fact that we have had this conversation shows you to be a truth seeker far more than many clever men and women I know." He laughed and we took our coats and left. My friend never went back to that restaurant again and our relationship was to gradually dry up thereafter.

I got the impression from this man (who it transpired was a Moslem, but could have been from any faith in view of the subject matter of our conversation) that he had done something "wrong" and that he was going to suffer punishment from God for it. He was in torment, but something of our exposition and exploration perhaps helped him see a different face of God, not least a reminder of the one that in his suffering he had seemed to forget but who is mentioned in the very words which open the holy Qur'an – about Allah being the merciful and compassionate. In the previous sections we have examined where this shaming and judging God arises and why. Yet this little vignette in a restaurant brought the false and the true God into sharp focus. In the popular press, the rather nasty character and his (and he usually is a he) followers seem to get a lot of attention. Religion though is a bit like a public swimming pool, for all the noise is at the shallow end. Meanwhile, that kind of God paradigm brings huge suffering to people across the world, when the world is already full of so much suffering.

I have been in places in my life and met people that would be described as evil, but I have never felt comfortable with the idea of pointy-tailed little beasties running rampant inside and outside our bodies. Describing people or places as evil may sidestep the responsibility to look at what makes people behave badly or to see what projections from deep in our own minds we are placing in the world around us. Evil can be a spiritual experience too. It can teach us what is false, but it can also seduce us without the presence of our soul practices, into believing that it is true. I remember reading an account of the life of a serial murderer who described how by killing he felt life had a meaning, a purpose, and gave him a sense of connection to life.[121] There are qualities here which fit with some definitions of spirituality as discussed in Part 2, but unless we have the insight in ourselves and guidance from outside ourselves, the shadows in the unconscious (some would see these as demonic by definition) pervert the search for Love into the way of destruction. Perhaps some persons are so wounded, so dark, so "evil" that they might not be capable of love. My heart tells me that in all human beings that same heart of love is there too, but there are many in whom it is buried so deep that we may wonder if it could ever be free at all, if it is even there. But then, maybe quite suddenly, that person can surprise us, when some glimmer of light in the eyes or a loving action makes us hope once more.

Is there, then, a separate evil one? A devil? A broken aspect of the Divine intent on subverting God himself? I know many people who believe so and see a Manichean struggle in the world between light and dark. There is indeed a struggle, a constant push and shove between the boundaries of shadow and light, fear and love at opposite extremes with all the gamut of the human experience sandwiched in between, anger, hate, resentment, kindness, compassion, forgiveness. I experience this breaking into three levels; first there is the Divine Will, the spirit, the power, the energy behind all things moving everything into wellness, into wholeness. Then we might see a second aspect of will, that of our own ego consciousness, which even if seemingly intended benevolently, is essentially self will and about seeking self-satisfaction and power over others and the creation. (Extremes of this, which we might see as evil, would be black magic and negative prayer - wishing for harm to come to someone). Such psychic energy is contrary to soul work, for the latter seeks to surrender to the will of the One, the ego wants to be the One. A further dimension of this might be that mass of swirling unconscious energy, individual and collective, that can result in individual and collective acts of great evil. Some traditions have it that anything that is not aligned with the will of the divine must ultimately come to grief, or is an opening for the personification of evil known as the devil, Satan, the enemy.

It is necessary to look first at the contents of our own consciousness, there is more than enough shadow there to deal with and perhaps as we enlighten the personal, then the transpersonal is transformed too on the principle of "as above, so below". The shadow side of ourselves, all the ignored and repressed aspects of woundedness, is the source from which the ego draws its dark behaviours, its anger, its hatred and so on. Of this repressed darkness and personal shadow, James

Hillman observes that there is "the archetypal darkness, the principle of not-being, which has been named and described as the devil, as evil, as original sin, as death, as nothingness."[122] The alchemical process of transforming the darkness into the light is what defeats it, by illuminating it rather than fighting it with its own weapons of violence or destruction the shadow, the place of not-being, is made light. The God I know is all, is one, there is nothing that is separate from God or not God, and far greater theologians than I have wrestled with the problem of evil, all I can do is address it where I can in myself and my sphere of influence, see it clearly, with help, and engage in its transformation. For even in the darkness, God is there too, and even the shadow has its own part to play in a consciousness both personal and transpersonal, the "plan" of which our egos can see but a small part, while the soul at Home sees it all. The shadow is full of potential but there is no spiritual "progress" without going down into it.

Diabolic and symbolic are related words both with Greek origins. They have more subtle meanings than the general use of them. The symbolic is that which draws things together, connects, makes things whole. The diabolic is that which splits apart, disconnects, destroys. In both we can find meaning, but only in a consciousness firmly founded in the heart, in the Divine, can we ensure that we follow a symbolic rather than a diabolic path. When Jesus taught in parables, as did so many religious founders, he rarely used literal truth but spiritual truth. He used the symbolic approach to draw people together with each other and in themselves into a new unity of understanding and connection of and in the Divine. The scriptures of all the great faiths are full of stories packed with symbolism, with spiritual truth while not necessarily being factually true. When Jim Jones led his people into massacre in the jungles of Guyana[123] in the name of God, he did so in a diabolic way, splitting them off from their common sense, from their love of their children, for God, into subservience to him and his version of God. His unhealed personhood was projected onto others where he used fear not love, the desire for power not surrender into the Divine, his own unchallenged view of the world instead of a deep and reflective experience of God to ultimately destroy himself and his followers. Such is the familiar pattern that the false guru can weave.

Much that is "wrong" in the world stems either from our egocentric belief that we are separate from the creation and that bad things like natural disasters should not happen. Or it happens through people who are in the shadow of disconnection from the love of God and who act it out on the world in destructive ways. Or perhaps, in the Jungian collective unconscious sense, a kind of vast negative prayer emerges that manifests in the world wearing many faces according to our projections, unravelling the connected threads that loves weaves. The shadow of evil that emanates from human consciousness is not in the God I know, but somehow in some way I cannot quite comprehend, God is there within it ultimately making all things whole. As the psalmist sang "If I make my bed in hell, you are there...... even the darkness is not dark to you" (Ps139:8-12). There is nowhere that God is not and all things are contained in God and that includes the paradox of evil.

Then there is another kind of darkness, not that of the shadow of suffering and evil, but the darkness of God of which the poets and mystics (such as Julian of Norwich) write, which has a very different quality to it and perhaps serves a different purpose. This sense of equanimity about good and bad, also reflected in the parable of Isa in Part 4, is also found in a short story of a man who was poor and lived on a small farm on the edge of a forest. One day he was in the woods and he found a beautiful big horse, brought it home with him and was looking forward to its help in ploughing. His neighbour came by, saying how fortunate the man was, how his labour would now be much reduced and he could become much wealthier. "Well, you never know," smiled the man. A few days later his son took the horse for a ride, fell off and broke his leg. The neighbour came by again this time to say how sorry he was that the man had now lost his main help on the farm, how he would now struggle to get the crops in to make ends meet. "Well, you never know," said the man once more. A few days later the army came through the village and forced all the young men into service and marched them off to war – except the son with the broken leg. The neighbour came by once more, full of sorrow for his own son had been taken. "How fortunate you are, had your son not broken his leg you too would have lost your son like the rest of us." But the man replied knowingly as before, "Well, you never know".

The following examples look to explore these themes, for part of our spiritual work on the way home is the process of integration, seeing the all as one, and that we cannot do unless we know the dark as well as the light.

I reported in Part 2 the story of the person with cancer who had seen her disease and dis-ease as a spiritual journey, in which the search was not just for a cure, but to find meaning and purpose in it. As a Christian she had revisited many aspects of her faith and found them wanting. How could Jesus in the beatitudes talk of those who mourn or being reviled being blessed? Her cancer had certainly plunged her into grief about the loss of her old lifestyle, her body image and the possibility of death. And perhaps there are more ways of feeling reviled than personal insults, for cancer can feel like a revilement upon one's own body.

In his poem "A sleep of prisoners" Christopher Fry[124] writes how even times of dark and cold are filled with potential, where we might take "the longest stride man ever took". The notion that suffering can be pregnant with the possibility of transformation is a spiritual truth. Yet it can be a real stretch for those of us caught up in the midst of suffering at the time. Many have demonstrated that even in the midst of great suffering, a deepening of faith is possible. Nelson Mandela showed how a man can come to fullness as a human being rather than diminish into resentment and bitterness despite a terrible prison sentence. Victor Frankl[125], Dietrich Bonhoeffer[126] and Etty Hillesum[127] were unbowed by the concentration camp nightmare.

The Sufi mystic Hafiz[128] seems to positively welcome suffering, using it as a means of releasing his attachments to ideas of body or personhood and thus set him free on the path to enlightenment. "Pour on more oil", he writes, to bring yet more flames to the place of suffering until all that keeps us from God is burned away. For most of us, suffering is something that we just want to go away. The word repentance has been rather reduced in some circles to saying you are sorry (to God) for being bad in the hope that He will forgive you and fix your life for you. But the original Greek source is *metanoia* and it means much more - to "turn around", to "transform". That is, to turn our way of seeing what was once judged bad into good, to change our way of being in the world, to make something that is fearful and threatening into a catalyst for change.

In soul works terms, this might mean looking at something that we see as bad or unforgivable in our lives and finding new dimensions to it, without which we might be stuck in our old ways. I have worked with so many people down the years who, much to my admiration, have taken something that hitherto they had fought to push away and instead embraced, explored, understood and integrated it and indeed found that they could change their lives with it and yes, even be grateful for it. That is a tall order for many of us, yet I think as I write of Mike who burned out and went through the pain of leaving his job but who is now glad of the experience because he is so happy in his new life and with more fulfilling family relationships. Of Christine, abused as a child and who now has turned her victimhood into a force for change and for helping others. Of Annie who has taken the suffering of the loss of her son and deepened her capacity to care for others so wounded. A wound is also a blessing. Suffering can be a source of fierce grace, as my teacher Ram Dass called it, as he passed himself through the shadow of having a life-threatening stroke.[129] It is interesting to reflect in these terms what kind of "life" is being threatened in the light of the discussion in part 2.

My dad spoke with pride of one thing in his life, his Royal Air Force (RAF) wartime service. Mention of it was sure to animate him with fond reminiscences and endless stories. I learned much later that the picture he painted was not entirely true. My relationship with him was a long and difficult one. Mine was a family where emotional intelligence was limited, and would probably nowadays be classified as dysfunctional. But it was working class and I got "good enough" parenting I guess, if somewhat limiting and loveless. Overt signs of affection were few – so few that I can count on a few fingers moments of loving physical contact, and no one in those years ever said "I love you". It was the way it was, and paradoxically a rich grounding for life in so many ways that I now look back on entirely with affection and respect. It was not always so.

The anger I had for my parents took a long time to heal, but when it did I set about learning more about my father and my mother although both were long gone. I had always until then rejected the biblical admonition to "honour thy father and thy mother". I have worked a great deal with people who were abused as children and had far more damaging childhoods than mine – how on earth could they be expected to "honour", let alone love? Yet I know that the wounds of childhood persist, and at some level the abuser still abuses, until we have come to forgive and let them go. The kind of forgiveness I mean takes us beyond statements of right or wrong, rather it requires us to stand back and see our histories from a grander perspective, to see ourselves in the long chain of the generations where each plays its part in making us who we are, as we do the next generations.

Honouring the father and mother is more than accepting everything our parents do as OK simply because they are our parents. It is about having the humility to see ourselves not as products of our individuality, but of the endless process of generation, and that sometimes things that we think of as black or white may in fact be much more mysterious and unfathomable. Purpose and maturation in life are not always arrived at in ways that are obvious to us. My childhood could be classed as deficient in so many ways, yet I bless each moment of it, yes even those parts that were filled with suffering. Why? – because I feel now at this point in my life profoundly OK, and the emerging picture of my life would not be as it is if everything had not been as it was. Judgements like good or bad are simply no longer relevant, they are the diabolic efforts of the ego to self justify, to separate and make unwhole that which seeks to be whole, holy. Stepping outside this way of thinking we find that integration and forgiveness are possible and that they set us free. The emotional shackles of unforgiving bind us and continue to wound us long after the original source of that wound. Until we come to forgiveness, the soul itself is not free.

I have worked with cancer patients who in the midst of their horror have found immense peace and even came to appreciate their disease for its transforming effect on their lives, with women who have been beaten and years down the line almost been grateful to their ex-partners for the part played in ultimately setting them free. Countless situations where what seems like a life tragedy at the time ultimately (and especially with the benefit of nurturing guidance) can be part of the *metanoia* – where that which was "bad" or "wrong" is transformed in us by a shift of consciousness around it. Put simply, it was Maya Angelou who said, "If you can't change a thing, change the way you think about it."[130] Thus by this process, the process of forgiveness, that which was once deemed harmful paradoxically helps make us more whole by being the catalyst for the search for Home.

The honouring of the ancestors is not just about our biological parents, for we have parenting in many spheres of life, including those who build society before us. (In my youth in the 60s I fashionably took part in denigrating everything that the older generation stood for!) Bright young moderns of every generation tend to see themselves as more scientific, more skilled, more knowledgeable than their forbearers. If we have a grand view of our world, it is because we are often standing on giant's shoulders. When we do not honour our roots, they shrivel, and a rootless community dies.

My sister and I took the trouble to investigate more of my dad's wartime life by contacting the RAF. We got access to his records and found among other things that the rosy picture he painted included not a few spells in the military prison. My sister and I suspect he must have been a difficult man to manage, wilful and disobedient to authority. "I wonder who he reminds me of?" she said. Perhaps sometimes we have "issues" with our parents because we are more like them than we care to think!

I have come to honour him now, and made the simple gesture of ensuring that his name is now written into the book of remembrance at St Clement Danes in London, the RAF church on the Strand. When I visited the crypt lately and saw his name in the big book in its glass case I was profoundly and joyfully moved. And I had the strangest feeling that my dad was too.

My mother too holds an honoured place in my life, though she was ever an enigmatic presence to me. She was a woman born into poverty, poor in schooling and like so many women of her time, of low expectations for herself. I remember her as forever cooking, cleaning, knitting or mending things, or reading romantic novels, the Mills and Boon type. I wonder if the books were her escape from a life of limited horizons. It may also be that through her I came to love books, words and working with words. Books in our neighbours' homes were as rare as hen's teeth in those days and indeed anyone who was bookish was suspect in some way.

I must have been a challenging kid to raise. At a time of life when most mums had done with childbearing, I was born from her when she was 45. She was in her fifties when I was passing through junior school and her 60s when I visited the horrors of my adolescence upon her. I don't remember her complaining. She just seemed to get on with life, deferred always to my dad, accepted what money he offered for housekeeping and dreamed a dream forever unfulfilled of living in a bungalow. "I could have had one but your dad sent it up in smoke or down the drain" – his daily diet of 60 Capstan full strength cigarettes and not a few pints of beer took a lot of resourcing.

And perhaps I inherit from her too a love of the land, of the countryside, of things that grow, and especially the cherry blossom tree in our back garden which she so admired. Its radiant pink flowers buzzed with the sound of bumble bees each spring, and its petals would shower like confetti across the back doorstep. She loved her garden and the outdoors, the long walks through the fields up Cemetery Road or to my aunt's farm a mile or so away; little escapes from the industrial red brick all around. She would adore where I live now with its wild hills and green fields and not a factory to be seen.

She left me with so many mysteries about herself; she is forever veiled to me now by death, but I planted a cherry blossom tree and I watch it grow as she must have watched the one grow in our garden back in Radcliffe, growing in tandem with my life with her. Perhaps my attempts at wordsmithery are also in part her legacy and her inclusion in my work her epitaph. I looked for a particular shrine to the feminine where I might remember and honour her. My dad has his place in the RAF church in London. But whither the feminine? She has her place too, not in one place but in all places, in the eternal unfolding of the creation that surrounds me, the cycle of the seasons and of birth and death. My mother's shrine is not in book of remembrance or building, but in the creation I see bursting all around me, town or county, field or factory, she is there. I see her and know her more as the years pass, both as her own person and as a representative of that primordial mother impulse, that Isis, that Mary. In forgiveness we draw all strands of our lives together, into the whole.

Sometimes that unwillingness to make whole is manifested in our spiritual work, a tendency diabolic to split ourselves into parts we judge good or bad, light or dark. But the Whole draws the whole unto itself. I am mindful of Julie, a woman with some years of spiritual experience, and an episode of visualisation we shared. She felt estranged from God and during the course of the session she became distressed, seeing herself forever on the threshold of a doorway into the light yet unable to step through it. In exploring this she described herself as standing by the door wearing a tatty hat and an ill fitting coat and socks that did not match. She had with her lots of polythene bags from upmarket shops, full of what she thought were the good and admirable bits about herself. Stashed well away from her in a darkened corner of the room, were old bags from cheap stores full of the nasty parts of herself she did not like. She became aware of what kept her from stepping through the door. She was holding back part of herself she judged bad. She realised that actually nothing less than all of her was called and loved by the Divine. Julie, my spiritual "bag lady", was able to gather up all that she had been and step through the door.

Another person I encountered in more recent years also had some lessons for me about forgiveness, suffering and shadow. The Keswick Convention attracts thousands of Christians every year to its three-week gathering. My friends encouraged me to go along to one of the meetings one evening, and we packed into the giant tent with several thousand others to hear one of the speakers.

Long years of spiritual seeking, and training as an interfaith minister, have brought the blessing of being with people of many different faiths and feeling comfortable with different ways of worship, although there are some that I am glad I do not have to participate in. This particular event had a decidedly fundamentalist element, and some of the speakers were pretty quick to identify whose "side" of Christianity they were on, not least by deploying those classic means of reinforcing group identity by suggesting that "their" beliefs were the only "true" ones and that they were under attack from "others". These are some of the oldest tricks in the book amongst fearful people for polarising society and excluding some in order to feel safe in the special group "in the know".

The main speaker got into his stride, drawing on Psalm 22, the one later used in the New Testament to substantiate the view that the manner of Jesus' death was foretold. By the time he had finished I felt I'd done twenty rounds of heavyweight boxing. I heard nearly an hour in which blood, nails, suffering, punishment, sins, broken bones, more blood, more punishment poured out from this man. I think the "love" of God got squeezed in a couple of times, but only in the context that God so loved his son that he decided to sacrifice him. Encouraging people to believe by making us feel guilty is not a healthy approach to spirituality and faith. This child-sacrificing, punishing, angry, sadomasochistic God is not the God I know 'though I accept that He is very real to some people. It also occurred to me that if the preacher had used the word sex in his talk instead of the word God, he'd have been arrested on the grounds of promoting sadomasochistic pornography.

The overwhelming impression I gained of this man was that he was a deeply wounded and angry individual who was projecting his stuff out onto the world. You didn't need a degree in psychology to see that maybe somewhere down the line this man may have had the kind of parenting or other life experiences where love and punishment, shame and affection, suffering and attention somehow got horribly mixed up. He seemed to be a classic example of the spiritual teacher who has done an awful lot of theological work and can quote and spin the holy books with great skill, but has not done the emotional work on him/herself to become a more whole and well rounded human being.

Part of me wondered if he is like this with his religion, what on earth would he be like without it? And I shuddered to think of the options – for history is littered with the damage and mass slaughter done to others by those who have not resolved their woundedness and instead have projected it onto the rest of the world. I got the sense that religion had provided this man with a kind of anger management course. It kept his woundedness well repressed, but had done nothing to resolve it. Anger and hatred come from fear, for they are responses to feeling that we are under attack, responses that can help us feel less powerless in the face of it. Revenge is likewise a use of ego power – the desire to get others to "see" us, how they have hurt us.

Angry men (and women) can be the most destructive beings on the planet, especially when they get into positions of political power over others. " Anger management" (arguably something of an oxymoron – can one really "manage" anger?) programmes are somewhat suspect if all they do is give us the tools to control/repress the anger as opposed to finding ways to acknowledge its existence, heal it, and find ways to channel the fiery energy in more positive ways. For example, many great spiritual teachers expressed anger at the human condition, but channelled that energy into working for public good. Ghandi, Martin Luther King, Aung San Suu Kyi are modern examples who offer a model of a healthy response to anger - acknowledge it (as opposed to repression, denial and bottling it up), work with it to see where it comes from in ourselves (usually a situation that provokes feelings of being helpless, unloved, unworthy, attacked etc.) and transform it.

The emotional energy of anger can be changed into something positive in our actions in the world and in changing parts of ourselves seeking to be healed e.g. dig the garden rather than beat your partner, work for a charity that helps victims of torture rather than be a suicide bomber. Jesus encountered his own demon, but refused to give way to it (Matthew 4:3). Notice he did not ignore, fight, repress or pretend that it did not exist but chose not to let it hold sway over him (restraint). When we "fight" evil on its own terms we feed it and it grows, even when we do so with good intentions. Those who "fight" cancer can bring an unhealthy imagery to their attempts to be cured. I was once confronted by a person of great evil, in whom the shadow was intimidating and strong; probably the most terrifying experience of my life. I sought to fight it with all the conscious means at my disposal yet its grip was relentless and seemed to grow after each apparent retreat. It is difficult; indeed impossible to put into words what happened here, for words would reduce it and would not make sense and after all it is just a story. Suffice to say one thing I learned about evil that night, and myself and my attachments, was that we cannot do battle with it on its own terms. Instead the struggle against evil must be in the opposite terms, by turning away from it, refusing to engage with it in like manner, by preferment of love. Thus it and its methods are rejected and surrendered into the power we do not own, surrendered instead to the Love and the source of that love in whose hands the evil is dissolved.

So many opportunities arose for transformation in suffering as I look back on my life. And I look back on them now with wonder, and compassion - how on earth did I miss that one? Where did that one come from? Thus the ongoing struggle to be ever more whole, more healed, more loving, more compassionate is part of our spiritual life and there is no end to it. This includes struggles with the shadows that come into our life in the present and the revisiting of those that arose in the past. I had a delusion that someday all that was in my past would be perfectly healed and whole, yet here I am, nearly sixty years down the line and I still find myself revisiting parts of my history, old hurts, old joys and seeing new facets of them, new teachings, new understandings and integrating them into the trajectory of my life. This is not a morbid dwelling on the past or picking over old sores, rather a conscious appreciation that our life experiences, even ones we think we have long left behind, are a rich seam for yet more knowing about ourselves and about God. To know ourselves more deeply is part of the essential teachings of all the great faiths and all modern psychotherapeutic approaches. Jesus for example taught the need to "bring forth what is within", drawing out from our shadow selves that which needs to come into the light to be healed. Otherwise we cannot be fully healed and truly know ourselves for "if you do not know yourselves then you are in poverty, and you are the poverty."[131]

Knowing ourselves includes knowing the nature of the reality we live in, the ordinary reality of the created world and its continuum into the invisible world of spirit, of expanded consciousness. I watched the horrific pictures of the Tsunami that devastated so many lives on Boxing Day 2004. Men (and they usually were men) of varying religions preached and pontificated about God's role when the wave hit. Some tied themselves in theological knots trying to squeeze out a rational explanation. Others lapsed into duality of good and evil forces, thereby inadvertently making the best case for atheism – if there is an all powerful God and he permits evil to exist while he has the power to prevent it then he is not worthy of worship; if he is not all powerful then he is equally unworthy of worship. Still others lapsed into sickly, repellent judgementalism - it's God punishing us for our sins (but then what kind of God is it who "punishes" "innocent" and "guilty" alike?).

In our egocentrism, our attempt to set ourselves apart from the natural world around us, we can forget that we are part of the cosmic order. The elements, earth, air, fire and water are just being themselves without regard to what we think of them. The primary forces in the world – creation, destruction and holding - are forever shifting margins between each other. That is the unfolding nature of the cosmos and we are part of it. We are in the real world where suffering-bliss exist side by side; some beliefs would say we have chosen to be here. So, all we can do is accept responsibility for the bits we can and work to relieve the suffering wherever we encounter it and where it is in our power to do so. All the great spiritual teachers put this among the foremost of their teachings. Jesus, the Buddha, the Prophet, Guru Nanak, Krishna these and others of all faiths urged us to spend less time judging people or tying to pin down God's will and rather more in being active compassionate helpers of others – at every level of life. Most of us could not help those involved in the Tsunami directly, but we could look at where our money and our lifestyles cause suffering in other ways. We can address the attention-commanding crisis when it arises, but we can also (perhaps more difficult) give ongoing attention to those sufferings which are lower profile yet equally relentless and tragic as well as the suffering in ourselves. Individually we can probably change very little, but it is important that we try nonetheless and Mother Theresa[132] reminds us that "In this life, we cannot do great things. We can only do small things with great love."

Not long after the Asian tsunami, my own locality was hit by flood and storm. We lost just a few slates and thirty fine old pines. Not far away many lost homes and livelihoods and a few their lives. Once again the judgements of God, or otherwise, were trotted out. But one man just turned to a TV interviewer and said, "It's nature isn't it? Simple as that. Get on with it." I was visiting a hospital at the time and watched nurses and doctors deal with the endless flood of suffering. It rolls up the corridors of our hospital wards and clinics. Spills through the doorways of our homes and health centres. I turned from the TV in the waiting room and went back to the bedside, and was deeply grateful for nurses and doctors and paramedics who just got on with dealing with what was before them. No judgements or attempts to rationalise or explain away the suffering, just dealing with it and seeking expertly, compassionately, the relieving of it. But against death, even they must at some time give way.

A recent death in my family caused me to reflect on this cycle of suffering. A death in the family knocks us into another reality; ordinary life with its passions and priorities is put on hold. But Western culture does not prepare us well for death, seeing it like old age as a time of loss or defeat. The spiritual search is about dying into life, in a sense, for we may wake up and become aware the kind of life that Jesus spoke of and on which we reflected in part 2. The kind of life that is present in the here and now as we plunge into Home, in God. Spiritual practice in all traditions has at least one common thread, the preparation "for our eventual encounter with death and what follows, whether this is conceived and experienced as heaven or some form of paradise, transcendence of the human condition subject to samsara or rebirth, or some other ultimate state of realisation."[133] The mettle of our faith and practice, of whatever tradition, is tested when we encounter in ourselves or others that point of crossover into the ultimate mystery. Religiosity and spiritual work contain the groundwork for that encounter.

Readying ourselves for our own death may be a lifetime's process, not a subject of morbid fascination, but a conscious exercise with both practical and spiritual implications as I have discussed elsewhere.[134] Doing so in order to make death and bereavement less painful for ourselves and others, such as sorting out practical things like finances or living wills, seems one level of approach. Doing so in order to deepen our awareness and annihilate the illusions of the self, or of mortality, quite another. We may come to live in each moment as if it is our last embodied moment that can make life seem supremely precious.

The disciples asked Jesus about death, and like all great spiritual teachers he did not provide a straight answer. In so doing, he completely subverted their existing notions of death: "The disciples said to Jesus: 'Tell us in what way our end will be.' Jesus said, 'Have you therefore discerned the beginning since you seek after the end? For in the Place where beginning is, there will be the end. Happy is he who will stand boldly at the beginning, he shall Know the end, and shall find Life independent of death." [135] He challenged the whole basis of our understanding of life itself, the contrast between the egotistic life and the soul life (Matthew 7:14 and 10:39 for example), asserting that we have to lose our lives (i.e. the limited way of seeing life) in order to discover true life, life lived in the Divine, immortality. Jesus in the beatitudes offered a further glimpse, specifically about how an encounter with bereavement however painful it might be, can also be a blessing. He said "Blessed are those who mourn, for they will be comforted." (Matthew 5:4) His announcement that eternal life dwelt in every person was reinforced by the gift of mourning. How can this be so – those in the midst of mourning and its agony can hardly be expected to see a blessing there? Mourning is not just an experience we have for a dead person, for our lives can be full of so many deaths – of expectations, roles and so on. Mourning can thus affect us at many levels, but the poet reminds us that in an ending is also a beginning. [136]

Sahajananda, synthesising a Hindu-Christian perspective writes that those who mourn may be brought to realise, if they do not already that much of their happiness is a passing happiness when it comes from others or material things – all these must pass away. People who "lose their earthly source of happiness may realise its passing nature and so find eternal happiness."[137] Thus the gift of death can be, paradoxically not just terrible loss, but also the potential for gain, a *metanoia* of our way of seeing the world that moves us from attachment only to the transient nature of life in this reality, to the possibility of life that is lived fully in the now coterminous with the life at Home. It is not a life to be found after death, but a life that can be lived fully in the moment.

To see death and loss as a gift, as having potential for more and not just less can be superhumanly difficult when we are caught up in the midst of them. That is why the presence of wise persons, such as soul friends, at the time of death can be so profoundly healing through the pain. That is why so many spiritual teachings in many faiths urge us to prepare for death now as part of life, not as means to avoid suffering but as a way of approaching it with greater awareness and equanimity.

For we teeter always on the existential edge. At any moment our quietly ordered lives can fall apart as we are robbed of all those things in which we invest certainty. Like thieves lurking in the night, the forces of chaos are ever present, waiting for the right moment to slip up behind and mug us of our precious possessions. I witnessed this recently after a delayed flight to Australia when, veering between resignation and fury, my fellow passengers sought to handle the countless disorders, missed moments and scuppered plans that now filled our lives.

The shambles at the airport mirrored the chaos into which my own body slipped a week later, when an unlooked for health problem laid me low, dangerously low, and I found myself in the Cairns Hospital emergency department. Far from home, exhausted, sick - I watched my fear shifting ground constantly as the twin poles of the terror of non-existence and the humour of the ridiculous pulled in opposite directions. Sometimes I felt my body giving way and my heart failing and I was plunged into a gut-stuck tremble, at others I lay there thinking of the utterly futile like "If I die and have to be sent back to England in a box, will somebody remember to cancel the meals on the plane?" or "Have I got clean underwear on?" (Mother, oh dear mother – what memories you have left me with!)   I was knocked off centre, into the abyss, into the place of forgetting by a combination of fear, pain and drugs. I was helpless and facing the helplessness and sometimes, during the long wait as machines clicked and hummed to tell me more than I knew myself of my own inner workings, quietly furious with God for letting me down. The possibility of death after decades of joyful and painful conscious spiritual awakening seemed damned unfair, I wasn't ready to die; it just wasn't in the plan!

And I also reflected on one aspect of this health crisis – I was not surprised. For, weeks before, I had been having strange and disturbing death dreams. The lecture tour, when requested over a year before seemed like a good idea at the time, but as the moment of travel drew closer, a steady and increasing series of mishaps occurred – emails going astray, arrangements falling through, problems arising one after another. Moments of prayer and contemplation were spiked with grim words and imagery. I had an overwhelming urge to make out my will, settle some affairs and phone the kids to say I loved them – all of which I did. And when people said "You must be looking forward to it.", I said, or thought, "My heart is not really in it." - words that rang with many meanings as I stared at the erratics on my monitor in the emergency room with the madness and distress of a busy department roaring around me. Somehow I knew there was something I had not paid attention to here, something missed, yet inevitable and unavoidable.

My interior struggle was not mirrored in the affectionate discipline of my doctors and nurses who were universally kind, attentive and practical. They were superb chaos managers – keeping all those forces of disorder, inside and outside my body, at bay by the quiet concentration on what needed to be done. One nurse with an unusual degree of spiritual intelligence held my gaze and said, "You need to be alone don't you? This kind of place doesn't lend itself to quietness, but I can tell you need some time to make sense of it don't you?" I was astonished by her sensitivity, not to say possible telepathy, and her practical response of shooing people away, partially drawing the screens to permit observation without obtrusiveness, and leaving me to drop within.

It was then a loneliness came upon me, the intensity of which I had never before known. Something deep and dark overwhelmed me as I passed from rage at God, to suddenly feeling the absence of God. Despair welled up. A feeling like drowning. An absence of breath. A lifeless, hopeless void. In this interior shadow I could "see" only one thing, a great black hole that was growing bigger by the second and turning into a vast vortex. Whirlpool-like it was drawing me in, to a place beyond terror, for this was death and it was headed my way and there was nothing I could do about it and I was on my own and God had left me and I didn't know which if any of these frightened and desolated me most. As I lay on that trolley, alone and desolate, that vast black vortex was set to overwhelm me. In the depths of my being I cried out within, after the fear and the fury were dissipated, "Where are you now, where are you now when I need you most?" And felt the wetness of tears.

After what seemed like a long age, but must have been no more than seconds, from the heart of the darkness came a still, calm, quiet voice – "I am here, I am here". The nurse returned behind the screens, the doctor arrived to do what he had to do. I opened my eyes to them and was at peace; ready to surrender into the hands of my carers and to the unknown. Perhaps those last words from the darkness were part of my nervous system seeking to reassure me, perhaps some conjured up voice I needed to make it all OK, perhaps a sudden chemical or electrical discharge I had triggered to make it all feel better and give me courage. I did not experience it that way. That loving "voice" was real to me, a new dimension of God in the dark as well as the light, something about God though perhaps not God who is beyond words or identity.

In the first part of this book I summarised some of the various explanations for God as a comforter. Some people get the God feeling from drugs and I can agree from my hospital experience that there's something to be said for them!. As I slipped effortlessly into unconsciousness as the white liquid slipped equally effortlessly down the intravenous line, I recall feeling, "this is just like God" as the anaesthetic and relaxant took hold. That same bliss swept over me that I have felt so many times before as I fell into mystical union. And another thought came – that underlying addiction (to drink or drugs) may be that same desire to fill the empty space, to drown the pain of existence, to seek the rapture that paradoxically is readily available within if we learn to receive it.

As Paul Tillich observes, belief in God or something else is what holds at bay the unconscious fear of non-existence. He writes; "The anxiety of meaninglessness is anxiety about the loss of an ultimate concern, of meaning which gives meaning to all meanings. The anxiety is aroused by the loss of a spiritual centre, of an answer, however symbolic and indirect, to the question of the meaning of existence."[138] As I lay in that emergency room, a collapse into uncertainty, anxiety and meaninglessness was more painful than anything that was going on with my body. Nurses kept apologising for sticking needles in me or scraping off my chest hair and all the other pokings and proddings – but I have no memory of physical pain. I have a memory of watching everything happening, feeling everything happening, but in some oddly detached way as if it was happening to some stranger who was yet vaguely familiar to me – that "haven't I seen you before somewhere?" feeling. Even the fear which swirled around between body and mind neither possessed nor was possessed by me. Some "I" was experiencing it all, in a way that was curiously interesting even though death was stalking around – an uninvited and invisible though not necessarily unwelcome guest. I wondered if this was some trick of the mind, a disassociation in order to detach from the pain and fear. Or perhaps it was a sign of mental collapse and irrationality. Or perhaps it was indeed the deep peace of letting go of who I thought I was and being at One. But the theorising soon fell away; the drugs took hold, and oblivion.

I love science. It's really useful. I like drugs, ECG machines, aeroplanes, roads, water supplies and countless other things in life that work because of science. Some aspects of New Age and indeed Old Age thinking envision a world without science. In this model we dream of going back to some happy, back to nature, primordial condition. In this harmonious, natural state we are at one with the creation and all is bliss. A reality check, based on the archaeological evidence indicates that our ancestors never lived in such a realm and life was often tough and short. I suspect the idyllic arcadia is really a reflection of our desire to get away from the difficulties of living in the present, or perhaps it is a collective unconscious urge to that lost imaginary Garden of Eden. Spiritual work teaches us that we cannot return to such a garden in historical terms, but must seek it in the here and now, in the liberation of the soul. In any case, I think it was Gore Vidal who, when asked for a good reason for not wanting to live in a past age replied "Dentistry!"

Science then is useful, but enter the realms of spirit, and the uses and claims of science begin to look a little frayed around the edges. The will for power of many in modern science, however it is dressed up (to know everything, to be certain, to find a solution) is sometimes rooted in very reductionist views of human beings, and a very irrational attachment to a faith position (that there is no God) as every bit as "irrational" to the faith position that there is. The scientific creed (and I use the word creed advisedly for it is just as absolute as any religious creed) goes something like this:

"I believe in a single substance, the mother of all forces, which engenders bodies and the consciousness of everything, visible and invisible.

I believe in a single Lord, the Human Mind, the unique son of the substance of the world after centuries of evolution: the encapsulated reflection of the great world, the epiphenomenal light of primordial darkness, the real reflection of the great world – evolved through trial and error, not engendered or created, consubstantial with the mother substance – and through whom the whole world can be reflected. It is he who - for we human beings, and for our use – has ascended from the shadows of the mother-substance.

He has taken on flesh from matter through the work of evolution, and he has become the Human Brain. Although he is destroyed with each generation that passes, he is formed anew in each generation following, according to Heredity. He is summoned to ascend to comprehensive knowledge of the whole world and to be seated at the right hand of the mother-substance, which will serve him in his mission as judge and legislator, and his reign will never end.

I believe in Evolution, which directs all, which gives life to the inorganic and consciousness to the organic, which proceeds from the mother-substance and fashions the thinking mind. With the mother-substance and the human mind, evolution receives equal authority and importance. It has spoken through universal progress.

I believe in one diligent, universal, civilising Science. I acknowledge a single discipline of the elimination of errors and I await the future fruits of collective efforts of the past for the life of civilisation to come. So be it." [139]

This somewhat tongue-in-cheek creed epitomised some of the hypocrisy of much of contemporary science – believing itself to be rational and objective, yet deeply rooted in its own articles of faith and dogmas. It says something once again about the egocentrism of human beings – placing ourselves at the centre of the universe and the creative process, of all that is known and knowable, of an essentially materialist and quantifiable cosmos with no room for mystery or the possibility of creative and conscious forces at work which may be beyond those produced by the human brain. In claiming to be the summum bonum of human endeavour, it omits one significant human quality – humility. It is noted, "Man's freedom requires a religious basis. Freedom only grows from participation in absolute truth, from the human being's bond with the divine mystery in life." [140] Public spats between prominent theists and atheists shed more heat than light on the debate, and often both parties are seen to be polarised in their own faiths. To seek the teaching of creationism alongside evolution, as is happening in some of our educational institutions under pressure from the religious right is nonsense. Faith comes from another domain of the human being and is not part of the scientific realm. The poet Tennyson wondered if anything provable was worth believing in. To match creationism with evolutionary theory arises from the error of mixing *mythos* with *logos* which we explored in Part 7, to confuse the nature of literal truth of facts and spiritual truth in scripture. This attempt to root religion in facts reflects once again not only a misunderstanding of factual and spiritual truth, but also perhaps a brittleness of faith that needs to feel something must be factually true in order to be believable. To seek to put them together demeans both the value of science and all that it brings us and the value of God who is precious simply because he/she/it transcends the definable, the factual. Science is debased by attempts to equate the faux science of creationism with it, and scripture falls foul of scientific rationale, reduced to fairy tale instead of its rightful place as the poetic, mythic, inspiration towards the Divine.

Thomas Merton[141] writes of a kind of faith that is not rooted in hopeful beliefs, but in a deep sense of knowing – the kind of knowing that we feel when truth touches us deeply (and certainly does not require or is indeed accessible to scientific validation). Yet what of my own experience in that emergency room, that stalking by death, the sense of a presence of the Divine even in the darkness? Was this to be distrusted because I could be loading it with all kinds of psychological baggage, or the effects of drugs, or the fear of the moment? If the evidence of religious experience has any meaning in the world, then surely it is its transformative power – to make us more loving, more conscious, more socially engaged, more connected to the world, more healed and whole, more able to relate to others, more empowered to relieve the suffering of others, more able to see clearly to truth. The "more", the expanded state of consciousness, of being-ness, is the product of these extra-ordinary human experiences. Indeed to me for many years now these things have not been extraordinary but ordinary. Looking at how common they are amongst human beings, to not having them is extra-ordinary!

Paul Tillich further writes that "The courage to be is rooted in the God who appears when God has disappeared in the anxiety of doubt."[142] It is said that in spiritual work the last thing we let go of is fear. Our lives are full of opportunities around fear, and perhaps we unconsciously summon them up, where we must confront it, and like confronting the enemy in the darkness, we may learn how to respond to it, to embrace it, to love our enemy and work with it. If fear was a herd of buffalo, death would be the biggest one that leads the lot and yet Joseph Campbell wrote that "One thing that comes out in myths is that at the bottom of the abyss comes the voice of salvation. The black moment is the moment when the real message of transformation is going to come. At the darkest moment comes the light."[143] Many of the people I have mentioned in this book tell their stories of their "black moments" – stories of feeling hopeless, spiritually arid, and suffering from disease or loss. Each in their own way experienced that darkness, but each too saw a light there at some point.

Thomas Merton[144] writes of "the God Who is God and not a philosopher's abstraction, lies infinitely beyond the reach of anything our eyes can see or minds can understand. No matter what perfection you predicate of Him, you have to add that He is not what we conceive by that term. He Who is infinite light is so tremendous in His evidence that our minds only see Him as darkness...to find God we must pass beyond everything that can be seen and enter into darkness." My friend said, "I'm surprised you were afraid – I thought you were supposed to be spiritual." I have often heard this from fellow seekers, taking on board some delusion that the spiritual search somehow loses our humanity. It is human to fear, to be spiritual is to know that we are not our fear, to not be imprisoned by it.

The toboggan of fear I rode on that occasion in the emergency room down the long dark slope took me to a place I had not expected, or would probably have gone willingly. And oh those angels, those doctors and nurses who rode down with me, those accompaniers in shadow, and those warriors against chaos - they stand with us like our soul friends and communities, on the existential edge being there with ropes and hooks to haul us back when it looks like we might teeter over. And what hidden, unknown power works its way in them too we might wonder?

...We rave at mountain views
Or the sun losing itself over Skye.
We see in the brief eagle's shewing
A high spot worthy of recounting,
Or perhaps it is the perfect womb
The sanctuary offers, which is cause for comment.
But this mighty crumpled landscape
Comes into its own
When enfolded by night
The time that Mars owns
And insists upon attention
The time Orion
Naked and belted
Calls to us to seek
Under the moonlight.
If we were to overturn convention
And let the balcony feel our flesh under starlight
Let the wet boards hold us
While a passing cloud
Prophesies the content of our dreams.
Then and only then
Stripped to the bare essentials
Like we were at the changing of the guard
Then, if we forget just a little
We may remember.
For this is a hall of remembrance,
The place of dis-covery
Of something we already know
And having hidden once
In a secret place for safety,
Safely hidden,
Even from memory.
Here lies the eternal invitation
Finally gathered up from the reading room floor
The one we always knew we would receive.
In the house of remembrance
Past sense and sensation
There is a kind of elevation

Above the rocky cliffs climbed
Perhaps over many decades
A history, walled and pacified,
In that solitary point beneath the procession.
The world turns
The stars turn
But on a quiet night by a solitary candle
We may find that we are simply
Here.
There are only three kinds of people,
Those who are awake,
And those who are sleep,
And those who are at some point of transition between the two.
The bridge is the metanoia, where meaning and experience
Collapse in transcendence.
Bell, book and candle, incense, calling home.
My mind is like Tarzan,
I swing through the jungle,
From experience to experience
From thought to thought I grasp and swing,
Until someday I guess, I swing
Slap bang into some big trunk,
Really big,
And cry out at last,

"Me Tarzan, You God!"...

Part 10

"Home is where the heart is"

Testimony

In my desire for finite goals some years ago a wise woman said to me, as I moaned about wanting a clear endpoint, that "If you really knew what it was you wouldn't do it." I think she was right and in more ways than one. If anyone had said to me a couple of decades ago that in this spiritual pursuit my value system, my way of being in the world, the work I do, the religious path I would follow would end up where they are now I would probably have told them they were crazy and opened another bottle of wine.

And who knows where the next step might be, for we never know which way the wind, the spirit, may take us. Coming Home is a call to a dynamic not static relationship with the Divine.

Ecologist and philosopher Brian Swimme[145] saw that "The great mystery is that we are interested in anything whatsoever. Think of your friends, how you met them, how interesting they appear to you. Why should anyone in the whole world interest us at all? Why don't we experience everyone as utter, unendurable bores? Why isn't the cosmos made that way? Why don't we suffer intolerable boredom with every person, forest, symphony, and seashore in existence? The great surprise is the discovery that something or someone is interesting. Love begins there. Love begins when we discover interest. To be interested is to fall in love. To be fascinated is to step into a wild love affair on any level of life." The exquisitely composed poem that is the creation calls us into love for it, cannot do otherwise, and in loving, falling into love, we participate co-creatively in the writing of that vast poem.

There is nothing new under the sun (Ecc. 1:9). For a moment, holding Rose my new granddaughter I felt this very intimately. I suddenly seemed to see the long trajectory of her ancestry of which I am but a small part She lay in my arms at peace, unaware of how deeply moved I was and just feeling her presence in the world. How she will live her life I do not know, but what I did feel then was that her unique life will be only an image of her true life, that beneath surface impressions, the whole of creation is an endlessly repeating pattern. There is, was, nothing new, all newness, innovation is but a surface impression, waves upon the still waters from which they arise only to return whence they came. The pattern is beautiful, rich and eternally shimmering and shifting in form, but the pattern is repeated, change is only part of the perception of time and space.

Beneath the surface the eternal now is as it always was, *isness* is the constant, in which time and space are contained. Rose as a baby is born into that isness. Somewhere along the way she will surely lose it, only to find her Way Home. It is an inevitable course. The isness of my beloved granddaughter and the exquisite journey of life she will make is made all the more exquisite by the constancy of what lies beneath superficial impressions of change and chance. And thus we come to know ourselves fully as we are already known by the source from which we sprang.

It begins and ends with God, where the beginning and the end are one. When we rediscover our Home we have a new place from which to bear witness to and participate in the world. Witnessing is not creating a separate entity, a duality, it is a quality of being of the Presence, it is the Self looking at and knowing the self.

We can return to Memphis (Part 4 – the metaphorical place of exhile) and embrace it with love, breaking through the dualistic perceptions of reality and work in and with and for the whole. All perceptions of this and that become one. *Aduaita*, the Hindu teaching of non-duality becomes a reality not a taxing concept to be grasped. We can approach our joys and difficulties in life with greater equanimity, wisdom, compassion and peace as Isa, Jesus, taught us in Part 4. We are less likely to be caught up in those legion tricks of the ego that can pull us away and cause us to fall into forgetting where we came from and who we are, into the delusion that God has left us. This Divine, this Absolute, this One, this God, this Great Friend whom we come to know is ever present no matter what thoughts or actions might pull us away from time to time. And if we do fall into forgetting our disciplined attention, our soul friends, our soul community, our soul works and our soul foods are there as helpers to bring us back into remembering. We live, move and breathe in the world with greater compassion, ability and willingness to serve without feeling that we are sacrificing ourselves, to love without grasping or feeling lacking, needy or unworthy.

These are the authentic fruits of the spirit by which we are known, unto God, ourselves, others. God, Home, becomes our still point in the turning world. We fall in love with God because we come to know that God is love (know it deeply, not as a hopeful belief or a theological deduction) and thereby are liberated from

172

the concerns of our little self to the concerns of God in the world and all of humanity. We learn to live in the eternal now, buffeted out of it far less by the relentless demands of the hungry ego. Love has taken control.

Love is the transforming fire that drives this whole spiritual awakening and powers the universe. It is the "intolerable shirt of flame"[146] that relentlessly burns off all illusion or restriction. It calls us to move beyond sympathy, where we can understand what another feels and feel it as if it were our own. It is beyond empathy, where we can identify with the other persons situation and really feel it as they might feel it themselves. It pours through compassion, which calls us to combine feeling with action, the heartfelt desire to care, to be of service, to alleviate suffering. Compassion arising out of this unconditional love spurs us to action, for it is "not simply a sense of sympathy or caring for the person suffering, or a sharp clarity of recognition of their needs and pain, it is also a sustained and practical determination to do whatever is possible and necessary to help alleviate their suffering"[147]. Spiritual awakening is about bringing more love and compassion into the world through the relief of suffering – of individuals, groups, and communities and indeed the whole of creation and not forgetting ourselves. It is compassion free of attachment, a way of being in the world that does not exhaust us with the burden of caring for others, but which liberates us to care from a place of resting at Home in the Source of infinite love. We do not burn out from this kind of caring, it is not from our own emotional ego batteries that we draw it; rather it is from that infinite source, a source so vast that it is willing to broadcast it wastefully.

It is not an emotion that drains us, but one that comes from the open heart, drawing after much emotional and spiritual work, upon its deepest resource unfettered by all kinds of emotional hang ups or ego attachments. It is not charged with the debilitating desire to fix everything - but rests in humility, deep awareness that we can change very little yet humbly play a part within our capacity. Sometimes we go the extra mile, but more often we simply travel the miles we can, through non-attached compassion that does not leave us depleted. However, to do so means that our own hearts must be open to the Source and healed of all that gets in the way, otherwise whatever love we express is always conditional. In the fairy story "the Snow Queen", Hans is unable to be loving until the splinter of ice is removed from his heart. Icy, heartless people are uncommon, but not rare and perhaps the inevitable products of unresolved wounds in our hearts or the waste land that does not value or foster compassion.

Love, the greatest of all human emotions as St Paul so perfectly expressed (Corinthians 13:1-13), is not something universally accepted or understood in the waste land. Yet this Love, this *agape*, is not associated with affection, lust or attachment to things or persons. It is a compassionate concern and action for another's and the world's wellbeing, indeed for all of humanity. It is uncluttered by value judgments and rooted in respect and equity. This love is unconditional, not one which says "I'll love you if you love me" where the undertow is really about meeting the ego's codependent needs for gratitude, power, worthiness or acceptance. As we have explored in this book, all our Soul Care approaches are grounded in the surrender of the ego will, of the alchemical transmutation of our way of seeing and being so that the soul, the very wellspring of love in the world is set free. Liberated into its true nature, to do and to be love. How could it not be so? For the soul is of God and God is Love. Therefore all that emanates from the soul cannot be but love and loving.

The ego cannot comprehend this love, although it may in time surrender to it. It sees and knows in a way that is alien to it, its values are an inverse of it. And yet it has a power and an energy of its own, unwilling yet waiting to be mastered by something other than itself. Its psychology has been mapped in Maslow's[148] classic concept of the hierarchy of needs – that familiar pyramid shape - with the basic needs at the bottom (food, shelter, safety etc.) which have to be met before we can address other needs rising above them in sequence to the pinnacle of self-actualisation. The latter is that place where "A man can be what a man must be" as Maslow put it. In egotistical terms this relates to fulfilling all our hopes, dreams and aspirations and making fullest use of all our attributes. An ego perspective as we have seen is somewhat limiting for the maximising of the ego is the opposite of the spiritual search. Indeed, spiritual seekers tend to subvert the hierarchy theory, often forgoing many aspects of need – wealth, security, sometimes food and so on – in the pursuit of higher goals, of getting to God. These "goals" as we have seen are diametrically opposite to the ego desires, for in spiritual terms we do not self-actualise; we self-immolate to find the Self. In that sense a person does indeed become what a person must be, but not in the terms in which I suspect Maslow intended that statement. The psychological pyramid with its peak is very different from the spiritual ladder of descent into the depths of being. The peak as the maximised ego is a world away from the depths of the boundless soul.

When we look at the great spiritual teachers down the centuries, they offer us shining examples of how to live our lives, to live in the world and be a living presence of that non-duality. This can sometimes seem like an impossible goal, to be self actualised beings like a Jesus or a Prophet, and it is, for the goal is not so much to strive to be them, but to be fully ourselves. In discovering our true selves then we find that we are like them. All the Soul Care work we pass through reveals truths like this to us. The work of opening fosters the inpouring of the Divine so that we come to realise that we do not master Truth, it masters us.

Some of the discussion in these pages has focussed on the merits or otherwise of a religion, a tradition, as part of our soul community, the participation in which is a spiritual practice in itself. There is no requirement to join a religion in order to get to God, but, as we have explored, all the evidence suggests that on balance it is better to have the strength (and weakness) of a tradition and an associated soul community to draw upon. How do we choose one? I cannot say for sure. Perhaps we need to be cautious of making it our choice at all. Perhaps we might feel called to one, as in my experience. Perhaps the dominant one of our childhood is the right one to return to, but from a very different place in ourselves. Or perhaps it is right and true to commit to another, maybe even radically different from our origin. Sometimes there might be signs along the way, the promptings from people, literature or events that reinforce a message - the metaphorical "angels" speaking to us. Drawing upon the discernment resources of our four Soul Care approaches we can be guided to discern our true course, following sometimes not what is our will but the Will. Sometimes of course there is a happy coincidence of the two!

Going it alone is hard work and for most of us may well be impossible if we are to approach the obstacles along the way safely and fruitfully. It is also a blessing to have others with whom we can share the bliss and joy of the journey too. What we bring to a community also influences what we get out of it. It is not for me to say that a particular way must be followed, but on balance the general principles that it is better to go deeper into one tradition rather than many and to do that in a soul community associated with it holds true.

Religion helps bind a community together, the waves on the ocean are countless but they are not self generated and they do not exist alone. A religion offers the rites of passage which bring meaning and belonging to our lives – the loss of rites of passage is arguably partly the cause of the socially atomised waste land. It is difficult if not impossible I believe to pursue the Way without the strength and challenge of a tradition in which to express and find it. A tradition offers the ground and the firm foundations often tried and tested over thousands of years of exploration in which all the mistakes and delusions have been mapped, responded to, and ways through found. The common notion that we can be "spiritual not religious" is suspect and often an excuse to avoid the difficult terrain of participating in a religious tradition/community, built on some delusion that spiritual exploration should be all about sweetness and light and exclusively nice people and experiences, or that it can be undertaken in solitude. The way religion is portrayed and distorted (by followers and observes alike) hardly helps encourage seekers and those in exile to return it is true. However, overcoming our hostility to religion and the religious, like overcoming the thought that we can "go it alone", are themselves subjects for rigorous discipline in spiritual work full of potential for surrender, humility and healing.

There is another aspect to consider when we shift from one religious tradition to another. It happens especially among Westerners who fall in love with some idealised image of the religions of aboriginal peoples. We pilage them for the bits that are alluring, project all kinds of notions of perfection onto them, abuse the originators by our exploitation of their beliefs and fail to "get" what they are really all about because we do not have the cultural backdrop and language. This tendency to project and to avoid our own cultural traditions reveals much about ourselves and is a product of spiritual uncertainty in the waste land.

There is wisdom in religious traditions which we are ill advised to reject out of hand. And the rejection is understandable in a world where so much of religion and those who follow it seems mean, savage, excluding and cruel (invariably the opposite of what the founder of that faith taught). Yet most people of faith are struggling to be the best human beings they can be, seeking to be inclusive, loving and kind and generous to themselves and each other as well as dealing with their own spiritual conflicts. Simply because such people tend to be unostentatious, quietly getting on with life and using their faith to inform a Way that is full of humility, love and justice we tend not to hear from or about them. Perhaps they are the majority, for whom faith and the holy book are open to interpretation, a food for the soul to be chewed over, reflected upon and used to transform the person, not to lapse into fearful dogmatism that is inflicted woundingly on the rest of the world.

For every hard liner there are people, far more people, whose approach to religion is open and loving, like the Divine. I recall being harangued by someone using a passage from the gospels where Jesus says he is the Way (John 14:6). In the hands of literalism there is not far to go with that, and at a stroke that phrase has been used to persecute and slaughter non-Christians and indeed many Christians down the ages. Scholars and teachers with richer interpretation offer greater hope [149] [150] when instead they peel back the layers of meaning and show breathtaking vistas (for example the deeper meaning of the use of "I am" in Aramaic) of possibility that include rather than exclude, enhance rather than diminish. It seems unwise to limit God and reduce or elevate facts and holy books to the level of the incontestable, for we then make the thing itself God not of God, a kind of idolatry and blasphemy.

I have learned too that embracing the truth in other faiths does not dilute a commitment to the one we follow ourselves. Quite the reverse, it can strengthen it. Only those whose own faith is built on fragile foundations of which they may not be fully conscious tend to see other faiths as a threat. With true faith, as we explored in Part 8, we are able to travel across boundaries to find the common ground, honouring and respecting those of other faiths while digging ever deeper into the well of our own. Diversity of perspective is strength not a weakness to faith.

Quoting scripture fluently and with apparent authority, can seem difficult to stand against, but it is, as Bonhoeffer remarked[151] a darkness masking as light, hiding shadows of fear, power-seeking and so on. When *mythos* gets buried by *logos*, when interpretation of scripture gets lost in literalism, then all faiths fail both seekers and God. I recall the challenge of the Dalai Lama at a meeting in Manchester nearly 20 years ago. Most at that meeting were like me exploring Buddhism but he was not interested (much to everyone's surprise) in gathering converts. Rather he threw out the challenge "Why are you interested in Buddhism? You in the west have all the spiritual answers you need in your Christian roots. There's no need for you to be a Buddhist, what you need is right under your own nose". Needless to say this caused some consternation, but his words have remained with me ever since, and eventually helped me make some difficult choices myself.

There are many people like me who have been in exile from Christianity for all kinds of reasons, not least the difficulty in reconciling what we know in our hearts to be true with what some religionists throw at us. The post-modern deconstruction and seperation of religion has worsened the disconnection. the familiar routines and rituals of a religion can become lost to us. The language ceases to be familiar and becomes alienating. Working with a group of seekers recently, few knew what words like "holy;", "sacraments", "worship", "communion" etc. meant anymore. None felt they would know what to do and how to behave in a religious service. Yet, also like so many I encounter, it is "in the blood" often since childhood.

The research evidence shows that huge numbers of people are seeking their way Home, but in the current spiritual supermarket we are either alienated, confused, spoilt for choice or avoiding the difficult and the deep. I have swum the length and breadth of the New Age river, encountered seekers along the way of many types, but plunging back into Christianity, following those callings that I outlined in Part 2, certainly offers many challenges. Friends ask, "How can you possibly be part of any religion, look at what they are doing to the world, how much suffering they cause" or "Look at all these Christians always fighting with each other or hating women or gay people or anybody – do you really want to be part of that?" Yet these past few years I have felt this calling, and when we hear that voice (duly checked and balanced by the methods suggested in this book) who can ignore it? And of course, there are closed hearts and narrow minds in all faiths as we have explored, but there are also people of big heart and open minds and examples of the latter in the case of Christianity include the Inclusive Church, the Progressive Christian Network, Accepting Evangelicals, the Modern Churchpeople's Union and so on, while other groups such as the Quakers have a long history of openness and inclusivity.

I offer my own story only as an example, not with any weight of recommendation of which faith you may or may not follow. Getting involved with any religion is by its very nature a strong spiritual practice. If we have a sense of "calling" is it a true one, is it really "in the blood"? Or is it clouded and influenced by all sorts of unconscious motives like a need to belong, avoid choice confusion, or to enter something tough because we feel we must suffer and religion is supposed to be like that. If we decide upon following a tradition, at least for a time, to strengthen our spiritual commitment then does this mean we have to be part of a formal religious organisation? Is it possible to go deeper into a tradition without joining one of its communities?

It is not impossible to get into serious spiritual work and Soul Care without a religious tradition, but to pursue our search without it as I have said is problematic and a matter for serious reflection and self examination of motives. Going it alone may indeed work for some people, although I have yet to come across any teacher or tradition that does not require at least at some point, the discipline of exploring a tradition with other people. Whether that is always an established religion or not is another matter, and certainly getting involved with one can be guaranteed to press every one of our buttons! It is packed with the raw material of spiritual awakening and one of the test beds of authentic spirituality. So we think we have become loving? Then try it in the real world of ordinary people. So we think we are so spiritually mature? Then try it in a religion full of difference and difficulty.

The walk to my local church is across idyllic open country. I enter a gathering where all sorts meet, though like most churches in rural communities there is a dearth of the young and those from ethnic minorities. Yet I have learned that all life is here. In microcosm are all the different views on Christ that wash around the Christian church right now. In the bible class, you can have ten people sitting around and there will be ten different perspectives on a single sentence. This is part of its challenge, and also its joy. Love does not require that we all agree, God moves in ways that we can barely touch upon – remember, "You never know!" Being and belonging are basic human drives, so it is natural that most of us seek to cluster with others, looking for that strength of tradition and community, and perhaps at first unconsciously seeking that idyllic community of perfect people. As I explored in Part 6, the whole point of a soul community is to help us shed the illusion that such a body of people exists. Like all families there is diversity of view and behaviour, good days, bad days, peace and conflict. The point is that we embrace those diversities and still eat together at the end of the day, still love each other while sometimes being disappointed. Just as mighty spiritual beings like Jesus seemed to be perfectly balanced human beings, so it behoves us to seek that balance in community, holding opposites together we hold the One. Thus in my case I have returned to where I started, perhaps to know it for the first time.

Each of us must follow our own calling, even if it means going into something fraught with difficulty, while placing that calling before the scrutiny of our soul friends and community and the discernment through our soul foods and works. In my case the calling and it was indeed a calling that I did not at first wish to hear, was back into the tradition of my childhood. Being called or drawn (either back to the old or towards the new) in this way of course raises the question of which religion if any we will follow that embodies the Homeward urge. In the case of Christianity we could justifiably get choice overload with many thousands of divisions and subdivisions to choose from, not to mention the tens of thousands of smaller sects that come and go.[152]

I need to emphasise again that what I describe here is my own recent experience and I offer it as an example for reflection on the value or otherwise of being part of a particular tradition and the religious communities gathered around it and as part of the process we may encounter along the way. You may find yourself doing likewise, returning to a faith that is familiar to you or venturing off into another that calls you, or maybe none at all. I have a hunch we will all end up in the same place anyway!

Even the thought of being part of religion is highly problematic for all sorts of reasons to many of us, but my own experience offers a case in point of making that resistance the subject of rigorous spiritual work. In an age of rampant individualism, there appears to be an aversion to clustering anyway, especially in something that seems to have rules and regulations (more spiritual practice!). For me that handbrake turn towards the Christian faith has been loaded with just about every spiritual conflict I can think of. A friend told me some years ago to "Be careful what you pray for, you might just get it!" Well, I made a promise to do and to be whatever it takes to get closer to the great Friend – little did I know that "whatever it takes" has included just about everything. Maybe I could have set some limits!

The God I know does not punish, so I asked in relation to church, why me and why here? I prayed upon it and sought wise council. The Anglican Church, bound to the establishment, riven with strongly held opposing views, in tension between *mythos* and *logos* – a softer landing could surely be chosen? This church full of charge and counter charge, with its historical exclusion of so many from left handed or black people to women and gay people. This church full of big hearted and bigoted. Why this church? – because I am called there, because the Love of God is here as much as anywhere, because I heard what my friend said about turning to Christ all those years ago, because of the enormous depth that a tried and tested tradition has to offer. Because here is a place like anywhere else, full of practical, ethical, spiritual and moral differences and concerns, struggles with diversity, and wonderful fellowship – in short the raw material of any spiritual community. Light and shadow exist in all religions.

When we feel drawn to a particular community it is important to examine the motives and intentions, to seek prayerfully to know if it is the right community where the Will calls, to discern if it is true. Personally that process has led me to feel at rest in the truth that where I am right now is true to myself, and to the Friend. At the same time we need to be aware that if the Will someday calls elsewhere then it must be followed, after due discernment, but followed nonetheless. Right now I find myself in a state of puzzlement, wonder, laughter that it should be this place for me: I did not think I would be here, in this church, my soul community in all its bittersweet love, in all its gifts, in all its potential for giving. It could have been anywhere I guess, some other faith or the bottom of a bottle, but it wasn't to be. It is here and now and I trust in it until God calls otherwise.

All we can do is follow what is true, and what is true is often something we may not like at first. In my example it has been a turning back to something lost in childhood and distorted by adult experience, and not allowing those distortions to keep me away from something precious. The surface layer in many respects may be unappealing, but beneath it lies a rich wisdom tradition that if we are willing to go there is a deep well of spirit. Here past all the superficial and distracting is the Christ, this man, this woman, this brother, master, teacher, friend in whom God broke into the world and called "this Way". It has been a deep breathless dive into the known and the unknown, into a tradition with all its spiritual riches and the poverty of its brokenness. Others get called to other Ways, I cannot say better or worse, and the Way once found must be taken and pursued with seriousness if we are to reap the blessings of all that it has to offer. There are no bypasses, no shortcuts, not if our hearts really long for a deep relationship with the One.

My spiritual life has been filled with immense highs and lows, and who knows, maybe all those theorists and scientists I quoted in Part 2 might be right – that God and the God experience is just a delusion? That all my experiences of good and evil, of God and spirit might all be mere fabrications of a mind or ego seeking meaning and significance in the world. And yet they have been tested, not least because I do not get the rewards that the ego would demand - more money, power, fame, pleasure, avoidance of pain – so they do not stack up on the score that God is just a comforter. Quite the reverse. And there has been testing through discernment by the processes described in this book which provide a framework for checking out the true from the false, tested by knowing their fruits. We can trust the process, but tie our camels! Thus in the pursuit of God and knowing that we will be called Home, still we have in place the four Soul Care approaches described in this book, just in case, to keep us on our way.

A curious and heart-warming fruit may also be noticed that is not often mentioned in the literature. This changed way of seeing affects every aspect of our lives, past and present. A scene we have looked at many times before suddenly seems more beautiful, more sacred. We linger where once we passed on. A song heard long ago, an ordinary song, is now replete with new meaning. I recall listening with my mum to Doris Day when I was a child and we sang along to "Once I had a secret love". Decades later I heard it not as a song about two people falling in love, but about the discovery of the divine love in the heart. "And that secret love's no secret any more." Coming Home the ordinary often becomes extraordinary.

The soul has descended into matter and longs for Home, but this does not mean that matter is bad, rather the soul on being liberated returning Home free of ego clutter, revels and serves in matter. Union of soul in the Divine after the long purgation of the ego is not disconnection from the world into God, but connection to God in the world. There is in some traditions a tendency to deem matter, physical reality, as an irrelevance, an illusion, something to be escaped. This does not seem to be spirituality, rather escapism, a symptom of the struggle to escape ordinary physical reality, the world of matter, because it is perceived as full of suffering. But matter matters, it is part of all that is not separate from it, it lives and moves and has its being in the Divine, and in most creation stories, such as the book of Genesis, the Divine creates the world of matter but does not condemn it, but sees it as "good". The alienation from matter is what feeds, for example, nihilism or sexual repression as we explored in Part 8. The Way Home allows us to embrace reality in its fullness, to participate in the world of matter and higher consciousness, heaven and earth, beyond these dualistic concepts.

I have encountered stuck and painful places with those I love, and all that spiritual work has stood me in good stead I know, allowing me to respond to that pain with more patience, love and understanding than hitherto, even when that old part of me would be screaming to have its own way. It has allowed me to function more fully and creatively in the world. It has also allowed me to experience the joy and the pain of the world more than ever before. Yes the spiritual path can lead us to know the bliss of the world and the love of God more deeply than had we remained closeted in the safe parameters of the ego, but we come to feel the suffering of the world and of God in the world more deeply too. We experience more of the world not less, how could we not do so if we are to be fully in this moment, in the world and to love it and serve it, not the self, more fully, authentically and effectively?

Arid and painful times are not just about loss and may include gain, part of the process as much as the pleasant and blissful ones; for in these we come to understand that the stuckness is a precursor to new breakthroughs, new insights, new and more expansive love. Coldness and aridity towards our soul efforts can be a sign that we need them even more, that the ego is still grasping for power and seeking to hold us in its thrall. The value of the "enemy", something inside us that makes us feel hopeless or stuck for example, or a person or event coming from outside that makes us feel within unseen or misunderstood or nor accepted – this enemy is a friend too, for he/she/it teaches us that we still have work to do, that we need help, that we have deeper to go into humility. It becomes clear then why Hafiz says "pour on more oil" or Rumi prays to "break my heart again" not because they are spiritual sadomasochists but because they know that drawing closer to God, to Love, is over the twin bridges of suffering and joy, both cross the chasm of time and space on the way Home.

Ah, but the faith, the knowing, the groundedness of experience – all tested in the fires of soul friends, soul foods, soul communities, soul works – pulls us onwards. The calling like so much true spiritual experience can feel just like that, a pull, a drawing out and towards something often against the will, as opposed to a pushing where it is often our will calling the shots. Pushing is an attempt to hurry and "he who is in a hurry delays the things of God".[153] What we come to know in the calling of God stands more true and outwith anything the rationalist debate can describe or change. After a while it may be that notions of spiritual work fall away, as we come to realise that we have been in charge of very little, if anything, it has been the spirit of God at work in us. The Way is quite simple you see – a dissolution of ego power, surrendering it (without punishing or blaming) into service, and losing self in Self and the realisation that we did not follow the Way, but it was the Way that was within us, working to bring us Home all along.

There is also laughter along the Way, in fact I have laughed more in this search than I thought possible. Soul Care is serious work, but it is playful and happy work too. Indeed the search without laughter is less than human and ought to be subject to some rigorous spiritual testing to see if it is indeed a true path, where the blockages are and what needs to change. For an ability to laugh, in love and joy, is a spiritual attribute too. Anthony DeMello[154] writes "The master was in expansive mood. So his disciples sought to learn from him the stages he had passed through in his search for the divine. "God first led me by the hand," he said, "into the Land of Action, and there dwelt for several years. Then he returned and led me to the Land of Sorrows, and there I lived until my heart was purged of every inordinate attachment. That is when I found myself in the Land of Love whose burning flames consumed whatever was left in me of myself. This brought me to the Land of Silence where the mysteries of life and death were bared before my wondering eyes." "Was that the final stage of your quest?" they asked. "No," the master said. "One day God said, 'Today I shall take you to the innermost sanctuary of the temple, to the heart of God himself.' And I was led to the Land of Laughter." The spiritual search is packed with conundrums, confusions and challenges, it is also replete with heart, humour and hilarity.

So often the great spiritual beings of history are portrayed as rather sombre people. Exploring the gospels anew I began to realise that Jesus told jokes, that a study of the Buddha illuminated a man who enjoyed a good belly laugh, that the prophet must have giggled away too. God-filled beings laugh as well, because they were fully human and it is human to laugh with the sheer fun and absurdity, the comic-tragedy of life. One of my early teachers set me a task of contemplation and began by saying "Imagine Jesus laughing". It seemed so ridiculous when I began the exercise, for I had projected onto Jesus all my own misconceptions and hang ups and all those images I'd seen or heard of a rather sweet man but always very serious one. I sulked and wondered and struggled my way through the meditation, only to burst into hysterical laughter myself at the end! It is useful to remember that laughter is part of spiritual awakening too, in fact any soul community or soul friend that does not laugh is probably best avoided. For a true community, a true soul friend, a true tradition, embraces all aspects of what it is to be human. We reach the "I am" by integrating fully our own "I am" – which is the same, at Home.

We can get stuck on words, not least our names and genders for God. Coming home we find they are pointers along the Way but they are not the way, God is beyond typecasting, beyond any labels of descriptions we care to offer, beyond theology. Even our desire to understand God is something through our spiritual work that we learn to put down on the Way. Our images of God, like the images we have of ourselves, have to die if we are to know God and ourselves beyond image. The old dies, into life. I have at home a beautiful statue of the walking Buddha. He has broad hips, full breast and soft elegant frame – conveying that aspect of our Buddha nature, our essence, our souls, that is integrative of both genders. Many of the great spiritual teachers, most of whom have been men, were profoundly feminine as well as masculine in their teachings and their behaviour. Integration, holding opposites in harmony, being with mystery, uncertainty and paradox lightly are hallmarks of a maturing spirituality.

All the four Soul Care approaches in this book are our conscious contribution to the work along the Way. They are not the Way itself, any more than a map is the real ground it describes. The work prepares us, purifies our consciousness so that we are readied to receive more and more of the Divine. Fighting or pushing or working with the ego are all traps that keep us attached to it. The purification from these heightens our receptivity to the Presence, to learn from it, to receive the inpouring of Divine Love, the Holy Spirit, Grace that draws us ever closer to Home. We are made free by Grace, not our own will. Our work is to refine, purify and prepare ourselves to receive this will through the dissolution of the power of the ego, of self-will into Self-Will. The heart, the seat of the Divine in us, is set free to be heart-felt and heart-full in the world, governing our identity as the servant of the Divine that it is. The heart's desire is the signal of God within, the beacon flashing out to us who we truly are and why we are here. Soul Care work opens us to that desire, sensitises us so that the inpouring of Divine grace strengthens and liberates it.

Jesus said, "My yoke is easy and my burden is light" (Matthew 11:30) and this is sound advice in our spiritual "work", as we come to find it less laborious, less effort-full and soften into the Divine Will which takes us and leads us onward. We may notice increasingly as we learn to let go into the Divine, that there is more joy and less suffering in our spiritual practice, that it tends to simplify into forms of "prayer and fasting" that do not require striving and sacrifice. The yoke no longer weighs us down or pulls us back, the burden is light, not just less heavy but light itself, the true light of the Divine shining more and more in our lives, and light is weightless, it is no burden at all. We can relax more into our life and practice along the Way, for God is taking care of us, drawing us Home with inevitable and unconquerable love.

God is faceless and formless, all the faces I see are just impressions, constructs of my mind that wants to make sense of God (my heart knows and does not bother with sense, but with the sensation of God by which it knows). Yet in my humanity it is hard to connect with the faceless and the formless, the eternal, the unknowable. It locks itself onto a shape or form. Some would argue that God in compassion presented himself in physical form so that we could see Him in the being of Jesus. Other faiths too have their images of God, sometimes in human form. Whether these gods we seek are true or false gods is why we need the discernment process mentioned in this book. Actually, one of the beauties of being in time and space is that we can have it both ways! We can experience God through our spiritual work as immanent and transcendent, personal and transpersonal.

In the Brothers Karamazov,[155] Therapont through his zealous effort is delivered from the world, but he does not break through to the next level of integrating the world. Instead his efforts lead him to be authoritarian and self righteous and to call God's curse down on the world of matter, of ordinary reality. The *Staretz* Zossima, he too has done the spiritual work, but properly nurtured and in contrast to Therapont, he becomes full of compassion and in his surrender to God seeks to call down God's blessing on the world. Leading the spiritual life teaches us that the limits of ordinary human life can be broken, that we can go beyond the boundaries set by our egos, by our cultures, even beyond death. In our spiritual work we come to know the realm of the infinite and eternal, and it is love, only love that breaks these rules. Inescapable love. Love sets us on fire, is fire. It is the primordial stuff of the cosmos, out of which the creation burst forth. That fire burns still, the whole universe is on fire with that creative force, and it burns in us too.

The density of ordinary reality, of ego consciousness, has a gravity all of its own. Soul work sets us free, gradually (if we are careful) of this pull in giving up to a new centre of gravity so that astronaut like we can soar to new levels of reality; become aware of all that is and not just the bit that first held us in its thrall. To use another metaphor[156] we learn to be amphibious, able to dwell in different aspects of reality, and all are part of one reality, it is merely a question of awareness and perception. Yet in leaving our first home we come to cherish and have compassion for it all the more, to be willing to take care of it and participate in it but from a completely different place of awareness in ourselves. And paradoxically, by thus being more connected to the earth (in love) we become more sacred, not less. Being led, by the Christ consciousness or whatever name we call it by, that which was "in the beginning", we are led more deeply into the creation not away from it. When we know the creation, we know the creator.

Jesus, like all the great spiritual teachers, showed us the meaning of true freedom, to be fully ourselves no matter what the circumstances, and that to be fully ourselves we dissolve the false self into the true Self. Being fully ourselves is beyond the freedom of identity, but to see that as the trap it is, what at first seems a liberation (I am gay, I am black, I am a woman, I am a man, I am a Christian, I am a Taoist, I am straight, I am a diabetic, I am ...) of definition is but a staging post along the way. In acquiring an identity, sometimes seemingly at great cost, the true spiritual seeker comes to know that there is yet further to go, perhaps even scarier, that of surrendering even that perhaps hard won label. In emptying himself of the self (the trial in the desert for example), Jesus opens to his true divine nature and thus being possessed fully of himself, he was able to give himself away completely, to live in the eternal now in, but not captured by, time and space.

Going Home is not a permanent retreat from the world; it calls us to action in compassion and love not to withdraw. It is to leave behind the withered and work with the growing. It is to be in the world more fully, how could we not be? For this is Home, there is no duality, no "other" it is all part of the one and if we cannot be at Home here there is no other place, just here and now. Thus we can come to know that "here and now" in all its magnificent, boundless, loving possibility. We do not make the darkness of the waste land light by remaining indoors with our torches; we have to take them out into the shadow, to participate fully in the world in whatever way we are called so to do.

The Sufi mystic Jalalu'ddin Rumi, currently one of the world's most popular poets, wrote of his religion; "Ours is not a caravan of despair."[157] Famously he fell ecstatically through love of his mentor into love with God – producing some of the finest love poems to his Beloved on the way. His hopefulness for God permeates his work, there is no despair for he sees God as embracing and welcoming all comers. A Sufi chant and sacred dance based on his words calls out, "Come, come, whoever you are, even though you've broken your vows a thousand times, come, come again." The unconditionally loving God that Rumi directly encountered constantly calls everyone of us Home, no matter who we are, no matter how often we might stray from our best intentions or our best selves. Rumi's God, and mine and that of millions of others is the same God and is holy – in the true sense of the word, which is deeply related linguistically (from the Teutonic haelan) to our concepts of hale, whole, healthy, hearty, holism; holy, embracing all that is in sacred unity.

Our task, those who are seeking Home, is to mirror and embody that holy Home here on earth, to create communities of heaven where the sacred principles are mirrored in each moment, here and now, as above so below; a world of love beyond irrelevant distinctions like age, race, sexuality, social class or personal history. A culture of dismemberment, dissection, disconnection, atomising – the waste land – fragments those who live in it. We are separated from each other, the creation and ourselves, and God. Spiritual work flows the opposite way. The spiritual life re-members, re-connects, makes whole and holy.

The way home draws us into a "wild love affair with life". Our spiritual work is not about weird and wonderful experiences or fixity in religion, but getting past these and seeing the world differently, truthfully, full of endless change, refinement, transformation; seeing, being anew in, becoming more sensitised to God. It is the *via purgativa*, cleansing us of our ideas of self in order to know Self; a way of seeing that like all love affairs is full of turbulence and calm, bliss and pain. Most of all it is replete with unfathomable, boundless, endlessly inbreaking love in the One in whom that wild love affair is both complete and never ending, still and still moving. Into ourselves, into life, into the God we know and love. Home.

...If we are lucky
Or patient
In sacred, silent solitude,
We may catch a glimpse of God
Meditating
In the timeless moment
Between the flashes of the lighthouse,
Or the split sunbeam in the waves.

The holy is not bound by altar
Or portal carved just so.
It is here, now.
Under the pine roof where
the mouse peeps through the knot hole,
Under the glare of strip lights
Illuminating the temenos of
The ecstatic ordinary.
If we will only look.
If we only look.

The mountains have their own deep thoughts
We cannot share them.
Like the Buddha under the Bo tree, they have gone, gone beyond,
Gone beyond the beyond of our reach.
But we can sit and pray
And in our waiting
The veil may lift for just a moment,
Just a moment.
And if we watch closely,
We might just see something.
Don't try to pin it down
It will move like quicksilver from our grasp
Lost
Down the drain of the unconscious.
But sit and pray for just a moment
And watch another universe come into being.
Boom!...

Part 11

"Home is the place where, when you have to go there, they have to take you in." [158]

Letter 2

Dear Unknown Friend,

I cannot say this is the Way, or that is the Way. In a sense the great Way is not difficult for those who have no preferences, for it is the Way that prefers us! As Hafiz reminded us, we are all invited, that narrows down the choice to going willingly or resisting. Yet with so many doors open to us, we are called to become clear, to make choices, to do the work, to celebrate every step of the Way. I hope the words in this book have helped a little in the choosing. And in making that choice, it is clear that the perennial guidance for following the Way is to ensure that you have in place the soul friends, works, communities and foods that will nurture the soul, keep you safe and bring you all the struggle and peace you will need in returning Home.

I trust these words have helped make clear the value of discernment in making your choices, when to stick with something and when to let it go depending on how healthy it is for your soul, when to go deeper into surrender so that the Way Home takes you, rather than you seek to command it. There is no requirement to hang on to a soul friend or a religious tradition just for the sake of it and especially if it is harmful, but it is necessary to be very clear about your intentions and consciousness if the time comes to say goodbye to something or someone. The Way is not travelled entirely alone or entirely in company.

The Way may seem far off with many miles to go. Yet, if we cannot find the One here and now, where do we seek? There is nowhere else we can be. My friend and teacher Ram Dass became ill a few years ago, yet his limited speech after a stroke seemed if anything to enhance rather than diminish his presence. On my infrequent visits to the USA there would be some precious time alone with him. As conversation ebbed and flowed there would be periods of deep silence with a profound sense of love and simply being in the moment as each moment slipped into the next. Words were few, but the feeling almost overwhelming. "This is what happens," he said, "when soul talks to soul."

When our deepest Self is set free, it has nowhere it needs to go, nothing it needs to say or do. It is simply free to be what it is, utterly present in the moment, sunbathing in, indeed becoming, the radiant light of Love, of the Presence of the Friend. In this Presence we know beyond doubt, in faith, that we are loved by God not because we are superhuman but because of our essential humanity.

The four Soul Care elements we have explored are not the Way in themselves, but they help us along the Way and open us so that it is the Way that takes us ever more, stripping us even of the idea that it is we who are doing all the work of following, seeking, effort-ing. They open us to that inner prompting, to the power that transforms within dissolving all obstructions. It is what some would describe as the bursting forth within of the light of the Christ consciousness, the inbreaking of the grace, the Holy Spirit of the Divine which ultimately is the power that is magnetically, forcefully, relentlessly bringing us Home.

The seed of that consciousness is in each of us. Our Soul Care work is designed to let that seed flourish and blossom, to justify and purify the ground so that these seeds of the Divine can grow. The pattern of the universe is printed on our hearts, Soul Care and the distillation of our egos opens us to the radiant beauty of that pattern, sensitises us to the Divine will so that it can draw out of us the essence of who we are and allow that pattern to flourish, to be revealed, to be harvested in all its glory.

Soul Care, dear Unknown Friend, is like being a constant gardener. We treasure the beautiful flowers and vegetables, but have to keep the weeds down. The weeding and cultivating never stops, but there are periods of rest, times of enjoying the fruits of our labour. My life like yours has been full of times of sorrow and joy, love and fear. There have been times when I have behaved well and risen to being the best I could be, times when I have behaved badly and wounded others and myself. But as we tend the garden of our lives, we learn to forgive, accept, integrate, heal, so the heart of the garden itself heals, flourishes and is made whole. In this life, dear Unknown Friend, there is no ordinary life and spiritual life, although it can seem so at times. It is all one, and as we continue our work the beauty of the whole, the perfect place of every part is revealed to us. If we apply ourselves to heartfelt soul work and play, then that treasure deep within that has longed to be fully and radiantly in the world is revealed. It is free and at Home.

Tend your garden, dear Unknown Friend, tend it well, there is nothing else!

Yours,

In

Love,

A Friend

Part 12

"Your word goes out to call us Home
To the city where angels sing your praise."[159]

Coming Home

You said "Home".
I drank the booze of hospitality in a stranger's house.

You said "Awake".
I slept on the hard mattress of my loneliness.

You said "Pray".
I bowed low in the temple of despair.

You said "Dream".
I wove nightmares from threads of steel.

You said "Light".
I snuffed out candles on the altar of my desires.

You said "Love".
I hunted bodies under dark lamps.

You said "Come".
I, deaf Icarus, took flight.

You said "Be Still".
I raced in the grand prix of my thoughts.

You said "Know Me".
I watched Eastenders instead.

You said "Hold".
I let go Your hand.

You said "Wait".
I got on the first bus that came along.

You said "Trust".
I betrayed my soul in a palace of mirrors.

When You caressed me for attention
I slapped You down.
When You tickled my chin
I punched You away.
When You plunged a fist into my heart
I took the hand of fear and ran away.
When You shook me — hard, and hooked —
The pain unmanned me.
I sat up and listened.

Sometimes.

Then slunk away down the long corridor of shadows.

You
Reeled me in.

My mother always said, "It will all end in tears".
Had I known she had the gift of prophecy
I would have bought her bibles
Or the black chocolate she loved.
Goddesses deserve worship
When their compassionate eyes stroke your soul
With the melting honey of love.

You said "Now, come closer".
I drew myself upon Your knee to await Your orders.
I asked "When?"
You said "Now"
And I
Fell asleep again.

In the forgetfulness of the Porsche
The rock concert
Or simply an overdrawn bank statement,
I had been offered the womb of Your love.
I self aborted.
Again

But always the hunger.

A bowel-less pain.
The hollow pitiless tomb.

Relentless.

You have sent me living angels down the years.
I pruned their wings and stuffed my duvet with their feathers.
Angels,
The kind who fasten your seat belt when you fall drunk in the back of a taxi.

When You sent the message
This time in an unlooked for brown envelope.
I could only smile.
It seemed simpler
To surrender.
Falling into book and prayer.

Years ago I said "What do You want of me?"
You said "Be My Voice".
Struck dumb by impossible visions,
I ordered another pint.

The Lord Shiva slaughtered the slimy frog of my unworthiness.
"Death is mine not yours to give" said he.
And I remember,
I looked him straight in the eye for the first time.

Spinning in the velocity of my own redemption
There was nothing left to do but fall
Dizzy
At Your feet.
From apogee to perigee
In the flick of the serpent's tongue.

In surrender is peace.
In trust is service.

I ask "What have I learned here?"
You say "Trust".

I ask "What do You want of me?"
You say "Wait".

I ask "Why offer Your hand?"
You say "Hold".

I ask "Where do I begin?"
You say "Know me".

I ask "How?"
You say "Be still".

I ask "Am I worthy enough?"
You say "Come".

I ask "Why?"
You say "Love".

I ask "What lies in this dark?"
You say "Light".

I ask "How shall I find You?"
You say "Dream".

I ask "How shall I stay with You?"
You say "Pray".

I ask "What have I become?"
You say "Awake".

I ask "What is this place?"
You say "Home".

References

All Bible references are from the New Revised Standard Version. 1999. OUP. Oxford

[1] Eliot T S 1944 The Four Quartets. Harcourt Brace Jovanovich. London
[2] In Wright S 1989 Nursing the older patient. Harper. London
[3] Heelas P, Woodhead l, with Seel B, Szerszynski B, Tusting K 2005 The spirituality revolution – why religion is giving way to spirituality. Blackwell. Oxford
[4] Weil S 2000 Waiting for God. Perennial. London
[5] From Listening 2004 Prayers for Conversations. p2.
www.salforddiocese.org.uk/listening2004
[6] Frankl V 1959 Man's search for meaning. Rider. London
[7] Palmer P 1993 To know as we are known. Harper and Row. San Francisco
[8] Heelas et al op cit 3
[9] Davie C1995 Religion in Britain since 1945. Blackwell. Oxford
[10] Finney J 1996 Recovering the past. DLT. London
[11] Douglas-Klotz N 1999 The hidden gospel. Quest. Wheaton
[12] Lee Peggy 1969 Is that all there is? Columbia Records
[13] Sogyal Rinpoche 1992 The Tibetan book of living and dying. Ryder. London
[14] Eliot op cit 1
[15] Doyle B 1983 Meditations with Julian of Norwich. Bear. Santa Fe.
[16] Koenig H, McCullogh M, Larson B 2002 Handbook of religion and health. OUP. New York
[17] Pargament K, Koenig H, Tarakeshwar N, Hahn J 2001 Religious struggle as a predictor of mortality among medically ill elderly patients Arch Intern Med 161 1881-85 2001
[18] Krause J. 2006 Church - based social support and mortality. Journals of Gerontology Series B. 61. S140-146.
[19] Tillich P 2000 The courage to be. YUP. Yale
[20] Macquarrie J 1972 Paths in spirituality. SCM. Trowbridge
[21] Wright S 2005 Reflections on spirituality and health. Wiley. Chichester
[22] Grof S. Grof C (eds) 1989 Spiritual emergency: when personal transformation becomes a crisis. Putnam. New York
[23] Dennet D 2006 Breaking the spell. Penguin. London
[24] Dawkins R 2006 The God delusion. Bantam. London
[25] Hitchens C 2007 God is not great. Atlantic. London
[26] Newberg A, D'Aquili E and Rause V 2001 Why God won't go away. Ballantine. New York
[27] Hamer D 2004 The God gene. Doubleday. New York
[28] Schultes R and Hofmann A 1992 Plants of the gods. Healing Arts Press. Rochester
[29] Jung C 1961 Modern man in search of soul. Routledge and Kegan Paul. London
[30] Underhill E 1993 (first published 1910) Mysticism. Oneworld. Oxford
[31] Maxwell M, Tschudin V 1990 Seeing the invisible. Arkana. London
[32] Dossey L 2007 PEAR lab and the nonlocal mind: why they matter. Explore (3) 3 191-196
[33] Wright S and Sayre-Adams J 2000 Sacred space – right relationship and spirituality in health care. Churchill Livingstone. Edinburgh
[34] Wright S 2005 Burnout – a spiritual crisis. Nursing Standard Essential Guide. RCN publications. Harrow
[35] Heinlein R 1961 Stranger in a strange land. Putnam. London
[36] Merton T 1949 Seeds of contemplation. Hollis and Carter. London
[37] Heelas et al op cit 3
[38] McGrath A 2004 The twilight of atheism. Rider. London
[39] Cited in Armstrong K 2001 The battle for God. Harpercollins. London
[40] Eliot T S 1990 edition. The Waste Land and other poems. Faber and Faber, London
[41] Gallup Organisation – survey cited in Hatfield D 1999 New research links emotional intelligence with profitability The Inner Edge 1(5) 5-9
[42] Lerner M 2000 Spirit matters. Hampton Roads. Charlottesville
[43] de Chardin P T 1959 The phenomenon of man. Collins. London
[44] Speck P 2003 Working with dying people, chapter in Obholzer A and Roberts V (eds) The unconscious at work. Brunner-Routledge. London
[45] Almaas A 2000 The diamond heart. Shambhala. London
[46] Almaas op cit 45
[47] Pennick N 1996 Celtic sacred landscapes. Thames and Hudson. London
[48] Pennick op cit 47
[49] Ray PH 1996 The integral culture survey – a study of the emergence of transformational values in America. Institute of Noetic Sciences. Sausalito
[50] Thomas R 1999 The I society. The Guardian (Archive). 17.9.

References

[51] Halevi Y (trans. Levin G) 2002 Poems from the divan. Anvil. London
[52] Merton op cit 36
[53] Easwaran E 1988 (trans) The Upanishads. Arkana. London
[54] Heelas op cit 3
[55] Grof op cit 22
[56] Guenther M 2002 Holy listening. DLT. London
[57] Tweedie I 1907 Daughter of fire. Golden Sufi Centre. Inverness, Calif.
[58] Riso D and Hudson R 1999 The wisdom of the Enneagram. Bantam. New York
[59] Leech K 2001 Soul Friend – spiritual direction and the modern world. DLT. London
[60] Caplan M 2002 Do you need a guru? Thorsons. London
[61] Eliot op cit 1
[62] Almaas op cit 45
[63] Lao Tzu 1994 (trans Legge J) Tao te ching. Little Brown. London
[64] Schumacher E 1977 A Guide for the perplexed. Abacus. London
[65] Wernham S 2003 personal correspondence
[66] Eliot op cit 1
[67] Guenther op cit 56
[68] Liebert E 2000 Changing life patterns. Chalice. St.Louis
[69] Leech op cit 59
[70] Whiteaker S 2004 The good retreat guide. Rider. London
[71] Guenther op cit 56
[72] Aronson H. 2004 Buddhist practice on western ground: reconciling eastern ideals and western psychology. Shambala. Boston
[73] Jones A 1982 Exploring spiritual direction: an essay of Christian friendship. Harper and Row. San Francisco
[74] Ball P 2003 Introducing spiritual direction. SPCK. London
[75] Nickalls J (Ed) 1997 The journal of George Fox. Religious Society of Friends. Philadelphia
[76] Newell P 1997 Listening to the heartbeat of God. SPCK. London
[77] Steven K 2000 Iona. St Andrew Press. Edinburgh
[78] Bradley I 2000 Colonies of heaven. DLT. London
[79] Wright and Sayre-Adams op cit 33
[80] Barth K cited in Underhill E 2000 The spiritual life. Oneworld. Boston
[81] Krause op cit 18
[82] Dossey L 1996 Prayer is good medicine. Harpercollins. San Francisco
[83] Ram Dass and Gorman P 1992 How can I help – stories and reflections on service. Knopf. New York
[84] Shakespeare W 1982 edition Anthony and Cleopatra. Complete Works Vol 2. Nelson   Doubleday. New York
[85] Storr A 1996 Feet of clay – a study of gurus. Harpercollins. London
[86] McGregor Ross H 1998 Jesus untouched by the church – his teachings in the Gospel of St.Thomas. Ebor. York
[87] Wright op cit 21
[88] Palmer G, Sherrard P, Ware K (trans) 1983 The Philokalia. Faber and Faber. London
[89] Merton T 2005. Contemplative prayer. DLT. London
[90] Lane B 1998 The solace of fierce landscapes. Oxford. Oxford
[91] Wright and Sayre-Adams op cit 33
[92] Rolt C (trans) 1957 Dionysius the Areopagite: On the divine names and the mystical theology. SPCK. London
[93] Newell J P 2000 Echo of the soul. Canterbury Press. Norwich
[94] Wright and Sayre-Adams op cit 33
[95] McTaggart L 2001 The Field. Harpercollins. London
[96] Harner M 1990 The way of the shaman. Harper and Row. San Francisco
[97] Mascaro J (trans) 1962 The Bhagavad Gita. Penguin. Harmondsworth
[98] Ladinsky D 2002 I heard God laughing – renderings of Hafiz. Sufism reoriented. Walnut Creek
[99] Huston Smith cited in Borg 1995 Meeting Jesus again for the first time. Harpercollins. San Francisco
[100] Martin L and Robinson J 2005 TV to push the boundaries of sex. The Observer 28th August 2005 p4
[101] Wright and Sayre-Adams op cit 33
[102] Leloup J-Y (trans Rowe J) 2004 The Gospel of Philip. Inner Traditions. Rochester
[103] Jamison C 2006 Finding sanctuary. Weidenfield and Nicholson. London
[104] Tyler P 2007 Divine unknowing: lessons from the Christian mystical tradition for healthcare today. Spirituality and Health International, 8 (2) 64–73)
[105] Eliot op cit 1
[106] McCabe H 2002 God still matters. Continuum. London
[107] Dossey op cit 82
[108] Merton op cit 89
[109] Eliot op cit 1

196

[110] Baker R, Henry G 1999 Merton and Sufism: the untold story. Fons Vitae. Louisville

[111] Tyler op cit 104

[112] Wright op cit 34

[113] Cassian J 1997 The Conferences (ed Ramsey). Newman. New York

[114] Wright and Sayre-Adams op cit 33

[115] Virgil 1963 The Aeneid. Penguin Classics. Harmondsworth.

[116] Ignatius of Loyola (trans Puhl L) 2000 The spiritual exercises of St Ignatius. Vintage. New York

[117] Davies O 1994 (trans) Meister Eckhart – selected writings. Penguin. Harmondsworth

[118] Eliot op cit 1

[119] Liebert op cit 68

[120] Eliot op cit 1

[121] Williams E 1967 Beyond belief. Pan. London

[122] Hillman J cited in Zweig C and Abrams J 1991 Meeting the shadow. Tarcher. New York

[123] Storr op cit 85

[124] Fry C 1951 A sleep of prisoners. OUP. Oxford

[125] Frankl V 2004 Man's search for meaning. Rider. London

[126] Bonhoeffer D (ed. de Gruchy J) 1987 Selected writings. Collins. London

[127] Hillesum E 1966 An interrupted life. Owl. New York

[128] Ladinsky op cit 98

[129] Ram Dass 2000 Still here. Hodder and Stoughton. London

[130] Angelou M 1993 Wouldn't take nothing for my journey now. Random. New York

[131] McGregor Ross op cit 86

[132] Mother Theresa cited in Kornfield J 1993 A path with heart. Bantam. New York

[133] Teasdale W 2001 The mystic heart. New World. Novato

[134] Wright op cit 21

[135] McGregor Ross op cit 86

[136] Eliot op cit 1

[137] Sahajananda J 2003 You are the light – rediscovering the Eastern Jesus. O books. Alresford

[138] Tillich op cit 19

[139] Anon 1991 Meditations on the Tarot. Element. Shaftesbury

[140] Pannenberg W 1977 Faith and reality.(trans Maxwell J). Knox. London

[141] Merton op cit 89

[142] Tillich op cit 19

[143] Campbell J cited in McLuhan T 1996 Cathedrals of the spirit. Thorsons. London

[144] Merton op cit 36

[145] Swimme B 1984 The Universe is a green dragon. Bear, Santa Fe

[146] Eliot op cit 1

[147] Sogyal Rinpoche op cit 13

[148] Maslow A 1954 Motivation and personality. Penguin Compass. New York

[149] Douglas-Klotz op cit 11

[150] Borg op cit 97

[151] Bonhoeffer op cit 126

[152] Barret D 2001 The new believers. Cassel. London

[153] Underhill E 2000 The spiritual life. Oneworld. Boston

[154] De Mello A 1996 Walking on water. Columba. Dublin

[155] Dostoevsky F 1880 (1993 edition, McDuff D trans) The brothers Karamazov. Penguin Classics. Harmondsworth

[156] Underhill op cit 152

[157] Rumi (trans Barks C 1997) The illuminated Rumi. Broadway. New York

[158] Frost R 1915 "The death of the hired man" in "North of Boston". Holt. New York

[159] The Archbishop's Council 2000 Common worship. Church House. London.

Bibliography, other sources of inspiration and recommended reading not otherwise cited in the text

Achterberg J 1990 Woman as healer. Ryder. London

Anon (trans Wolters C) 1978. The Cloud of unknowing. Penguin. Harmondsworth

Armstrong K 1993 A history of God. Ballantine. New York.

Austin R (trans) 1980 Ibn Al-Arabi - the bezels of wisdom. Paulist. Mahwah

Benson H 1996 Timeless healing. Schuster. London

Borg M 1997 The God we never knew. Harpercollins. San Francisco

Borg M 1989 The heart of Christianity. Harper. San Francisco

Bradley I 2003 The Celtic way. DLT. London

Bruce S 2002 God is dead – secularization in the west. Blackwell. Oxford

Buber M 1937 I and Thou. Clark. Edinburgh

Dalai Lama 1996 The good heart. Wisdom. Somerville

Darbandi A, Davis D (trans) 1984 Attar F ud-din - the conference of the birds. Penguin. Harmondsworth

Douglas-Klotz N 2003 The Genesis meditations – a shared practice for Christians, Jews and Muslims. Quest. Wheaton

Douglas-Klotz N 2005 The Sufi book of life. Penguin. London

Eliade M 1966 Shamanism. Bollingen. Princeton

French R (trans) 1973 The way of the pilgrim. Harper. San Francisco

Gibran K 1994 The Prophet. Mandarin. London

Halevi Z 1991 Psychology of Kabbalah. Gateway. Bath

Holden M 2002 Boundless love. Rider. London

Holden R 1996 Happiness now. Coronet. London

Huxley A 1945 The perennial philosophy. Harper and Row. San Francisco

James W 1985 Varieties of religious experience. Penguin. Harmondsworth

Jones J 1996 In the middle of this road we call our life. Harpercollins. London

Julian of Norwich 1997 (trans Skinner J) Revelation of love. Image. New York

Jung C 1961 Modern man in search of soul. Routledge and Kegan Paul. London

A Kempis T 2004 (Croft A trans) The imitation of Christ. Hendrickson. Peabody

Kornfield J 2000 After the ecstasy, the laundry. Rider. London

Lawrence, Brother 2004 (trans Klein P) The practice of the presence of God. Hendrickson. New York

LeShan L 1974 How to meditate. Harpercollins. London

Levine S and Levine O 1995 Embracing the Beloved. Doubleday. New York

Lewis C 1952 Mere Christianity. Harper. San Francisco

Longaker C 1998 Facing death and finding hope. Arrow. London

Lynch G 2002 After religion – generation X and the search for meaning. DLT. London

Maimonides 1190 (Trans Rabin C 1952) The Guide for the perplexed. Hackett. Cambridge

Main J 1988 The inner Christ. DLT. London

Mascaro J (trans) 1973 The Dhammapada. Penguin. Harmondsworth

Matt D 1983 Zohar. Paulist. Mahwah

McGrath A 2004 The twilight of atheism. Rider. London

Mishra P 2004 An end to suffering. Picador. London

Muller W 1999 Sabbath: restoring the sacred rhythm of rest. Bantam. New York

Newell P 2000 1999 The book of creation. Canterbury. Norwich

Newman L 1963 The Hasidic anthology: tales and teachings of the Hasidim. Schoken. New York

Nouwen H 1994 The wounded healer. DLT. London

Nouwen H 1997 The inner voice of love. DLT. London

O'Malley B 2005 Lord of creation. Canterbury. Norwich

O'Murchu D 2003 Evolutionary faith. Orbis. New York

Pagels E 2006 The Gnostic gospels. Phoenix. London

Parsons S 2000 Ungodly fear. Lion. Oxford

Qur'an (trans Dawood N 1991) Penguin. Harmondsworth

Ram Dass 1971 Be here now. Crown. New York

Religious Society of Friends 1998 Quaker faith and practice. RSF. London

Robinson J (Ed) 1996 The Nag Hammadi library in English. Brill. New York

Rodegast P, Santon J 1987 Emmanuel's book. (also books 2 and 3, 1989 and 1994) Bantam. New York

Roth C (trans) 1993 Gregory of Nyssa - on the soul and the resurrection. St Vladimir's Seminary. New York

Scott W (trans) 1997 Hermetica. Solo. London

Shah I 1973 The way of the Sufi. Penguin. Harmondsworth

Singh P 2002 Guru Granth Sahib. OUP. London

Smith H 1991 The world's religions. Harper. San Francisco
Spong J 1998 Why Christianity must change or die. Harper. San Francisco
Spong J 2007 Jesus for the non-religious. Harper. San Francisco
St John of the Cross (trans Zimmerman B) 1973 The dark night of the soul. Clarke. Cambridge
St Theresa of Avila (trans R van de Weyer) 1995 The interior castle. Harpercollins. London
Sri Aurobindo 1970 The life divine. Sri Aurobindo Ashram. Pondicherry.
Streep P (Trans) 1994 Tao Te Ching. Bullfinch. London
Jewish Publication Society 1992 The Torah. JPS. Jerusalem
Vaughan F 1995 Shadows of the sacred. Quest. Wheaton
Wilber K 1995 Sex, ecology and spirituality. Shambala. Boston

Index